THE WORLD OBSERVED

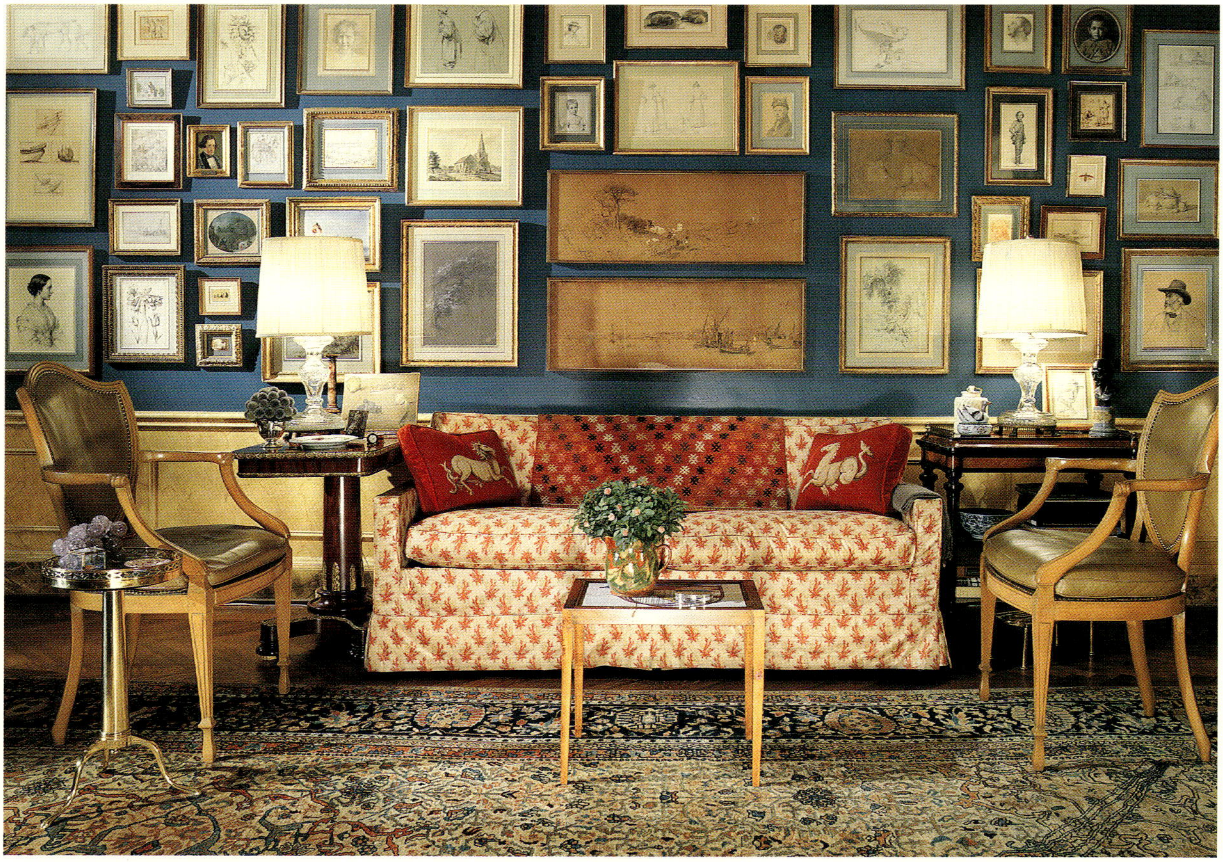

Part of the long wall of Charles Ryskamp's living room in New York. The four central works just above the sofa are by Edward Lear; the two long views of Naples are Mr. Ryskamp's earliest drawings acquisitions. Among the other sheets here are sketches by John Linnell, Paul Sandby, Christen Købke, Eugène Devéria, and William Blake Richmond.

THE WORLD OBSERVED

FIVE CENTURIES OF DRAWINGS FROM THE COLLECTION OF CHARLES RYSKAMP

FOREWORD BY *Charles E. Pierce, Jr.*

INTRODUCTION BY *Charles Ryskamp*

CATALOGUE BY

William M. Griswold · Cara Dufour Denison
Kathleen Stuart · Jennifer Tonkovich

THE PIERPONT MORGAN LIBRARY

NEW YORK

Exhibition at The Pierpont Morgan Library, New York
January 25–May 9, 2001

Generous support for this exhibition was received from S. Parker Gilbert, Janine Luke and Mel Seiden, Mrs. Vincent Astor, Diane A. Nixon, Mrs. Oscar de la Renta, Eugene V. & Clare E. Thaw Charitable Trust, Mrs. Charles Wrightsman, and Mr. and Mrs. James R. Houghton.

Library of Congress Cataloging-in-Publication Data

The world ob[s]erved: five centuries of drawings from the collection of Charles Ryskamp / foreword by Charles E. Pierce, Jr.; introduction by Charles Ryskamp; Cara Dufour Denison . . . [et al.].
p. cm.
Catalog of an exhibition held at the Pierpont Morgan Library, New York, Jan. 25– May 9, 2001.
Includes bibliographical references and index.
ISBN 0-87598-131-3 (pbk. : alk. paper)
1. Drawing, European—Exhibitions. 2. Ryskamp, Charles—Art collections—Exhibitions. 3. Drawing—Private collections—United States—Exhibitions. I. Denison, Cara D. II. Pierpont Morgan Library.
NC225 .W665 2000
741.94 074 7471—dc21 00-046530

ISBN 0-87598-131-3

Front cover: William Henry Hunt, *A Doorway in Bushey Church* (No. 93)

Back cover: Anthony Claesz. II, *Seven Tulips with Three Ladybugs* (No. 18)

CONTENTS

Foreword

CHARLES RYSKAMP's intense involvement with literature and art began in his youth and culminated in a distinguished career as a professor at Princeton University and as director, first of the Morgan Library and then of the Frick Collection. He started to collect books and art at an early age, and during the past several decades he has energetically enlarged and refined the splendid group of drawings of which the present selection is but a relatively small part. Working closely with dealers and studiously avoiding any conflict of interest with the institutions that he served, he pursued the acquisition of works by artists whose drawings were, for reasons of geography or chronology, not actively collected by the museums he directed. More recently—and especially since his retirement—he has expanded his collection, intentionally choosing sheets that might complement the holdings of the Morgan Library.

His collection is thus highly personal. While every major European school and many well-known artists are represented in the exhibition, the present selection is unusually rich in drawings of the golden age of Danish art, in sheets by Dutch and German draftsmen of the nineteenth century, in natural history studies, and in the depictions of everyday objects that Charles has collected with particular sensitivity and enthusiasm. Moreover, while the earliest sheet in the exhibition is datable to the sixteenth century, the latest—by Andrew Zega and Bernd H. Dams—was executed as recently as 1999, revealing a commitment not only to the art of the past but also to that of the present.

I would like to thank the group of friends who have so generously underwritten the exhibition and catalogue: S. Parker Gilbert, Janine Luke and Mel Seiden, Mrs. Vincent Astor, Diane A. Nixon, Mrs. Oscar de la Renta, the Eugene V. & Clare E. Thaw Charitable Trust, Mrs. Charles Wrightsman, and Mr. and Mrs. James R. Houghton. The selection of drawings was made by Charles Ryskamp and William M. Griswold, who wrote the entries on the Danish and Italian drawings; Cara Denison, Kathleen Stuart, and Jennifer Tonkovich contributed the other entries in the catalogue. Special mention must be made of Marilyn Palmeri, who coordinated the photography; of conservator Patricia Reyes and her staff, who examined all the drawings and provided invaluable assistance installing the show; of Lucy Eldridge, registrar; of Karen Banks, publications manager; and of Patricia Emerson, editor. Above all, I am grateful to Charles for agreeing to share his collection with others who love master drawings as well as for his pledge to give or bequeath all his Danish drawings and all but two or three of his Dutch and German drawings to the Morgan Library, where they will join some one hundred twenty works he has previously given.

Charles E. Pierce, Jr.
Director

Acknowledgments

SPECIAL THANKS are due to W. Mark Brady and Laura Bennett for their ongoing assistance at every stage of the preparation of this exhibition. We are also grateful to the following individuals: Hervé Aaron, Noël Annesley, Angelika Arnoldi, Luca Baroni, John Baskett, Timothy Bathurst, Katrin Bellinger, Jaap Bolten, François Borne, Martin Browne, Eric G. Carlson, Arturo and Corinne Cuellar, Bernd H. Dams, Roy Davis, Richard Day, Gertrude W. Dennis, William Drummond, Lydia Dufour, John Edmonson, Rhoda Eitel-Porter, Chris Fischer, Sebastien Goetz, Margaret Morgan Grasselli, Martin Grässle, Poul Grinder-Hansen, Bob P. Haboldt, Nicholas Hall, Stefaan Hautekeete, Egbert Haverkamp-Begemann, John Herring, Paul Herring, Niall Hobhouse, Sarah Hobrough, Paul Huys Janssen, Jennifer Jones, Anna Jozefacka, Robert Kashey, Richard Knight, Ruth Kraemer, Inger Krog, Armin Kunz, Fransje Kuyvenhoven, David Lachenmann, Cecily Langdale, Thomas le Claire, Bruce Livie, Erik P. Löffler, Anne-Marie Logan, Rupert Maas, Benjamin Antoine Maisani, Stephanie Maison, Kurt Meissner, Stig Miss, Martin Moeller, Priscilla Muller, Peter Nahum, Gabriel M. Naughton, Lisa O'Connor, Flavia Ormond, John Reed, Inge Reist, Simon Reynolds, Robert-Jan te Rijdt, William Robinson, Gregory Rubinstein, Francis Russell, Paul W. L. Russell, Marianne Saabye, Alan Salz, Pietro Scarpa, William H. Schab, Kate Schaeffer, Peter Schatborn, Rita Selle, Bonny van Sieghem, Stephen Somerville, Don Swanson, Yvonne Tan Bunzl, Eugene V. Thaw, Mary Ann Trulli, Jane Shoaf Turner, Frank van der Velden, Thomas Williams, Linda Wolk-Simon, Andrew Zega, and Laura Zukerman.

On Collecting Drawings

IS THE DRAWING GOOD ENOUGH to hang at the Morgan Library? That is a question I and so many others have often asked ourselves. The drawings illustrated in this volume are unlike those customarily exhibited at the Morgan Library: we expect the galleries to be filled with masterpieces by the greatest artists, whether Pisanello or Picasso. I was, therefore, altogether hesitant about presenting a group that I, by necessity, had gathered on a very modest budget; if any drawing proved to be remarkable, it came because of unusual good fortune.

It was decided, however, that the present exhibition and catalogue might be an inspiration to young collectors and to those who grow discouraged when they read of extremely high prices paid at sales in New York, London, Paris, wherever. I personally hoped to encourage new collectors, who would, as I have, discover areas that are not as yet fashionable, and they might be comforted to know that almost every year, including the last one, I have come across drawings that cost less than a thousand dollars yet could well accompany those illustrated here.

In addition to my financial constraints, during the nearly eighteen years when I was director of the Morgan Library, I had to avoid any conflict of interest in my purchase of drawings. I therefore first of all looked for works made after 1820, which was (when I came to the Library) the normal chronological cutoff of drawings for acquisition. Fortunately the nineteenth century was a rich period of draftsmanship, and many thousands of drawings survived. It was not my favorite century, but it deeply interested me because of its variety. I also sought schools not represented at the Library or in other American public collections.

In 1987 I left the Morgan Library to become director of the Frick Collection. Since 1997 I have been Director Emeritus and an Honorary Fellow of both institutions. In the past dozen years I have therefore had few considerations of conflict of interest, since the Frick for the most part does not collect drawings. Through all of these years, from 1955 to the present, I have held a position at Princeton University, and recently I also was associated with the Institute for Advanced Study in Princeton. In my early years of teaching, devoted largely to English literature, I frequently held classes on prints and drawings at my house, to discuss the works of art and how to acquire them.

A most important area of collecting for me in the last twenty-five years has been the golden age of Danish art (1800–1850). I had long admired these works but did not know them well. Paintings of this age, and especially drawings, were extremely rare in the United States. I decided that I would be unable to enjoy Danish art, as well as some other aspects of European drawing, unless I personally acquired the works. Thus, barriers became not only challenges, they created new worlds for me. I believe that there are still such possibilities for collectors—and museums;

in reality, the shutters may become "Charm'd magic casements" opening on new worlds. Such windows of opportunity are not often opened by a chance find at a flea market. In my experience, and as the provenances listed in the catalogue will make plain, fine drawings may more likely be found at the best dealers and auction houses. I have always kept a close relationship with them and relied not only on their notices and catalogues but also on frequent visits to keep them constantly aware of my interests. Acquisitions depend on determination, study, and old-fashioned connoisseurship. Chance or luck come, if at all, after much looking and caring.

My collection has always been fluid. I sometimes had to sell art I highly prized in order to pay for basic living expenses, and there has rarely been money for more costly purchases. The acquisition of a number of the finest drawings was possible only through exchange: four or five works by minor masters or prints that I had bought many years earlier were traded for one much more significant drawing. Further, my collection is always changing because I have made gifts every year to public collections with which I have a special association. Giving, as much as acquiring, has been a principle of my collecting. I gave to family and friends as well as to museums. I have received such an important part of my education in various institutions, and so much pleasure, that it is a joy to return some part of their gifts to me. Most of the drawings I have given away have gone to the Morgan Library; a few of them have been borrowed for the present exhibition. I am at this time pledging all of my Danish drawings and all but two or three Dutch and German drawings as gifts or bequests to the Library.

* * *

I SUPPOSE that I have always been a collector. By the time I was seven or eight I had assembled a small library in a red bookcase in my bedroom, and in every one I had placed a simple kitchen label on which I had written my initials and an acquisition number. Only one work remains from that library, a cyclopedia of flowers, 1933; cost, $1.98: it helped me to understand botanical identification as well as being of practical use in gardening.

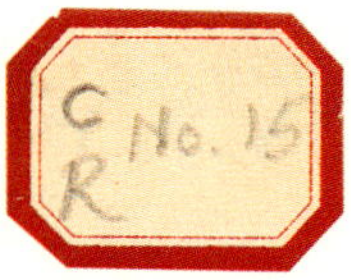

When I was thirteen, at home in Michigan, I ordered two contemporary etchings from a gallery in New York. But my interest soon turned to earlier periods of art. Mine was a professorial family, and we subscribed to New York and international newspapers; from an early age I knew about auction houses and art galleries, and I often sent for sales catalogues, which were usually free. One Sunday, as we were all lined up for church, a special delivery envelope arrived from Parke-Bernet in New York. My father assumed it was for him; when he discovered that it was for me, he told me that this had to stop because I could not possibly afford to buy at auction. I was giving the auction houses a false impression, so I no longer could send for catalogues. Admittedly, my youthful purchases were on the whole of no great value and little discrimination, but they were made with passion. In my early twenties, I bought a few prints by Rembrandt and Dürer. They were not very fine impressions, but for the first time I lived with original works by great masters. I had become a student at Cambridge University, and the prints were hung in my college rooms.

In the summer before going to Cambridge I had taken time off from my studies at the British Museum to visit print shops, galleries, and rare book dealers in London. All were wonderfully welcoming to me, and I established a life in which I learned almost as much from dealers as I had in my formal studies at universities or in my many visits to libraries and museums. My academic career included very few courses in art history. A turning point in my life came when I had the courage to enter the celebrated gallery on Bond Street, Colnaghi. The name was already legend to me. I was greeted warmly, and I asked to see etchings by Rembrandt. To my delight they had boxes containing many dozens of his prints. Members of the staff, including Mr. Harold Wright, the head of the department, spent hours with me studying each one.

For the only time in my life I had money in the bank for the year ahead. Despite that I had already spent part of a year's allowance on an engraving by Rembrandt and a woodcut by Dürer—and had no right to buy anything at all—I told them at the end of the afternoon that I wished to purchase an inexpensive etching by Rembrandt, and that I could write out a check at once. To my amazement, Mr. Wright said he would not sell the print to me. He politely declared that I had enthusiasm and curiosity but insufficient knowledge and discernment. He asked whether I could get an admission card to the print room of the British Museum. I said that I was fortunate enough to have such a card for the library (I was still rather young for admission), and I thought that with that I could get a similar pass for the print room. Mr. Wright told me to study all of the hundreds of Rembrandt prints there, and when I had done so, if I still wished to have the etching I had chosen, he would sell it to me.

Having secured my card, I studied the Rembrandts day after day when I should have been preparing for my literary program at Cambridge, and, of course, I did not buy the print at Colnaghi. Mr. Wright's advice, however, began my self-education in prints and drawings in earnest. I did not know it, but I was following the classic curriculum for scholars, curators, dealers, and collectors in the graphic arts. Great print rooms—especially those of the British Museum, the Fitzwilliam, the Ashmolean, Yale, the Fogg, and Princeton—became my haunts and my homes; the keepers and curators became my good friends. The result may be seen in this catalogue and exhibition.

While a student at Cambridge, I bought my first drawings. A former ballet dancer, Gabor Cossa, had an antique shop across from the entrance to the Fitzwilliam Museum and a few hundred yards from my college, Pembroke. I visited his intriguing place every week; it was an easy stop after studying at the Fitzwilliam or even on my way home from the more distant university library. I might buy a small piece of china or a bit of eighteenth-century silver. On one occasion I found, and bought (for £10), two large pen-and-wash drawings of the Bay of Naples, from the sea and from land, by Edward Lear. They were my first drawings and still hang one over the other above the sofa in the living room of my apartment in New York. In each of my homes, I have found that these drawings must occupy a similar position in my sitting room; when the two drawings by Lear have thus been hung (after having been tried in many other places), I can begin to hang the other works of art.

* * *

GRAPHIC WORKS ON PAPER, those that reveal the line rather than shading or coloring, have been from the first my principal passion. Gradually, however, I turned away from etchings, engravings, or lithographs to drawings. From my first summer in London, I had sought prints by Rembrandt, Dürer, and Blake, and after Pieter Bruegel, or by other celebrated masters; but later, in my first years as a teacher at Princeton, these became too expensive. I also began to prefer the immediacy, the quick and direct observation I found in drawings; I added other British drawings to the two by Lear.

Each year I spent about three months in England, mainly in London, and I grew to know many dealers in English drawings; some had become, like the curators, my friends. The sketches I bought were a natural extension of my formal studies and my professional life: English literature between 1750 and 1850 was the subject of my writing and much of my teaching. I did not, however, wish to collect professionally. The art that hung on my walls was bought simply for my pleasure and that of others. It brought back memories of trips throughout Europe and America. Drawings often marked special occasions; some were gifts or bequests. They were souvenirs of my life, and they did not for me form a collection. I hesitated to use the words *collector* or *collection* in referring to myself or to them. But I came to know and accept my taste and to act upon it—often very quickly. I was not afraid to buy anonymous works, and a number of the best works I bought seemed unidentifiable. After years of living with them, I might suddenly realize who the artist was; others I have looked at for decades and still have no precise idea of who may have executed them.

Some book dealers were early on important sources for my knowledge and for purchases of drawings: John Fleming, Walter Schatzki, and H. P. Kraus in New York, Rosenkilde and Bagger in Copenhagen, August Laube in Zurich, and Christian Nebehay in Vienna. I bought most of my drawings during the summertime. Naturally it was easiest for me to visit dealers when I was on vacation or when I was doing research and writing in London. But when I was teaching at Princeton, I went into New York almost every week, to see theater, hear opera, and explore book shops and galleries, mainly those showing contemporary art but also a few that had earlier drawings for sale, such as Helene Seiferheld, the Este Gallery, and above all, that Aladdin's lamp on Lexington Avenue, the bookshop and gallery of E. Weyhe. There was, however, much looking but not much buying during my early years of teaching. At any price, Mr. Weyhe was reluctant to part with his treasures, such as prints after Bruegel (a special interest of mine) and albums of Dutch and French botanical watercolors. Only after Mr. Weyhe's death was I able to purchase from his daughter Gertrude Dennis a number of Dutch seventeenth-century naturalist watercolors, some of my favorite acquisitions.

The first drawing by an important old master artist I tried to buy was that by Jan Brueghel of the *Castle of Tervueren*. It was in the major summer sale at Colnaghi in London in 1963. I was unsuccessful in purchasing it, but many years later it came to me as a bequest from a friend who knew of my early disappointment. This attempt to break into a world of master drawings led to friendship with James Byam Shaw of Colnaghi, as brilliant a scholar of drawings as anyone I have known. A few years after I failed to buy the Brueghel drawing (actually I intended to acquire it with a friend), I went to Mr. Byam Shaw and told him that I wished to exchange all of my prints and drawings for one drawing by Rembrandt—any drawing, no matter how small. With masterful diplomacy, and in his slow, deliberate way, he assured me that I would probably not be able to obtain even one of postage-stamp size. The Rembrandt school drawing reproduced in this volume is undoubtedly as close to the master as I shall get.

Gradually, by the mid-1960s, I was looking for drawings of various European countries; not until I came to the Morgan Library, however, did I actively pursue artists of the Continental schools. My chief concern, of course, had to be the collections of the Library. On occasion I would come upon a drawing that appealed greatly and helped to open a new world for me but did not seem appropriate for the Library's collections nor its limited purchase funds. My accumulation of drawings, many of which were therefore quite different from those at the Morgan, increasingly became an educational experience, a way of extending my knowledge. Although over these years I wrote more about art as well as literature, I nevertheless did not write about the objects around me.

I have never sought a focus for my collection; I did not wish to say I *must* have that. Yet, not surprisingly, I do have some peculiarities of taste and bias. Portraits and landscapes fascinated me more than historical, mythological, or religious compositions. This is one of the reasons that the Frick Collection has always been my favorite museum. I like very early landscape drawings and immediately react to a scene of an artist sketching in a landscape, especially if it was made about the year 1800. Studies of solitary trees always attract me, so do those of sailboats, beached boats, and boats on land or under construction. Botanical or animal sketches, studies of implements, still lifes, simple objects of work or play—whether quickly noted or carefully and fully delineated—intrigue me. I have always keenly sought after Dutch naturalist watercolors of the seventeenth century, as I have said, and among precise studies of fruit from all countries and times—above all, pears. Interiors, not the literal rendering of an interior, but those that reveal an inner life—*innenleben*—remain important for me, and, for some unknown reason, I buy sketches of unmade beds. I like preparatory drawings for paintings or prints in which the artist has observed from the model, the studio, or the scene before him only a bit of what he needs for the larger, final work. Most of these kinds of drawings will be seen in the following pages.

It was not, however, until I began to help select works for this publication that I realized there really was a focus for the larger part of my collection. William Griswold and I discovered this simultaneously when we together for the first time looked at all of the drawings. The title came to us at once: *The World Observed.*

* * *

THE ARTIST'S literal recognition and documentation of the exterior world is not characteristic of every work represented here. From my youth I have been attracted to some of the stranger shores of art, to the paintings of Bosch and Bruegel as well as to the prints associated with those artists. The drawing by Arent van Bolten in this catalogue represents a different order, sixteenth-century fantasy, rather than direct observation. Blake has also long been a special, intense interest, and I collected his prints, including his commercial engravings, drawings, books of his poetry, and drawings and prints of his associates. These artists so fully created their own world, each has such a precise vision, that one can, I think, continue to speak of a world observed. This also can be discerned in the drawings of Blake's contemporaries, such as Fuseli or Rehbenitz. Sometimes a drawing so sharply registers the original observation that even if it portrays a story or legend, one feels a direct projection from life. In the Rembrandt school drawing of Jacob's dream, that is true of Jacob's face, the way his head rests on the stone he uses as a pillow. It is the expression of the face, the weight of the head, that move me more than the vision itself.

I learned to appreciate these things principally alone, but my knowledge of art not only owes much to curators and dealers but also to collectors, as I have written. In my pursuit of certain artists, I was also encouraged by collectors who played major roles in my life. The two Lear landscapes brought me the friendship of two great collectors of Lear, Philip Hofer and Donald Gallup. My love of Blake, as well as other poets and painters of his time, helped to establish many friendships. In the beginning, from my early days in Cambridge, there was Geoffrey Keynes. Not long after I came to Princeton, I met Paul Mellon. As close friends and guides, both continued to play an important part in my collecting and career through my years at the Morgan Library and until their deaths. From Paul and Bunny Mellon, among many other things, I learned to treasure very small drawings, more intimate in scale, often more intense in impact. In addition, I had such friends as Benjamin Sonnenberg, Rudolf Heinemann, Janos Scholz, and Eugene V. Thaw—amazing collectors of drawings. The joy of collecting continues to be a bond with Gene Thaw, as does the satisfaction of building a private collection in relation to a public one. In recent years I have turned, as he has, for new challenges and pleasures to oil paintings on paper. Of course, I have, year after year, been deeply influenced and helped by my colleagues at the institutions I have served. Books foster special, strong friendships; so do drawings.

* * *

THE DRAWINGS shown here span five centuries and constitute approximately one third of those I now have. They are arranged in roughly chronological order, except for multiple works by a single artist, which are grouped. They may be divided into three sections: 1500–1790, 1790–1850, 1850–1999. At least half are European works from that second, short period, from the end of the eighteenth century to the middle of the nineteenth. They fall between two quite different revolutions, those of 1789–99 and 1848, a period of change and ferment but also one of peace and achievement. There is a wide variety of styles: classical, neoclassical, Gothic, sentimental or austere, Biedermeier or rustic or courtly, and finally, the beginnings of realism. The artists come almost exclusively from north of the Alps but a number of the drawings were done in Italy, though there is only one by an Italian artist. My ideal would have been to concentrate on Northern artists in Italy during the first half of the nineteenth century, but I was unable to focus my collecting that precisely or to find enough drawings to satisfy me.

For this period, the English artists are represented most fully because I have collected this school for the greatest number of years; they are followed by the French, German, Danish, and Dutch. I have not been successful in finding other Scandinavian drawings or eastern European or Spanish works. I have had to depend on associations I have made and have had virtually no opportunity to come across drawings from some of those countries that pleased me. Yet what I have acquired provides a more comprehensive picture than can usually be seen in America of draftsmanship across much of Europe during that extraordinary time.

It is now widely recognized that at the heart of this period, in the two decades preceding the invention of photography, many European artists portrayed the reality, the factuality of daily life. The high art of the previous century, or centuries, was deliberately avoided. The new art was one of modest analysis rather than of idealization or synthesis. In fact, artists often sought a fragmentary subject. They created a simple record of their observation, of the scene before them. It was intimate, unself-conscious documentation.

This clearly defined, narrow pictorial view is especially evident in the works of Danish artists, although among others shown here, from Bidauld in France, to Friedrich and Menzel in

Germany, to Constable and Linnell in England, there may be a similar concern for straightforward statement. This period has been admirably described and illustrated in *Before Photography*, that outstanding exhibition at the Museum of Modern Art and its catalogue by Peter Galassi. They had a profound influence on me, although I had been looking for this kind of art for years, long before I saw the exhibition in New York. (If I could only have owned a Thomas Jones sketch of a wall in Naples!)

Bits of artists' letters, notebooks, and sketchbooks from the early nineteenth century also capture the kinds of images that so greatly appeal to me and are typical of an aspect of drawing and painting between the two European revolutions. A favorite passage of mine is from a moving letter of Constable to John Fisher of 23 October 1821, when he wrote at length about the difficulty of painting skies and the "accidental Effects of Sky—because they always attract particularly." He goes on to recall rivers in the New Forest, parts of the landscape that he cherished there: "Willows, Old rotten Banks, slimy posts, & brickwork. I love such things. . . . As long as I do paint I shall never cease to paint such Places. . . . But I should paint my own places best—Painting is but another word for feeling. I associate my 'careless boyhood' to all that lies on the banks of the Stour. They made me a painter (& I am grateful) that is I had often thought of pictures of them before I ever had touched a pencil. . . ." Many of my early-nineteenth-century drawings were obviously documentary in purpose, but some, I believe, also were done to express the joy of the artist, as Constable expresses it. They show that drawing was an inescapable part of life and feeling. I wish that my collection represented more moods, from ecstasy to despair; I now especially look for works that, unlike sundials, show more than sunny hours.

* * *

To COMPLETE the catalogue, we have one or two drawings from recent years, even the last few months before this volume went to press. I never particularly sought out contemporary works but was happy when I found a drawing, oil sketch, or watercolor that excited me. The most extraordinary aspect of my life since I left the Frick Collection has been my close association with a number of young artists. Most have to live in a way that makes the garrets of *La Bohème* look like rooms at the Ritz. Some of these artists I have known for a few years; others, for only a few months. On occasion I have commissioned something in order to help pay their rent, or I have suggested a subject that I thought might be rewarding for them and for me. The benefits for me have been great.

When all of my time was devoted to teaching and scholarship, I kept most of my drawings and prints in portfolios. When I began to live a good part of the year in New York, I hung more and more of my drawings in an apartment there and kept out the light by shutters and ultraviolet-filtering Plexiglas. Finally my walls were covered, from top to bottom, with no consideration of school, type, size, or medium. There may be as many as seventy drawings on one long wall. A few are changed almost every week, as one goes out on loan, or a new one is acquired, or one might be moved so that I will see it better and afresh. But the two Lear landscapes remain firmly in their place.

In the end is my beginning. My latest acquisition shown here (I only hope that it is not my last) is *Warren Hastings,* a watercolor by George Stubbs. I had never before seen a Stubbs drawing for sale and never expected to own one. My earliest recollection of art—or science—is when I was three; it was probably reinforced by stories from my elder brother. I was looking at a copy of George Stubbs's *Anatomy of the Horse* with my brother in the attic of my grandfather's house in Grand Rapids, Michigan. I later searched for years before finding that work but finally bought a copy once owned by the dukes of Westminster. Now I also have the small portrait of Hastings. Forty years ago, in my first book, I had written about his school days and his famous trial.

The present book and the exhibition it accompanies will, we hope, stimulate an interest in drawings among those who mistakenly feel that it is no longer possible to collect them. Those who love drawings should be encouraged to make them part of their lives.

Charles Ryskamp

CATALOGUE

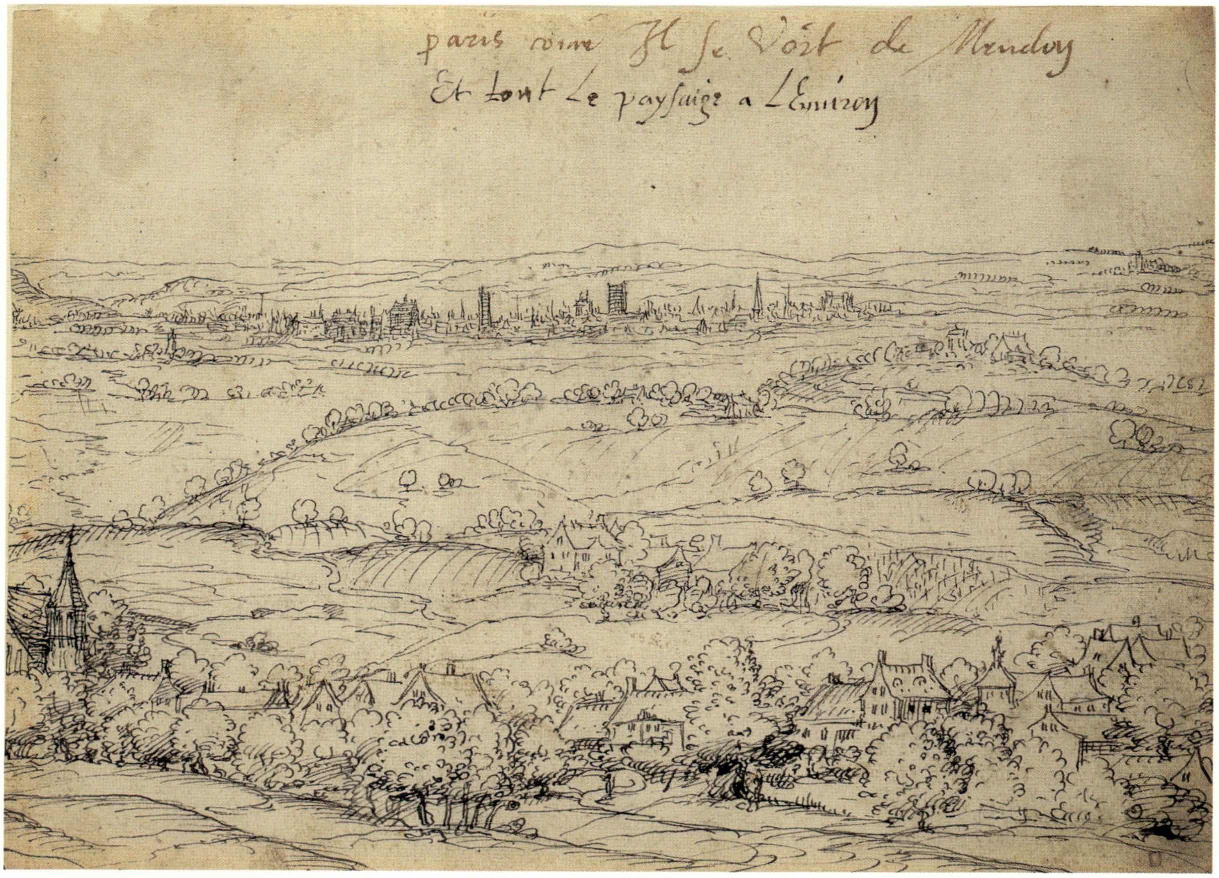
paris come Il se Voit de Meudon
Et tout Le paysaige a LEnviron

I

FLEMISH SCHOOL, SIXTEENTH CENTURY

I

View of Paris from Meudon

Pen and black ink.

5¾ x 8 in. (146 x 203 mm).

Inscribed at upper center, in pen and brown ink, *paris comme Il se voit de Meudon;* in pen and black ink, *Et tout Le paysaige a Lenviron.*

PROVENANCE: François Desmarais (his mark at lower right; not in Lugt); Same Art, Ltd., Paris, 1985 (as French school, 1600); Ian Woodner Family Collection, New York, 1985; sale, London, Christie's, 2 July 1991, no. 137 (as French school, ca. 1600), repr. (not sold); William H. Schab Gallery, Inc., New York.

EXHIBITION: New York 1994, no. 3, repr.

Opinion on the authorship of this drawing has been divided between the French and Flemish schools. Currently thought to be a work of an artist of the Flemish school, the sheet has been linked with the drawings of Cornelis Massys (ca. 1510–1556/57), the son of Quentin Massys and one of the first Netherlandish artists to devote himself to the depiction of landscape. It also has been suggested that the drawing is related to the works of the Master of the Errera Sketchbook, the name applied to as many as three different artists who, in Antwerp in the 1530s and 1540s, contributed to a sketchbook now at the Musées Royaux des Beaux-Arts, Brussels (Washington and New York 1986–87, under no. 8).

Comparing the present work with examples by Massys and the Master of the Errera Sketchbook, neither proposal is entirely satisfactory. Whereas Massys's landscape drawings are distinguished by a delicate handling of the pen and precision in the rendering of details, such as thatched roofs (Zwollo 1965, pl. 4), the present drawing is executed much more freely, with rapid notations of the pen, the rooftops defined with only a few cursory strokes. As for the landscape drawings in the Errera Sketchbook thought to be by an artist in Massys's circle, the careful recording of architectural and topographical details, as in the drawing that appears on page 130 of the sketchbook (Dunbar 1972, fig. 5), connects the Errera landscapes more convincingly with Massys than with the author of the present sheet. KS

JAN BREUGHEL THE ELDER

Flemish, Brussels 1568–1625 Antwerp

2

The Castle of Tervueren

Pen and brown ink and watercolor, over graphite; graphite marks at left probably added by a later hand; ruled border in pen and black ink.

7¼ x 13⅜ in. (185 x 340 mm).

WATERMARK: Grapes (Heawood no. 2154: Antwerp, ca. 1580–90).

PROVENANCE: Colnaghi, London, 1963; W. R. Jeudwine, London; Alice Tully, New York.

LITERATURE: London 1966, under no. 31; Paris and elsewhere 1979–80, under no. 6; Stampfle 1991, under no. 77, fig. 59; Haverkamp-Begemann et al. 1999, under no. 35.

EXHIBITION: London 1963, no. 27 (as Jan Breughel the Elder), pl. IV.

The son of Pieter Bruegel the Elder (ca. 1525/30–1569), Jan Breughel is known for his small-scale history paintings, exquisite flower still lifes, and various types of landscapes, both imaginary and drawn from life. Most of his numerous drawings that have survived are landscapes in pen and ink, often with applications of blue and brown wash.

The view depicted here is of Tervueren, near Brussels, in present-day Belgium. The first castle on the site was built around 1200, and it was rebuilt over the course of six centuries before being demolished in 1781. When Breughel made this drawing, about 1605, the castle was a principal residence of Archduke Albert and his wife, Isabella, the Habsburg regents in the Spanish Netherlands. In 1606 Brueghel was appointed court painter to the archduke, a position he held until his death.

Among drawn versions of Tervueren is a group of three works thought to depend upon a common model executed in the manner of Pieter Bruegel the Elder about 1600 (Haverkamp-Begemann et al. 1999, p. 149)—a drawing by Hendrik Hondius (1573–1650) in the Morgan Library, dated 1605 (acc. no. 1978.40; Stampfle 1991, no. 77, repr.); an anonymous sheet in the Lehman Collection, dated 1604(?) (Haverkamp-Begemann et al. 1999, no. 35, repr.); and an anonymous, undated sheet in Berlin (Kupferstichkabinett, acc. no. 4527; Stampfle 1991, fig. 58). In all three works, the forms of the architecture are massed, the foreground is abbreviated, and the castle is depicted from a vantage point that shows only a portion of the compound along a line from the entryway. In the present drawing, by contrast, the castle is viewed from a greater distance, with the foreground deepened and the composition broadened, recalling the panoramic world landscapes of Pieter Bruegel that were often adopted by his son Jan (Washington and New York 1986–87, no. 22, repr.).

The watermark on the present drawing also is found on sheets printed with the maps of Gerard de Jode (1509–1591), who, after Abraham Ortelius, is regarded as the most important Northern publisher of maps and atlases of the sixteenth century. Breughel may have had access to the same type of paper used by de Jode because in 1599 he married de Jode's daughter Isabella. KS

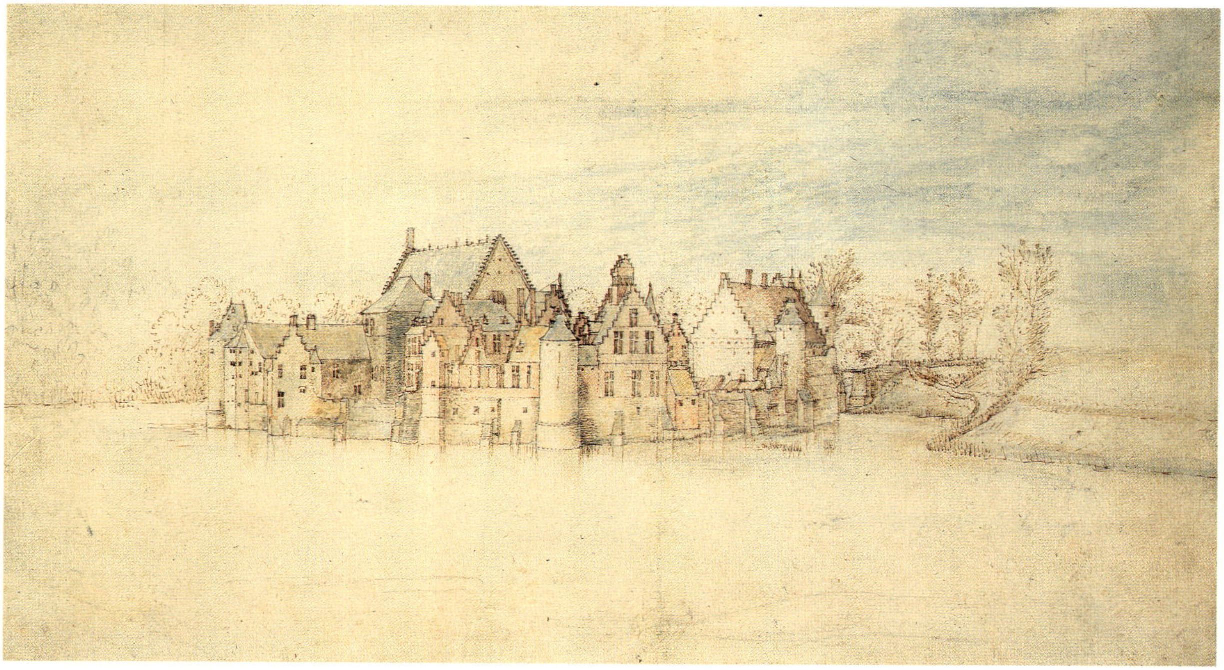

2

ABRAHAM BLOEMAERT

Dutch, Gorinchem 1566–1651 Utrecht

3
Study of Drapery on a Seated Figure

Red chalk, pen and black ink, heightened with white; framing lines in pen and black ink.

7¾ x 6⅝ in. (200 x 170 mm).

WATERMARK: Fragment.

PROVENANCE: Claude Kuhn, Basel, 1987; Kunsthandel Bellinger, Munich, 1987.

EXHIBITIONS: Basel 1987, no. 23, repr.; London 1987, no. 9, repr.

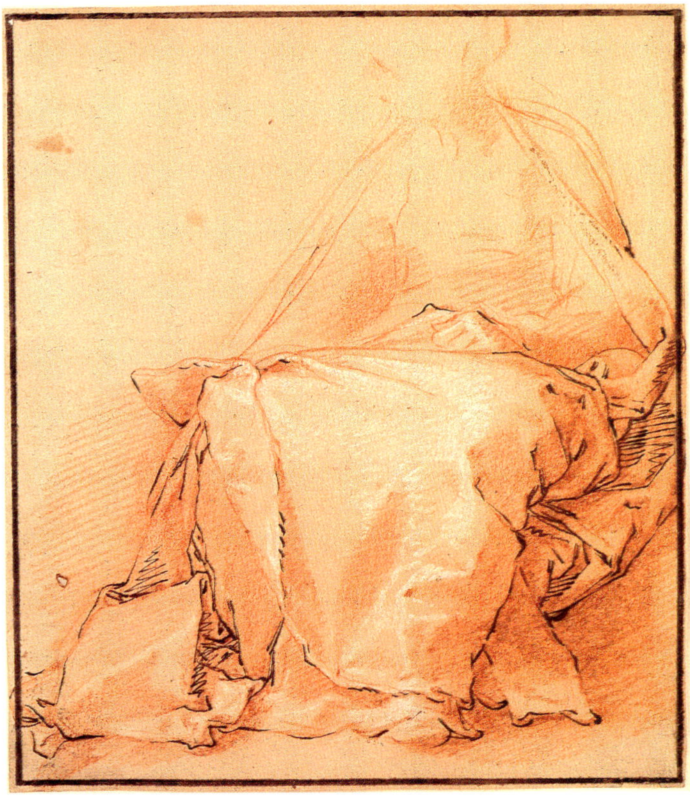

3

This drawing is preparatory for *The Temptation of Christ,* plate 1 of Bloemaert's most widely published series of engraved prints, *The First Series of Hermits (Sacra Eremus Ascetarum),* published by Boëtius Adams Bolswert in 1612 (Roethlisberger 1993, no. 164, fig. 265). While the forms of the top half of the figure and the head are suggested in a series of rapid strokes of the chalk, the treatment of the drapery is fully worked out, as is evident from the close correspondence between the drawing and the print. A drapery study in red chalk formerly with Thomas le Claire (Hamburg 1987, no. 17, repr.) is close in style and motif to this sheet and may also be connected to Bloemaert's preparations for the *Hermits* print. Another red chalk drapery study, recently with Flavia Ormond (New York 2000, no. 6 verso, repr. frontispiece), while not connected directly with the present sheet, may have been executed around the same time. Jaap Bolten suggests that the three studies may share a common French provenance (correspondence, 8 February 2000).

Several highly finished preparatory drawings for Bloemaert's *Hermits* series have survived, among them the group of sheets in Vienna executed in pen and brown ink and brown wash (Benesch 1928, nos. 424–27, pl. 108). An unpublished drapery study in red chalk that is preparatory for *Macarius of Egypt*, plate 9 of the *Hermits* series (information provided by Jaap Bolten; private collection, Paris), may represent a stage in Bloemaert's preparations for the print close to that of the present drawing. KS

ATTRIBUTED TO ALESSANDRO ALLORI

Italian, Florence 1535–1607 Florence

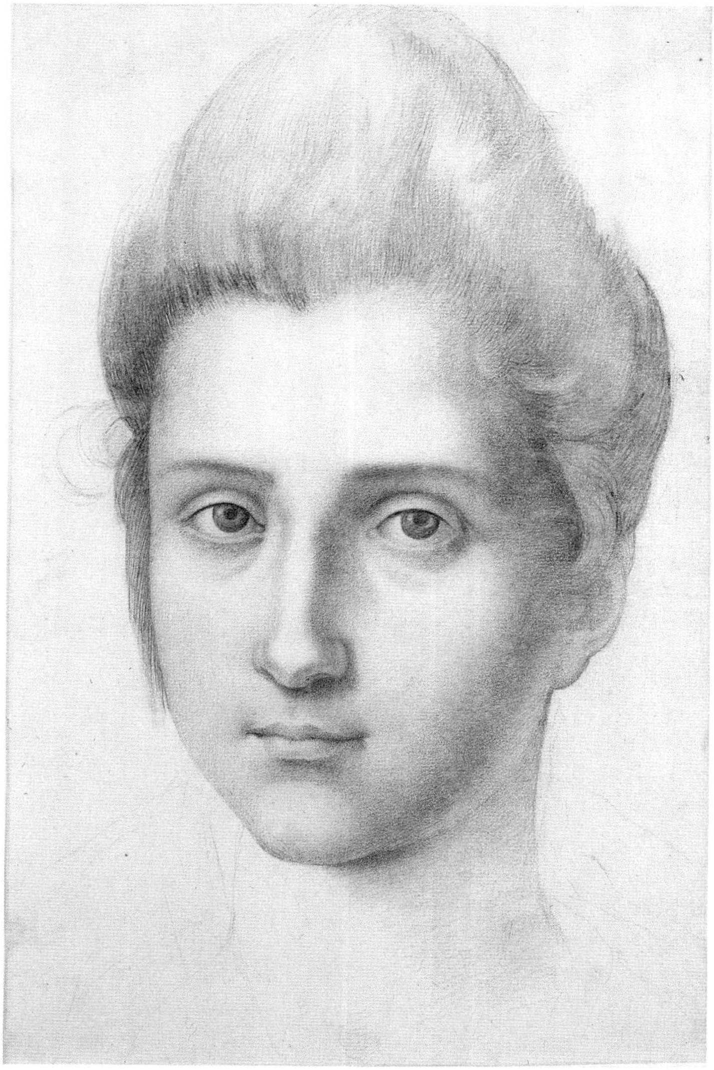

4

4

Portrait of a Woman

Black chalk.

13¼ x 9¼ in. (336 x 235 mm).

WATERMARK: Shield with letter *M* surmounted by a star (similar to Heawood 3026: Rome, ca. 1580).

PROVENANCE: Hans Calmann, London; Colnaghi, New York.

LITERATURE: Smith 1994, p. C29, repr.; De Grazia 1995, p. 175.

EXHIBITIONS: New York 1987, no. 20, repr.; Griswold in New York 1994a, no. 30, repr.

This impressive sheet was attributed to Allori by Jean-Luc Baroni, no doubt because the features of the sitter are similar to those in many of the artist's paintings of contemporary Florentine noblewomen. Nevertheless, few comparable drawings survive from the last quarter of the sixteenth century. Among the portrait studies by Allori that may be adduced in support of the attribution of this drawing are a portrait of a man in the British Museum, London (Giovannoni 1991, no. 177, fig. 411), and two sheets in the Gabinetto Disegni e Stampe degli Uffizi, Florence (Giovannoni 1980, no. 365, pp. 68, 70, pl. 61), and the Frits Lugt Collection, Institut Néerlandais, Paris (Byam Shaw 1983, I, no. 33, III, pl. 42), both of which are concerned primarily with details of costume. However, none of these is as large or highly finished as the present sheet, which—if by Allori—must have been made as an independent work of art rather than as a study for a painting. The hairstyle of the sitter would suggest a date close to 1600. WMG

ALESSANDRO CASOLANI

Italian, Siena 1552–1606 Siena

5
Figure Studies

VERSO: *Male Nude and Three Studies of an Ecorché*

Pen and brown ink, brown wash, over black chalk. Verso: Pen and brown ink.

10¾ x 8 in. (272 x 204 mm).

Inscribed on verso, in pen and brown ink, *buono da questa parte,* and, *vanni.*

PROVENANCE: Private collection, Scotland.

EXHIBITION: New York 1994a, no. 98, repr.

Along with Francesco Vanni (1563–1610) and Ventura Salimbeni (1568–1613), Casolani was the most important and successful painter of late-sixteenth-century Siena. Although this spirited sheet of studies is not directly related to a known painting, it is characteristic of the artist's work as a draftsman. The sketches on the recto may be preparatory for a battle scene, while the handling of the musculature of the standing figure depicted three times on the verso suggests it may be an écorché, an effect reinforced by the pose. Nevertheless, it is by no means clear that the figure has been flayed; the drawing may instead have been made from a live model or from the artist's imagination.

Comparable works include a study of *Hercules* in the Gabinetto Disegni e Stampe degli Uffizi, Florence (Chatelet-Lange 1972, p. 464, fig. 12), and *A Seated Woman and Study of an Ecorché* on the verso of a sheet formerly on the art market in New York and London (New York 1995, no. 11, repr.). WMG

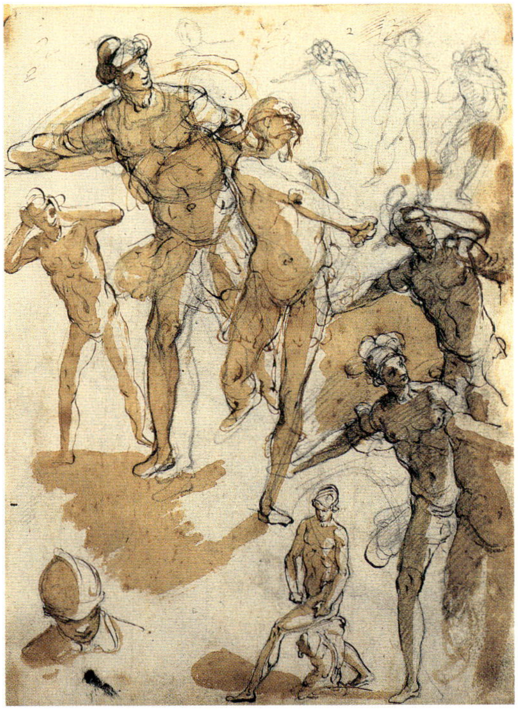

5

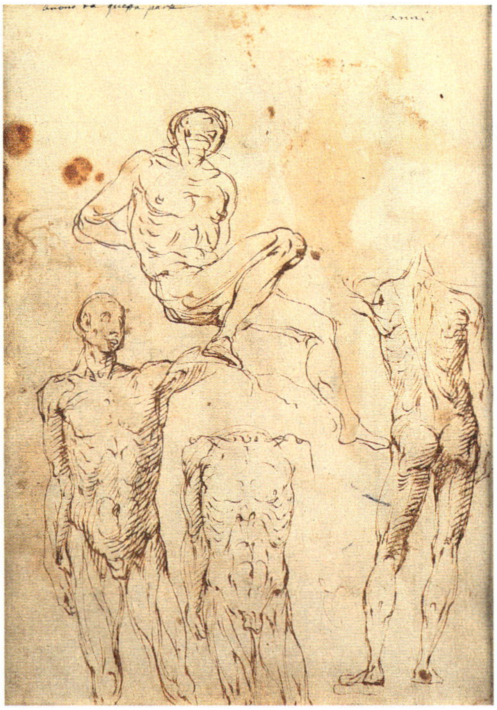

5v

ATTRIBUTED TO AGOSTINO CARRACCI

Italian, Bologna 1557–1602 Parma

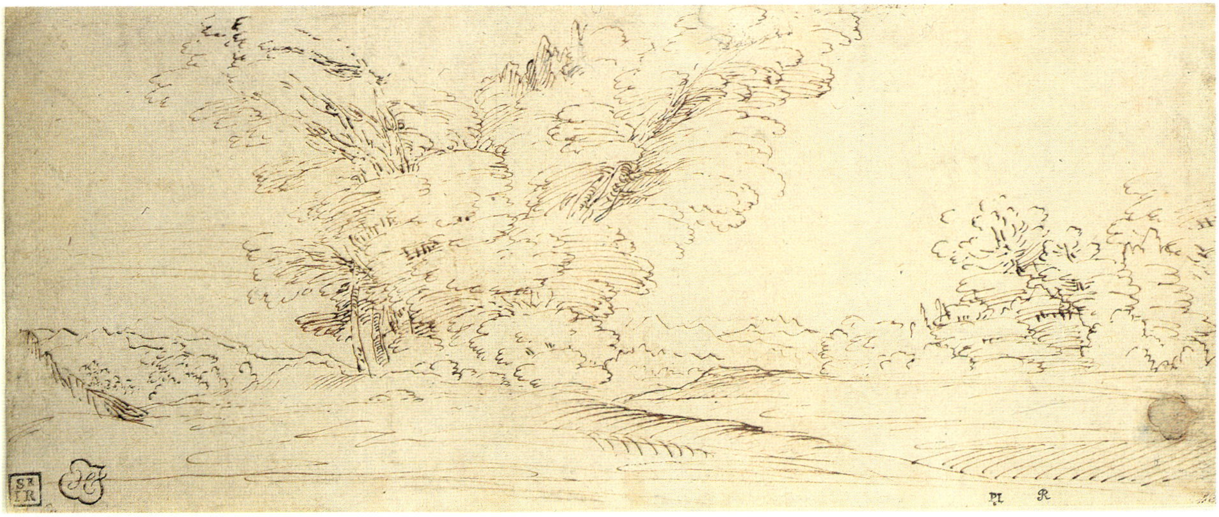

6

6

Extensive Landscape with a Clump of Trees

Pen and brown ink.

VERSO: *Studies of a Seated Male Nude and of a Shoulder and Upper Arm*

Pen and brown ink (the studies of a male nude); black chalk (the study of a shoulder and upper arm).

5½ x 13 in. (139 x 330 mm).

Inscribed on verso, in pen and brown ink, *A. Carra.io.4; Sir* [?] *J. Reynolds coll*^{n} */ WE P 187* (effaced) *27; Formerly in the coll*^{ns} *of S*^{r} *Peter Lely & Jon*^{n} *Richardson Senior.*

PROVENANCE: Sir Peter Lely (Lugt 2092); Jonathan Richardson, Sr. (Lugt 2184); Sir Joshua Reynolds (Lugt 2364); William Esdaile (Lugt 2617); Hamilton Easter Field (Lugt S. 872a); Mr. and Mrs. Lester Francis Avnet; sale, New York, Sotheby's, 18 January 1984, no. 183, repr.; Pietro Scarpa, Venice.

6v

Despite extensive recent scholarship, the attribution of drawings to Agostino Carracci, his brother, Annibale, and their cousin Ludovico remains exceedingly problematic. This is especially true of the landscape drawings, which are among the most innovative of their works on paper but can be deceptively similar in style—not only to one another, but also to works by such slightly later artists as Domenichino (1581–1641) and Francesco Grimaldi (1606–1680).

This sheet seems more likely to be by Agostino than any other member of the Carracci family or workshop.

Indeed the delicacy of the penwork and treatment of the foliage may be compared to those in such drawings customarily given to Agostino as *Landscape with the Rest on the Flight into Egypt* in the British Museum, London (Oxford and London 1996–97, no. 27, repr.).

The cross-legged youths with arms raised above their heads on the verso of the sheet are reminiscent of the Atlas figures that separate the scenes from the story of Romulus and Remus in the frescoed frieze of the *salone* of the Palazzo Magnani (now Credito Romagnolo), Bologna. While Annibale may have worked out the overall decorative scheme of the frescoes, all three of the Carracci collaborated on their execution, which seems to have taken place in 1589–90. The majority of the landscape drawings that have been attributed to Agostino and Annibale Carracci also would appear to have been made during the late 1580s or early 1590s; it seems likely that the present sheet, with its possible connection to the frescoes in Palazzo Magnani, should be dated about 1590.

WMG

FILIPPO LIAGNO (D'ANGELI), CALLED FILIPPO NAPOLETANO

Italian, Naples or Rome ca. 1587–1629 (?) Rome

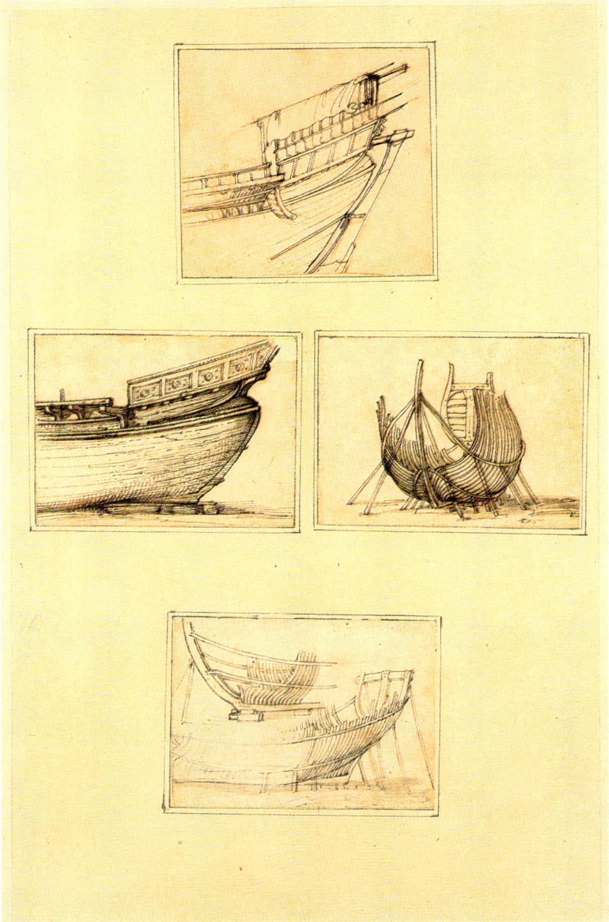

7

7

Four Studies of Ships Under Construction

Pen and brown ink (all four drawings), brown wash (two drawings), over red or black chalk; all four sheets laid down on one mount.

4 x 4½ in. (103 x 113 mm); 3⅜ x 4⅝ in. (86 x 118 mm); 3⅜ x 4¾ in. (85 x 119 mm); 3¼ x 4¾ in. (84 x 119 mm).

WATERMARK: None visible through lining.

PROVENANCE: Lord Northwick; his sale, London, Sotheby's, 24 November 1919, part of no. 21; private collection; sale, London, Christie's, 7 July 1981, no. 91, two of the drawings repr. (attributed to Salvator Rosa).

A pupil in Rome of his father, who seems to have been employed in the great decorative projects commissioned by Pope Sixtus V (r. 1585–90), Filippo Napoletano worked in Naples from about 1600 to 1614. By 1618 he was in Florence, at the court of Grand Duke Cosimo II de' Medici, after whose death the artist returned to Rome. During the mid-1620s, he was again in Naples. Like many other facts concerning his life, the date of Filippo's death is uncertain, but it appears likely that he died in Rome, probably about 1629.

Considerable confusion surrounds the attribution of works to Filippo Napoletano. That he was a painter of battle scenes, marine subjects, and landscapes is certain, but his paintings and drawings often have been erroneously assigned to his contemporary Agostino Tassi (ca. 1580–1644). These four drawings have affinities with the work of both men, but the assured, calligraphic penwork, perhaps inspired by that of such artists as Jacques Callot (1592–1635), has more in common with the style of Filippo than with the draftsmanship of Tassi. The subject, a favorite of both painters, reflects a fashion for marine subjects that was to influence the work of the somewhat younger Claude Lorrain (1600–1682). WMG

SINIBALDO SCORZA

Italian, Voltaggio 1589–1631 Genoa

8

A Guinea Pig

Pen and brown ink.

4 x 7⅞ in. (101 x 189 mm).

Inscribed on verso, in pen and brown ink, *AB / 1730 / In Roma con Licenza / de Superiori / Mio C;* in pencil, *Beaver Anib. Carracci.*

PROVENANCE: Wolfgang Ratjen, Munich; Flavia Ormond Fine Arts Ltd., London.

EXHIBITION: New York 1997, no. 6, repr.

The inspiration for Scorza's carefully observed depictions of animals was the work of Jan Roos (1591–1638), an animal painter who was born in Antwerp and educated by Frans Snyders (1579–1657). Roos moved to Scorza's native Genoa during the 1610s and was active there until his death some twenty years later. Animal painting rapidly became popular in Roos's adopted city, where it was enthusiastically taken up, not only by Scorza, but also by his gifted pupil Giovanni Benedetto Castiglione (1609–1664).

In addition to paintings, Scorza executed numerous drawings. Flavia Ormond noted the similarity of this sheet to a study of a wolf in the British Museum, London (acc. no. 1926-12-14-1). Other comparable drawings are in the Palazzo Rosso, Genoa (Genoa 1990, figs. 22–23), and the Ashmolean Museum, Oxford (Parker 1956, no. 949). In each of these works, the animals are neatly delineated as isolated motifs that might eventually be reused in other contexts. Although the animal in the present sketch does not correspond precisely to a passage in any of the artist's paintings, similar creatures, including other guinea pigs, populate much of his oeuvre (compare, for example, the guinea pig that appears on the right in Scorza's painting *Tortoise and Hare,* in a private collection, Genoa; Bonzi 1964, pl. 1). WMG

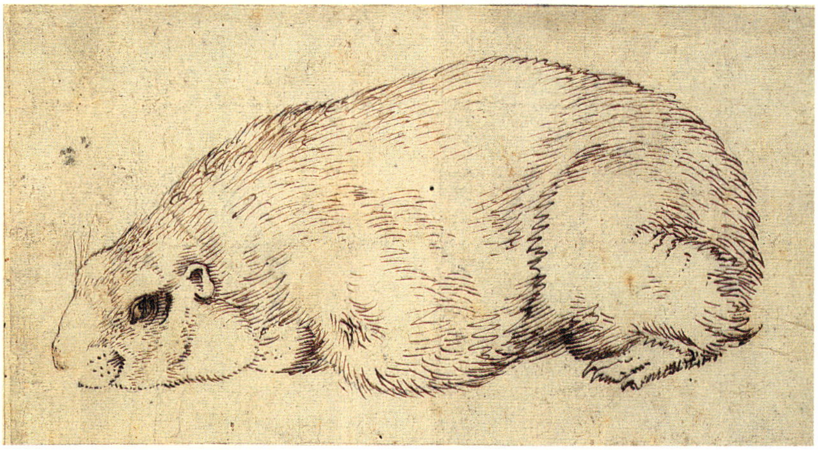

8

ITALIAN SCHOOL, SEVENTEENTH CENTURY

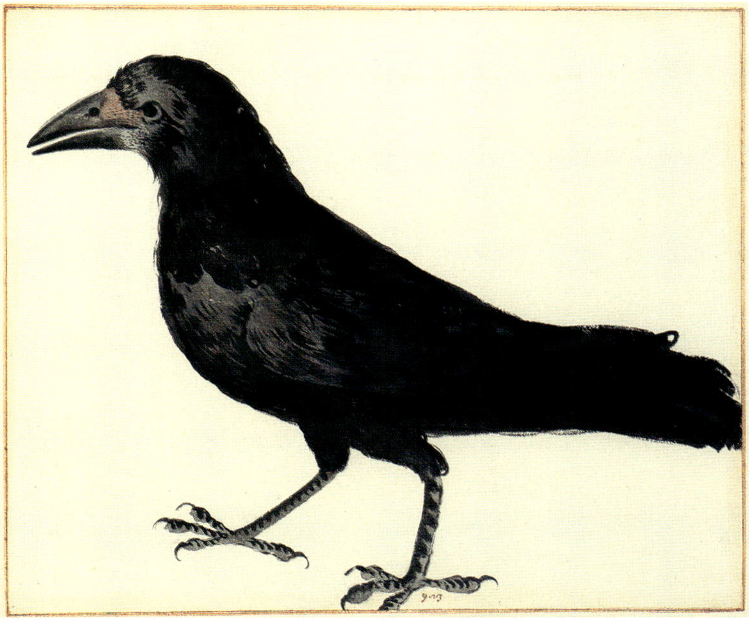

9

9

A Crow

Watercolor and gouache; laid down on old mount.

11 x 13⅜ in. (278 x 337 mm).

WATERMARK: None visible through lining.

Inscribed at lower center, in pen and brown ink, *983*.

PROVENANCE: Cassiano dal Pozzo; by descent to Cosimo Antonio dal Pozzo; Pope Clement XI; by descent to Cardinal Alessandro Albani; King George III; by descent to King George V; William Drummond, London.

LITERATURE: Haskell and Montagu (forthcoming).

EXHIBITION: London 1996.

Among the most remarkable figures of his age, Cassiano dal Pozzo (1588–1657) was for many years a member of the household of Cardinal Francesco Barberini (1597–1679), the powerful nephew of Urban VIII (r. 1623–44). A close friend of Galileo Galilei, Cassiano attained great prominence as a scholar and collector, and his library and private museum were admired throughout Europe. Although never a rich man, he commissioned from Nicolas Poussin (1594–1665) the series of *Seven Sacraments* now divided between Belvoir Castle and the National Gallery of Art, Washington, D.C., and he assembled an extraordinary collection of more than four thousand drawings of antiquarian, architectural, and natural history subjects, which he called his Museum Chartaceum (Museo Cartaceo, or Paper Museum). Cassiano commissioned most of these drawings, either directly from such major artists as Pietro da Cortona (1596–1669) and Pietro Testa (1612–1650), or from other, in many cases now-anonymous, draftsmen.

After his death Cassiano's vast collections passed first to his brother and then to his nephew and grandnephew, who in 1703 sold the Museum Chartaceum to Pope Clement XI (r. 1700–1721). Most of the Museum Chartaceum eventually was acquired from the pope's nephew, Cardinal Albani, by King George III (r. 1760–1820) and is now in the Royal Library at Windsor Castle. Shortly after World War I, however, a number of volumes were sold and eventually dismembered, as a consequence of which many sheets formerly in the Royal Library are now in public and private collections in Europe, the United States, and elsewhere.

The mount and characteristic number inscribed in pen and brown ink on this imposing study of a crow identify it as having belonged to the Museum Chartaceum, which included no fewer than four large-folio volumes of drawings of birds (see McBurney 1989, pp. 549–53). WMG

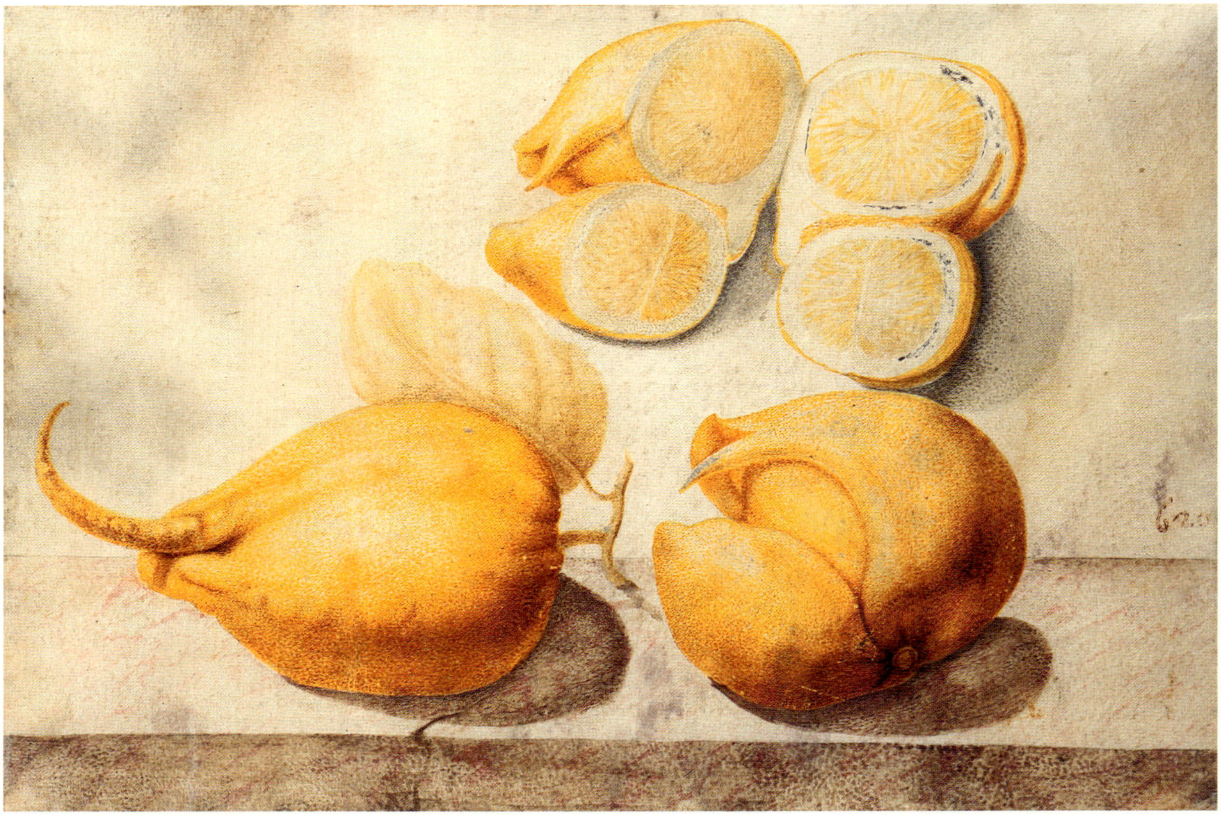

10

GIOVANNA GARZONI

Italian, Ascoli Piceno (?) 1600–1670 Rome (?)

10

Lemon, Citrus limon *(L.) Burm. f.: Two Twin-Fingered Fruits*

Watercolor and bodycolor, heightened with lead white (partially oxidized), over black chalk, on vellum; perimeter mounted.

5¾ x 8¾ in. (145 x 221 mm).

Inscribed near right margin, in pen and brown ink, *620*.

PROVENANCE: Cassiano dal Pozzo; by descent to Cosimo Antonio dal Pozzo; Pope Clement XI; by descent to Cardinal Alessandro Albani; King George III; by descent to King George V; Jacob Mendelson, London; Niall Hobhouse Ltd., London (Italian artist, ca. 1630).

LITERATURE: Haskell and Montagu 1997, no. 98, repr.

This drawing represents two twin lemons and two transverse sections of a third. Hybrid and misshapen fruits were of particular interest to Cassiano dal Pozzo, as they were to many of his contemporaries. The digitated double lemons in the present example belong to a sizable group of such fruit recorded in the Museum Chartaceum. See also No. 9.

While the vast majority of the drawings that belonged to Cassiano dal Pozzo remain anonymous, some can be attributed to artists of considerable distinction. Pietro da Cortona and Pietro Testa contributed drawings to the Museum Chartaceum, and so, too, did the peripatetic still-life painter Giovanna Garzoni, who is perhaps best known for the detailed watercolors of fruit, vegetables, and flowers that she executed on vellum for the Medici. Many of these survive in the Palazzo Pitti, Florence. The present sheet, unquestionably from the Museum Chartaceum and convincingly ascribed to Garzoni by Charles Ryskamp, is one of very few works by the artist to have entered an American collection. WMG

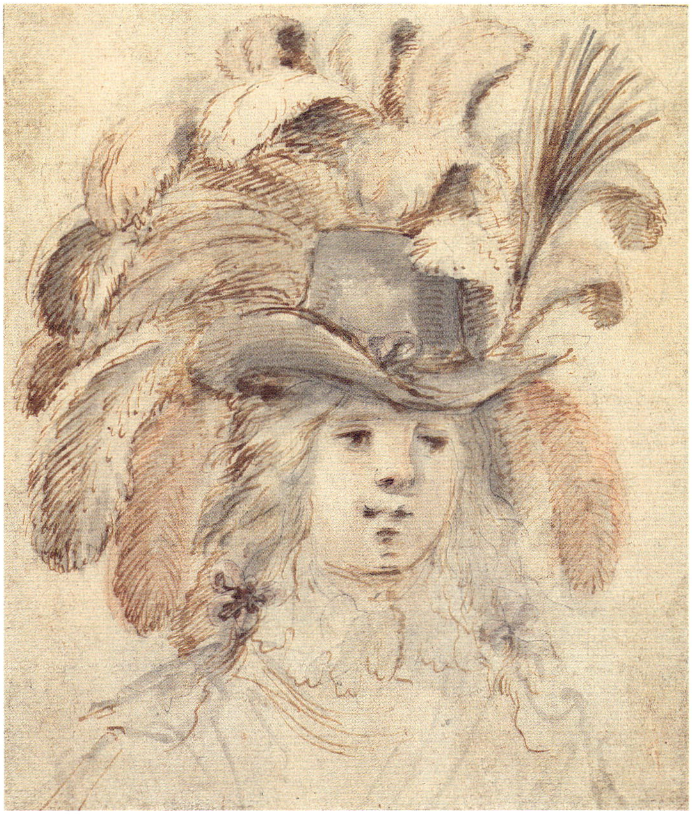

11

STEFANO DELLA BELLA

Italian, Florence 1610–1664 Florence

11

Young Cavalier Wearing a Plumed Hat

Pen and brown ink, watercolor, over traces of graphite. Lined.

5⅝ x 4⅞ in. (144 x 123 mm).

PROVENANCE: Edward Croft-Murray, London; by descent; Smithson and Williams, London; Hazlitt, Gooden and Fox Ltd., London; Thomas Williams Fine Art Ltd., London; private collection; sale, New York, Sotheby's, 12 January 1994, no. 173; Thomas Williams Fine Art Ltd., London.

EXHIBITION: London 1989, repr. on cover.

As a young man, della Bella taught himself to draw by copying the prints of Jacques Callot (1592–1635). In 1633 he traveled to Rome, and six years later he moved to Paris, where he was to remain until 1650. After returning to his native Florence, he worked extensively for the court of the grand dukes of Tuscany.

During a career that spanned less than forty years, della Bella produced more than a thousand etchings, as well as several thousand known drawings, most of which are studies in pen and ink for his prints. Other sheets can be connected with his activity as a designer of costumes for the theater and for the festivals that were so much a part of seventeenth-century life. Such drawings include full-length costume studies (see Massar 1970, pp. 243–66, pls. 1–21) as well as a number of bust-length sketches of figures in elaborate headgear, drawn either in chalk or with the pen, in most cases with the addition of watercolor.

This drawing is close in style and motif to two bust-length studies of cavaliers in plumed hats in the City Museum and Art Gallery, Plymouth, which, like the present example, probably were made in connection with festivals (London 1979, nos. 46–47, repr. p. 64). All three drawings may be dated to the period of the artist's maturity, when the influence of Callot that permeates his early work had given way to a freer, more personal style. WMG

ATTRIBUTED TO CORNELIS DE VOS

Flemish, Hulst ca. 1584–1651 Antwerp

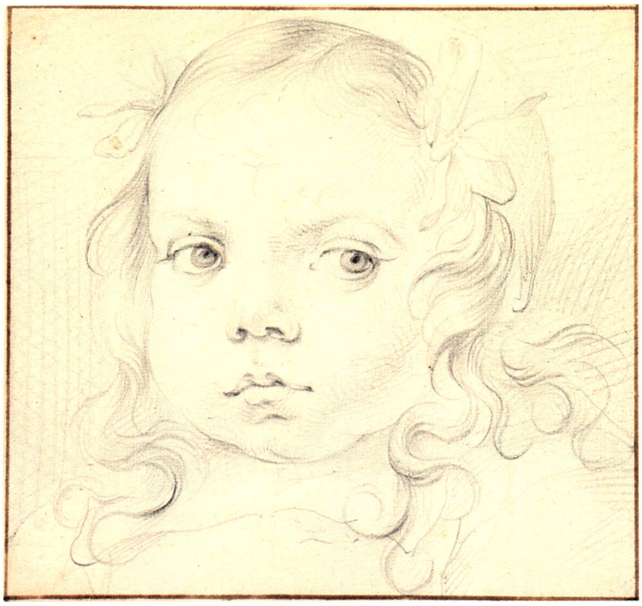

12

12

Head of a Girl

Graphite, extraneous touch of red chalk (at corner of figure's right eye); framing lines in pen and brown ink.

4½ x 4⅞ in. (115 x 124 mm).

WATERMARK: Eagle in a wreath (close to Churchill no. 499: 1631).

PROVENANCE: Unidentified Dutch collector; Jane Cleaver, 1789; by descent to A. C. M. B. Scott, Esq.; his sale, London, Christie's, 8 October 1974, no. 158 (as Netscher; this information according to Richard Day); Richard Day Ltd., London.

EXHIBITION: Munich 1995, no. 1, repr.

De Vos, considered one of the best portrait painters of Rubens's school, is known for his life-size portraits of the wealthy families of Antwerp. He made something of a specialty of children, representing them in accordance with the new attitude toward children—that is, not as miniature adults, but as individuals with distinct personalities (see, for example, *Portrait of a Family,* Koninklijk Museum voor Schone Kunsten, Antwerp; Van der Stighelen 1990, no. 63, repr.).

Drawings by de Vos—mostly portrait heads of children, in chalk—are rare, and apparently only one (formerly Deiker collection, Kassel; Kassel 1930–31, no. 247) can be directly connected with a painting by the artist (*The Artist's Two Daughters*, ca. 1622, Gemäldegalerie Staatliche Museen Preussischer Kulturbesitz, Berlin, acc. no. 832; Greindl 1944, pl. 4). Moreover, there is a lack of consensus on many of the sheets attributed to the artist. Among the drawings securely ascribed to de Vos—for example, *Head of a Young Girl,* in the Lugt Collection (acc. no. 4787; London and elsewhere 1972, no. 118, pl. 75), and *Study for the Heads of Two Boys,* in the Musée du Louvre, Paris (acc. no. 20.200; Van der Stighelen 1989, fig. 6)—the handling is different enough from that in the present sheet to cast doubt on the attribution. In both the Lugt Collection and Louvre studies the features of the faces are more freely drawn, with swift strokes of the chalk imparting a freshness and vitality lacking in the present sheet.

The subject of this work, which was included in an album of drawings compiled by an anonymous Dutch collector in the early eighteenth century, bears a resemblance to the young girl depicted in *Portrait of Mathilde Lintermans, the Wife of Jan Bierens, with Two of Her Children*, a painting by de Vos, dated ca. 1630, in the Los Angeles County Museum of Art (Glück 1933, p. 338, repr.). The girl in the painted portrait, who faces left, appears to be the same age as the present subject. The form of her chin and mouth are very close to the present sheet, and the steady, unsmiling gaze and broad, flat planes of her face are to be found there as well. The similarities suggest that perhaps a pupil of de Vos recorded the likeness of his master's subject. KS

ATTRIBUTED TO HENDRICK AVERCAMP

Dutch, Amsterdam 1585–1634 Kampen

13

Fishing Boats in an Estuary

Pen and black ink and watercolor over black chalk; framing lines in pen and brown ink. Verso: preliminary compositional sketch, in black chalk, of a riverfront townscape.

4½ x 7¼ in. (115 x 184 mm).

WATERMARK: Horn (similar to Churchill no. 316).

Inscribed on verso, at lower left, in graphite, *vliger fé*.

PROVENANCE: Johann Conrad Spengler, Copenhagen (1767–1839; Lugt 1434); his sale, Copenhagen, 8 October 1839, no. 1544? (as Abraham Storck); a nobleman, according to an inscription on the old mount; Richard Day Ltd., London (attributed to Simon de Vlieger).

This drawing probably was made in preparation for a finished work in pen and watercolor or gouache, either as a detail in a larger composition or fully worked up unto itself. Avercamp was one of the first Dutch artists to execute large numbers of finished landscape drawings, and as early as 1613 he is known to have sold watercolor landscapes to collectors (Brussels and elsewhere 1968–69, no. 2, cited in Amsterdam and elsewhere 1991–92, under no. 25). A drawing closely comparable to this sheet is *A Fishing-Smack Frozen in the Ice* at Windsor Castle (White and Crawley 1994, no. 285, repr.), in which a boat of a type almost identical to that in the present sheet occupies the near foreground, while houses sketched in outline in graphite are set directly behind.

Fishing Boats in an Estuary, which evinces a muted calm characteristic of drawings by Avercamp, was formerly attributed to the marine painter Abraham Storck (1644–1708), whose coastal scenes bear only a superficial resemblance to the work of Avercamp—for example, *Coast Scene with Numerous Ships* in the British Museum (Bernt 1958, no. 555, repr.), in which the boat at the center of the composition is similar in form to the boat at the right of the composition of the present drawing. KS

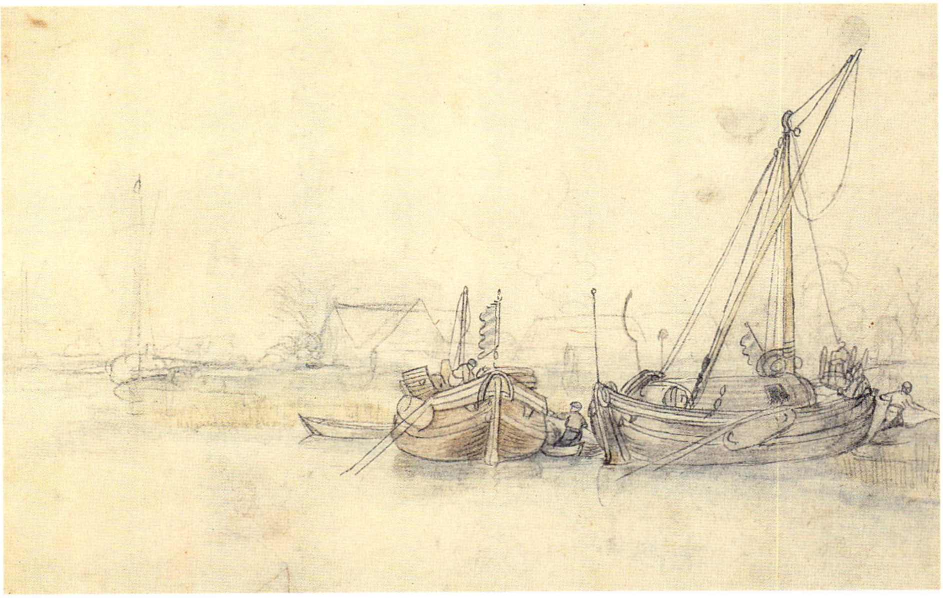

13

JAN VAN DE VELDE II

Dutch, Rotterdam or Delft ca. 1593–1641 Enkhuizen

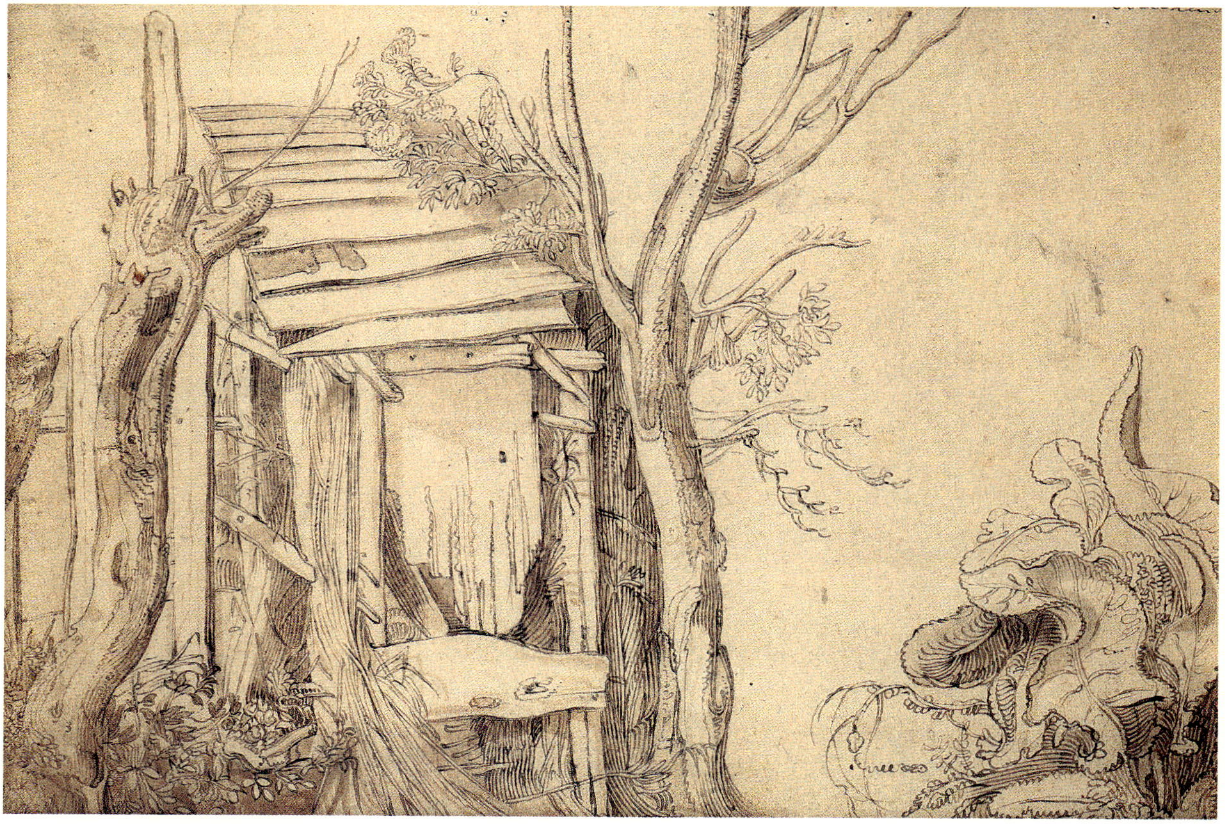

14

14

Dilapidated Hut; Plant Study to the Right

Pen and brown ink, brown wash; extraneous dot of red sealing wax at lower right; the hut incised for transfer.

7 3/16 x 10 5/8 in. (183 x 270 mm).

Inscribed at upper right, in pen and black ink, *Mechlin;* on verso, at center, in graphite, *e* [*c*?]; at lower right, in black chalk, *Sp. 20* [*25*?] *CXI;* and at lower right corner, in graphite, *15*.

PROVENANCE: E. V. Thaw and Co., New York.

Van de Velde the Younger was a member of the circle of artists working in the Netherlands in the early seventeenth century—including Hendrik Goltzius (1558–1617), Claes Jansz. Visscher (1587–1652), Willem Buytewech (1591/2–1624), and van de Velde's cousin Esaias—who are credited with establishing the Dutch landscape as a subject worthy of depiction in art. Following an apprenticeship with the engraver Jacob Matham (1571–1631), a pupil and stepson of Goltzius, van de Velde enrolled as a master engraver in the Haarlem artists' guild, prior to 1618 making prints mostly after his own designs.

Although some five hundred of van de Velde's prints are known and a considerable number of his drawings—mostly landscapes—have survived, few of the artist's extant drawings were made into prints and few designs made for his early prints survive. This drawing, which Charles Ryskamp identified as the work of van de Velde, is thus an important addition to his oeuvre because he engraved it in reverse in a print (Hollstein XXXIII, no. 327) that includes at the left a man fishing from a boat after a drawing by Willem Buytewech in the National Gallery of Art, Washington, D.C., *Woodland Pond with Fisherman* (acc. no. 1979.76.1; New Brunswick 1983, no. 22, repr.), dated ca. 1617. The print reproduces only the dilapidated hut of the present sheet and not the plant study at the right; indeed, only the hut is incised for transfer.

The print is one of a suite of four landscape designs said to be after Pieter de Molijn (1595–1661; Hollstein XXXIII, nos. 324–27). Although the first print in the group is inscribed *P Molijn. jnv. J. v. velde. excu*, and it and the succeeding two prints form a stylistically coherent group notable for their refined execution, the print that reproduces the present drawing displays van de Velde's characteristic vigorous penwork.

Dilapidated structures were favored elements in landscape drawings and prints by Northern artists beginning in the late sixteenth century, continuing in the vernacular the Italian tradition of depicting antique architectural ruins. In an important early work by van de Velde—*Amoenissimae aliquot Reginunculae, et antiquorum momentorum ruinae* (Some Most Pleasant Landscapes and Ruins of Ancient Monuments), a series of eighteen prints published by Claes Jansz. Visscher in Amsterdam in 1615 (Hollstein XXXIII, nos. 178–95)—the juxtaposition of landscapes and ruins suggests the stature beginning to be accorded the Dutch landscape. KS

ARENT VAN BOLTEN VAN ZWOLLE

Netherlandish, active before 1637

15

Man Astride a Fantastic Animal

Pen and brown ink and brown wash, over traces of black chalk, on tan paper.

4 7/16 x 4 13/16 in. (112 x 122 mm).

WATERMARK: Arms of Wurzburg, partially cut off (Churchill no. 274: 1622).

PROVENANCE: Lord Mark Kerr (1776–1840); by descent to his daughter Letitia Louisa Kerr; by descent to Lord Mark Kerr's granddaughter Lady Helen McDonnell; private collection, Netherlands; sale, Amsterdam, Christie's, 25 November 1991, no. 18, repr.

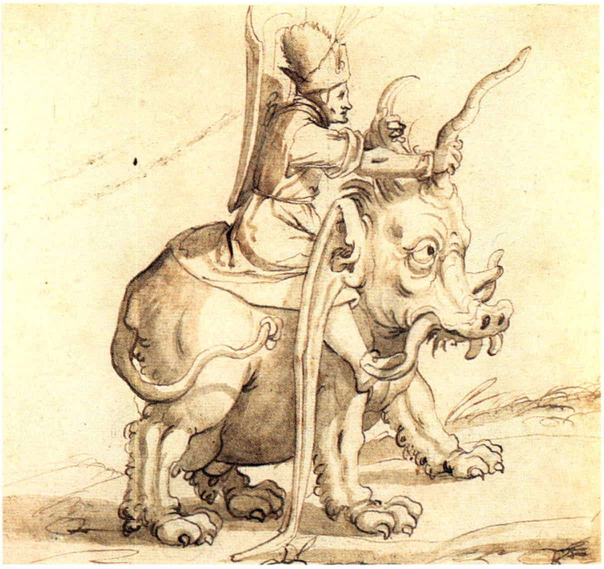

15

A goldsmith and draftsman from Zwolle, a medieval town in the northern Netherlands, Bolten is known today from the over four hundred of his drawings assembled in an album that was acquired by an unknown collector in 1637 (Leeuwenberg 1966, p. 276) and is now in the British Museum (Sloane album 5217; Popham 1932, pp. 97–136, pls. LXI–LXIV). Among the drawings in the album—which include designs for ornament, biblical and mythological subjects, nude studies, figures in contemporary costume, and portraits—are seventy-three drawings of fantastic creatures (Popham 1932, nos. 139–211). One of the many examples that are comparable to the present sheet is *Two Monsters Fighting*, which depicts two birdlike figures with dragons' heads (Popham 1932, no. 185, pl. XLII). Twenty-four prints after Bolten's drawings of monsters are known (Popham 1932, pp. 110–17).

The present sheet was part of an album of Dutch and Flemish drawings assembled in the nineteenth century by Vice-Admiral Lord Mark Kerr and inscribed on the flyleaf, *140 Drawings Collected together by M. Kerr some very valuable,* and, *Letitia Louisa Kerr left to her by her Father.* KS

ATTRIBUTED TO PIETER HOLSTEYN THE ELDER

Dutch, Haarlem 1580/90–1662 Haarlem

16

Lizard and Scorpion

Watercolor and gouache, over black chalk.

8 1/16 x 12 1/2 in. (205 x 318 mm).

WATERMARK: Arms of Amsterdam (Heawood no. 434: Holland, ca. 1685).

Inscribed at lower right, in graphite, *Peter Holsteyn le vieux;* at upper left, *59;* on verso, at lower left, in graphite, *holstein;* at upper right, in black chalk, *84.*

PROVENANCE: E. Weyhe, Inc., New York.

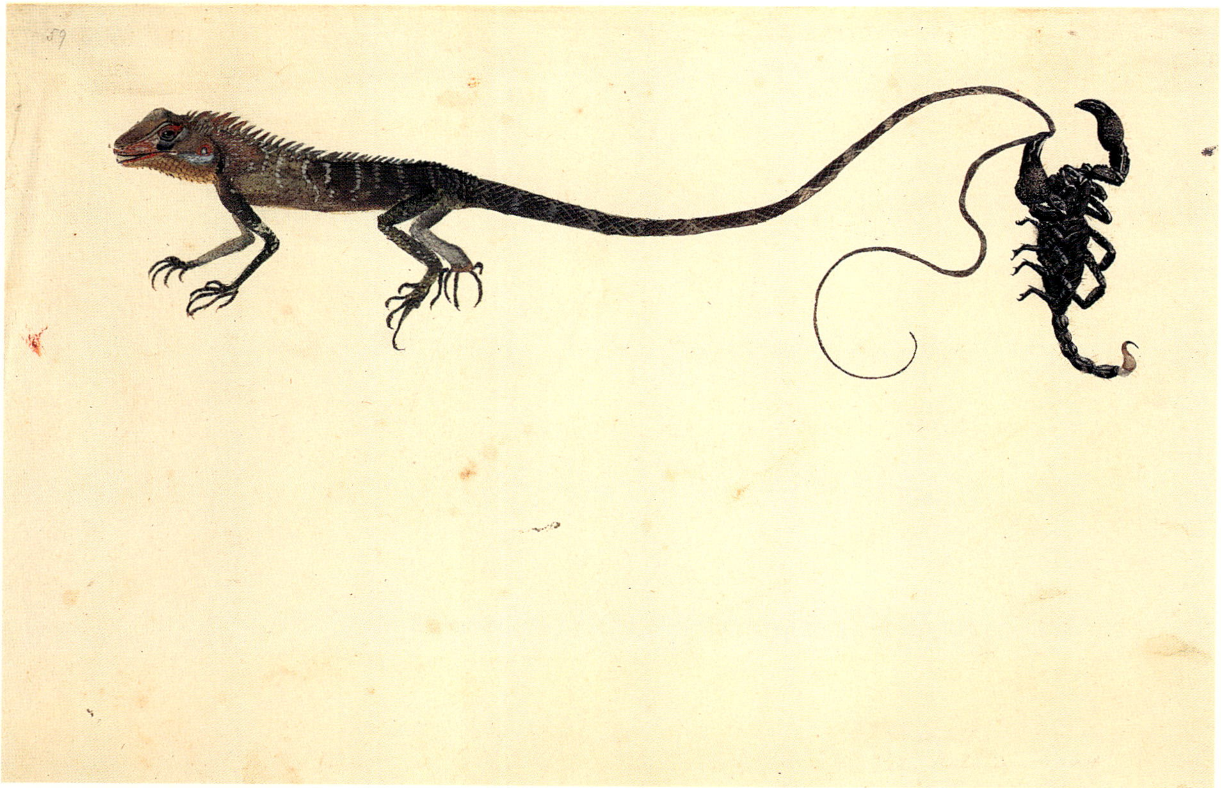

16

Lizards were a popular subject for artists (see No. 24), their patterned forms lending a decorative touch in the margins of medieval manuscripts and still-life paintings with Vanitas themes. In this drawing a scorpion grasps the tail of a lizard in its claw and snaps it to breaking, a life-and-death struggle worthy of Darwin (before the fact).

The drawing, which was part of an album of natural history subjects (see Nos. 24 and 26), has been attributed to the Haarlem painter and draftsman Pieter Holsteyn the Elder presumably because of the inscription, but the different handling of media and space in the depiction of each creature suggests that the sheet was executed by two different artists, neither of whom may be Holsteyn. While the lizard is rendered in an almost folk-art style—its body inert, the forms flattened, its legs dangling unnaturally—the scorpion is more expertly drawn: the rounded form of the claws defined by dabs of color in a stippling effect; the overlapping plates of the carapace defined by chromatically close strokes of dark olive green, dark gray, and black; the hairlike projections on the surface of the body described by exceedingly fine brushstrokes; and the legs on the right side of the creature receding into depth. While the lizard is pictured in profile, rendered horizontally across the sheet, the scorpion is meant to be viewed from slightly above, with the sheet turned ninety degrees to the left. One imagines an artist encountering the drawing with only the lizard depicted, its tail ending (more naturalistically) just at the break, and deciding to alter the composition by elongating the tail and adding a scorpion to battle its prey.

Neither figure is particularly close in style to other works by Holsteyn—for example, *A Lizard,* recently with Hazlitt, Gooden and Fox (London 1990, [n.p.], repr.), and *Studies of Moths and Other Insects,* on the art market in 1988 (sale, Amsterdam, Sotheby's, 14 November 1988, no. 141, repr.), both notable for their naturalism but neither approaching the sophistication of execution of the scorpion. KS

ATTRIBUTED TO DIRCK HALS

Dutch, Haarlem 1591–1656 Haarlem

17

Studies of a Glass Bowl, Baskets, and a Wooden Implement

Oil and watercolor over black chalk, heightened with white, on tan paper; ruled border in pen and brown ink.

8⁹⁄₁₆ x 7³⁄₈ in. (223 x 188 mm).

WATERMARK: Fragment.

PROVENANCE: H. Baron di Triqueti (Lugt 1304); Mr. and Mrs. Hugh Squire; Sven Gahlin; G. S. Abrams; Mr. and Mrs. Winslow Ames (their mark on recto); Baskett and Day, London.

EXHIBITION: London 1981, no. 48, repr.

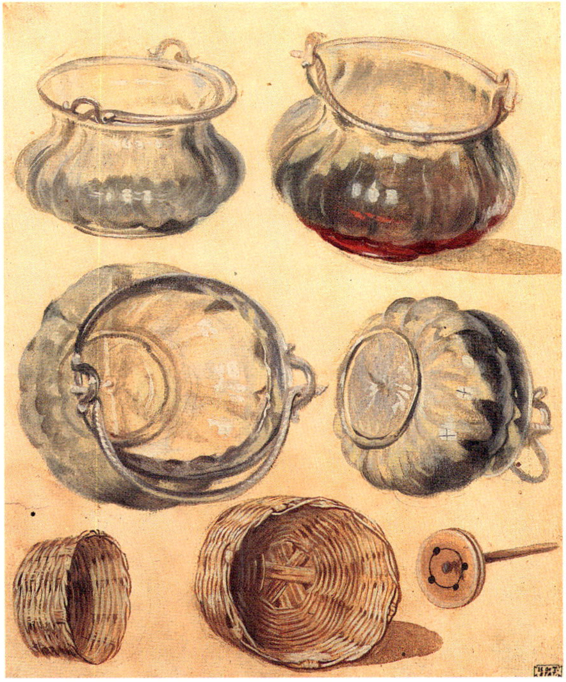

17

As Peter Schatborn has noted, Dirck Hals, the younger brother and pupil of the portrait painter Frans Hals, was one of the few northern Netherlandish artists to make oil sketches, of which thirteen—all figure studies—survive (Amsterdam 1993–94, under no. 298). The present work has been attributed to the younger Hals because of the similarity of handling of the oil paint observed in this sheet and that in two sketches securely attributed to the artist (London 1981, under no. 48): *Sketches of a Man Smoking* in the Rijksmuseum, Amsterdam (Schatborn 1973, p. 111, fig. 9), and *Standard-Bearer* in the Fondation Custodia, Institut Néerlandais, Paris (Amsterdam 1993–94, no. 298, repr.). Known for his paintings of interiors and fêtes champêtres, Hals may have employed the sketches on the present sheet for later use in such works (see, for example, *Elegant Gezelschap*, Frans Hals Museum, Haarlem; Schatborn 1973, p. 110, fig. 5). KS

ANTHONY CLAESZ. II

Dutch, Amsterdam ca. 1616–ca. 1652

18

Seven Tulips with Three Ladybugs

Watercolor and bodycolor.

15 11/16 x 9 11/16 in. (399 x 247 mm).

PROVENANCE: Sale, New York, Sotheby's, 13 January 1993, no. 60, repr.; Thomas le Claire, Hamburg.

EXHIBITION: New York 1994b, no. 26, repr.

This drawing, which Dr. Sam Segal has called a "characteristic work" by the artist (letter to Thomas le Claire, 1 March 1993), probably served as the title page to an album of drawings of tulips, the so-called tulip books that were produced mainly between 1635 and 1650 in the Netherlands. These volumes, of which nearly fifty survive intact, initially were made as sale or auction catalogues for the frenzied business of trading in tulips when bulbs of the most prized specimens commanded prices that exceeded those of Amsterdam's grandest canal-front houses. Later, tulip books recorded the contents of celebrated collectors' holdings (Segal 1998, p. 11).

Such was the popularity of drawings of tulips that seventeenth-century originals routinely were copied by later artists well into the eighteenth century; see, for example, *A Sheet of Studies of Six Tulips*, dated to the eighteenth century, recently on the art market (sale, Amsterdam, Sotheby's, 10 December 1998, no. 123, repr.), which closely follows the present drawing in composition, in the form of the petals and leaves, and in the inclusion of ladybugs on the leaves. KS

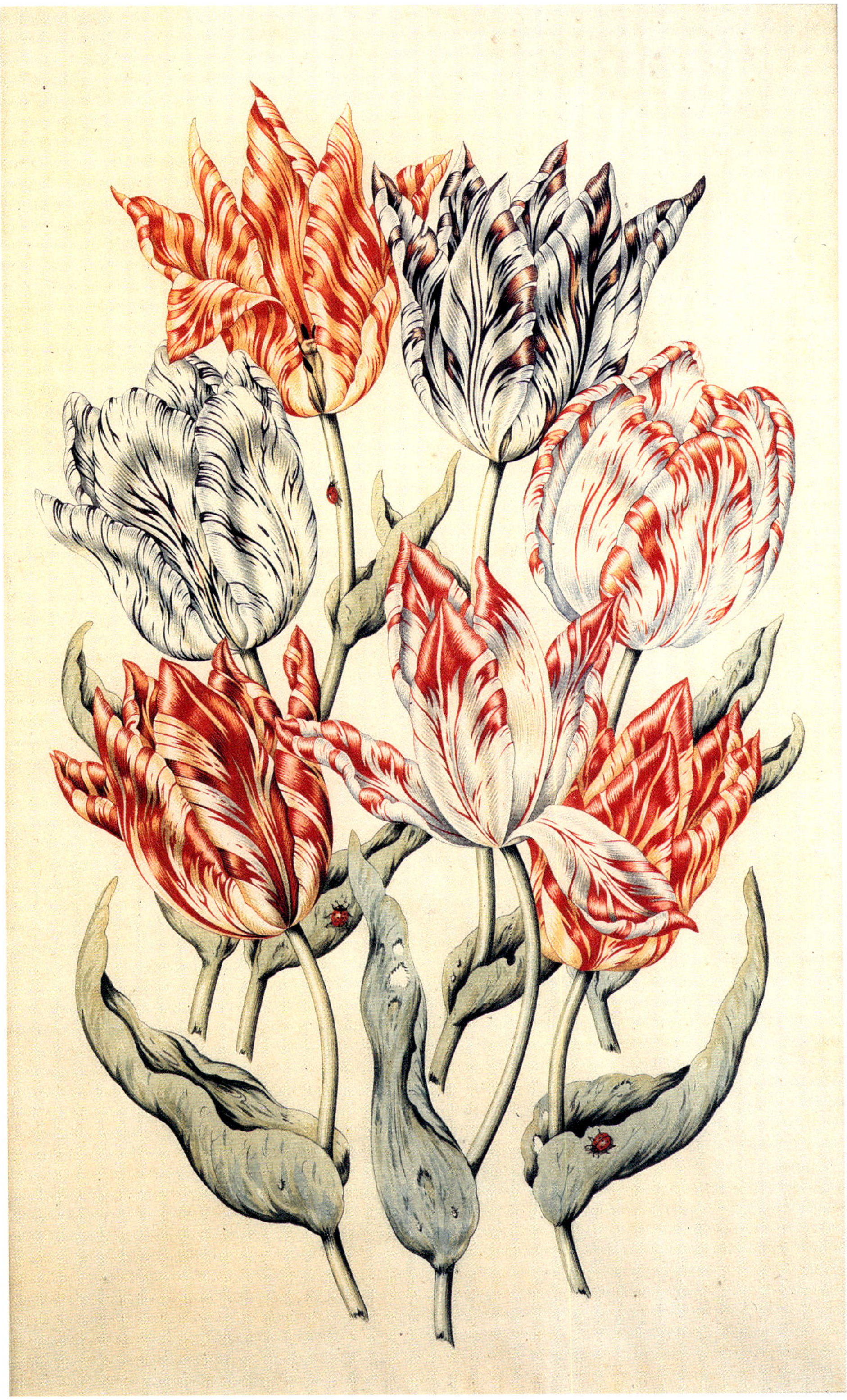

18

NICOLAS ROBERT

French, Langres 1614–1685 Paris

19

An Amaryllis and Two Tulips

Pen and black ink over black chalk; double ruled border in pen and brown ink.

11 x 7⅞ in. (280 x 200 mm).

Inscribed on verso, at lower left, in black chalk, *9* [paraphe? *NR* monogram?]; at lower center, in pencil, *Or. Zeichg v. Nicolas Robert*; at lower right, in pencil, *links unter / nummeriert: 9 / und Signatur?*; at upper left, in pencil, *18 x 26*; at upper right, in pencil, *18.6 x 26*.

PROVENANCE: Niall Hobhouse Ltd., London, 1984.

EXHIBITION: London 1984, no. 3.

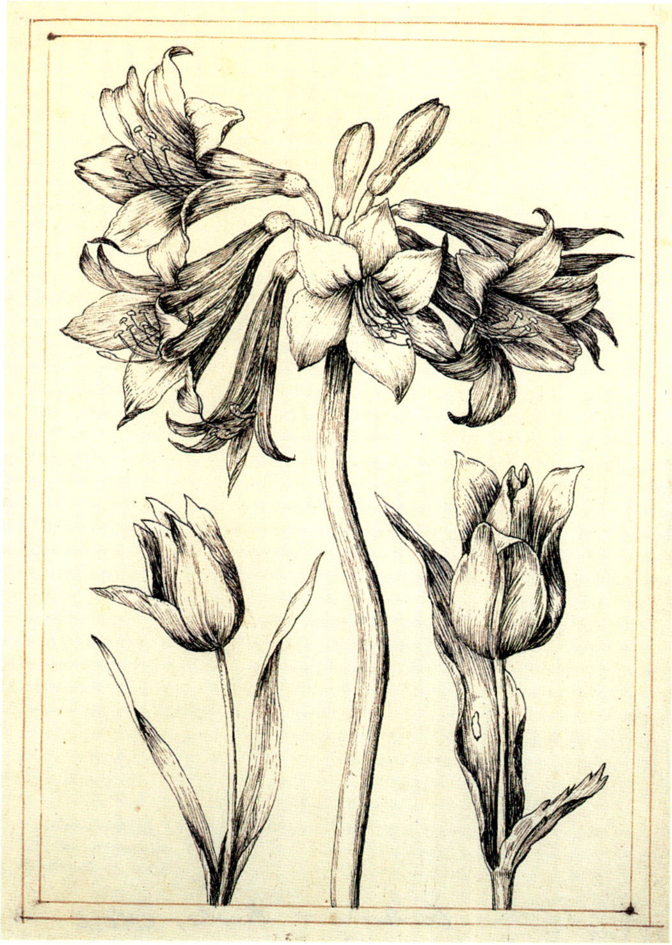

19

It has been suggested that this drawing may have been made in preparation for the artist's book of engravings after his own designs of flowers, *Variae ac Multiformes Florum Species: Diverses Fleurs*, published in Paris in 1660 (collector's files). However, none of the prints reproduces the drawing exactly. Two related works, also possibly made in connection with *Diverses Fleurs*, are *Daffodils and a Lily with a Dragon-Fly* and *Three Irises* (formerly with Niall Hobhouse; London 1984, nos. 4, 5, repr.). The present sheet follows upon the tradition of monochrome drawings in pen and ink of natural history subjects executed by Antonio Pisanello (1397[?]–ca. 1455) and Leonardo da Vinci, works that also may have been made in connection with prints (Blunt and Stearn 1994, pls. 13, 15).

The most famous natural history artist of the seventeenth century and finest of the French flower painters, Robert was commissioned about 1650 by Gaston d'Orléans, brother of Louis XIII (r. 1610–43), to execute a series of drawings in gouache on vellum of the flowers and animals in the royal gardens and zoo at Blois. These works formed the core of the collection known as the *Vélins du Roi*, to which, in a tradition maintained until the French Revolution, the king added twenty drawings each year (Scrase 1997, p. 20). KS

SIR PETER LELY

British, Soest, Westphalia, 1618–1680 London

20

Portrait of a Young Girl

Black and red chalk, heightened with white, on light brown paper.

10 x 7½ in. (255 x 191 mm).

Inscribed on original mount, *Sr. Peter Lely.*

PROVENANCE: Jonathan Richardson, Jr. (Lugt 2170); Sir Robert Price; Thomas Williams Fine Art Ltd., London.

The natural successor to Anthony van Dyck (1599–1641), Lely quickly established himself as mid-seventeenth-century London's preeminent portrait painter. He is also known for a less formal, though sensitive, series of chalk portraits made during the 1650s and 1660s. Executed with great delicacy in black, red, and white chalk, such drawings were not made as preparations for paintings but as independent works of art. A contemporary inventory of his studio made after Lely's death mentions that these subtle portraits or *"craions"* were meant to be put into ebony frames and displayed. Most of the artist's drawings of this category are in English collections, notably six in the British Museum and three at Windsor. In 1983 the British Museum was able to acquire an additional, particularly fine example on the London art market (London 1987a, no. 88, repr.). The Morgan Library has an attractive portrait of a young woman with a cloak lightly draped over her head and shoulders (acc. no. III, 201; New York 1998, no. 8, repr.). While she dreamily gazes into the middle distance to her right, the young woman in the present drawing engages the viewer with an uncompromising stare. Her identity, like that of the young woman in the Morgan drawing, has yet to be determined. CDD

20

AEGIDIUS TILBORCH

Flemish, Brussels ca. 1625–ca. 1678 Brussels

21

Dog Lying by an Oak Chest

VERSO: *Head of a Woman*

Metalpoint on prepared vellum (?).

Sight measurements: 2¼ x 3¹¹⁄₁₆ in. (57 x 100 mm).

PROVENANCE: Sale, Amsterdam, Sotheby Mak van Waay, 21 March 1977, part of no. 104; Richard Day Ltd., London.

A student of the genre painter David Teniers II (1610–1690), Tilborch produced scenes of peasant life and, later in his career, group portraits and interiors of Kunstkammern. In 1654 he became a member of the painters' guild in Brussels, and he ran a busy studio, although no students are known. In 1666 he was appointed keeper of the picture collection at Tervueren Castle, near Brussels, formed under the reign of the Spanish regents (see No. 2).

This work belongs to a traditional type of drawing called *tafeletten,* which are done in miniature on both sides of small tablets of prepared paper or vellum whose surfaces could be reground for subsequent use. Hendrick Goltzius (1558–1617) was among the most famous practitioners of these drawings (Reznicek 1961, no. 321, pl. 433), which were done quickly, on the spot, and meant to be incorporated later into paintings or more finished drawings. Once the surface of a tablet had been prepared for reuse, often only the impression of the earlier drawing remained. Such impressions on the surface of the support may be observed in the present drawing.

Neither the recto nor verso of this work has been connected to a painting by Tilborch, but both subjects are familiar in his oeuvre and often appear in the same painting (see, for example, *Peasants Before an Inn*, present whereabouts unknown; Legrand 1963, pl. 58).

KS

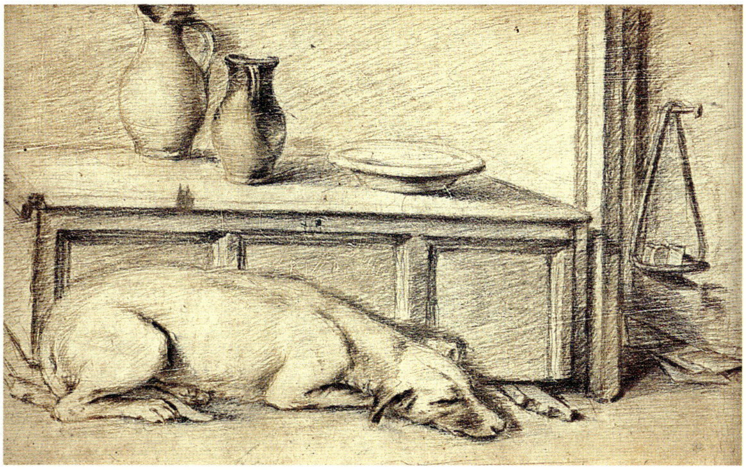

21

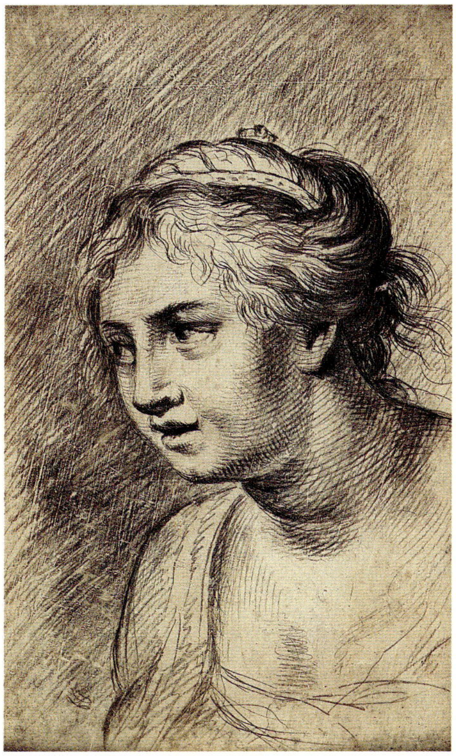

21V

ATTRIBUTED TO WILLEM DROST

Dutch, Germany (?) ca. 1630–after 1680 Amsterdam (?)

22

Dream of Jacob

Pen and black ink on tan paper; ruled border in pen and black ink; miscellaneous marks on verso in pen and black ink.

8 13/16 x 6 1/2 in. (224 x 165 mm).

PROVENANCE: Sir Joshua Reynolds (Lugt 2364); sale, Amsterdam, Christie's, 21 November 1989, no. 35, repr. (as Rembrandt school, ca. 1650); Richard Day Ltd., London.

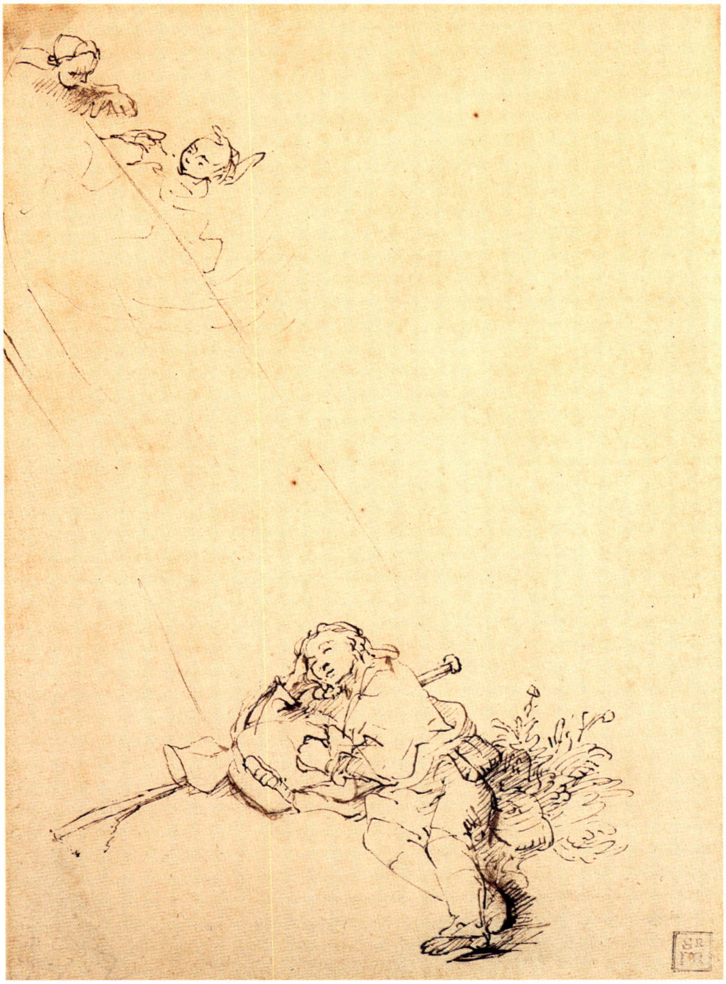

22

First attributed by Werner Sumowski to the school of Rembrandt, 1650 (sale, Amsterdam, Christie's, 21 November 1989, under no. 35), an opinion he has maintained (letter to Richard Day, 6 December 1993), this drawing has been attributed by Martin Royalton-Kisch to the Dutch artist Willem Drost (according to Richard Day, letter to Charles Ryskamp, 16 January 1992).

As Jane Turner has pointed out, an attribution to Drost is highly plausible because of the distinctive parallel hatching for which drawings by Drost are known (verbal communication, June 1999). A closely comparable sheet by Drost is *Hagar and Ishmael in the Desert* (Berlin-Dalem, Kupferstichkabinett; Sumowski 1980, no. 551^{x}, repr.), which bears not only the signature parallel hatching but also the same alternating heavy and light penstrokes as in the present sheet as well as a similarly empty composition.

The subject of the present drawing, which derives from the Old Testament (Gen. 28:10–22), relates the story of Jacob, who, stopping to rest for the night on his way to the home of his uncle in Mesopotamia, where he is to take refuge, falls asleep on some rocks and dreams of a ladder to heaven. The story is a popular one, first appearing in early Christian art. In the present drawing, the ladder is represented simply by two parallel strokes of the pen.

Otto Benesch (1973) notes six versions of the subject by Rembrandt (B.125, B.555, B.557, B.558, B.996, B.1381). In each there is a slight variation in the pose of Jacob, whose head leans variously on one arm, on both arms folded, on arms folded with fingers interlaced, or directly on the rocks. Jacob's pose in the present sheet, leaning on his upraised right arm, is not found among the variations by Rembrandt. KS

VALENTIJN KLOTZ

Dutch, ca. 1650–after 1718 The Hague

23

View of a Fort

Pen and brown ink, on tan paper.

3⁷⁄₁₆ x 5¹³⁄₁₆ in. (87 x 148 mm).

Inscribed and dated by the artist at upper right, *a[e]n d'Kruijsdyck den 27.sbr 1672* (the *7* subsequently altered to a *3*); inscribed at upper left, partially cut off, *44*; on verso, at upper left, in pencil, *F25;* at center, *15*.

PROVENANCE: Sale, Amsterdam, Sotheby Mak van Waay, 18 November 1985, no. 88, repr. p. 104.

In the 1670s Klotz traveled as a topographical draftsman with the army of the northern Netherlands under Prince Willem III of Nassau during the campaign against Louis XIV of France in the southern Netherlands. As Jane Turner has noted (Stampfle and Turner, forthcoming), perhaps it was during this assignment that he acquired the habit of carefully inscribing his drawings as to their date and location.

The view in this drawing is unidentified, but because of the similarity between the fort depicted here and that recorded in two drawings by Klotz inscribed by the artist *Bergen-op-Zoom* (Noordbrabants Museum, Hertogenbosch, acc. no. 27c[1–2]; Mosselveld and van Ham 1973, nos. 97 and 98, repr.), it was thought to be of this Dutch town, located near the border of present-day Belgium. However, Klotz's further inscriptions on the drawings in Hertogenbosch identify the location of the fort as *Kyck in de pot*, which, as may be seen in a military map of 1622 engraved by Claes Jansz. Visscher (1587–1652; Hollstein XXXIX, no. 43), is a steep, bowl-shaped crater at the top of a hill along the river some distance from Bergen op Zoom. The terrain is different enough from that in the present drawing to cast doubt on Bergen op Zoom as the likely view.

Dr. Paul Huys Jannsen has proposed more plausibly that the view is of a gunpowder tower in Schoonhoven, a former military site near Rotterdam that Klotz visited in September 1672 (correspondence, 19 July 1999). An engraving of a ground plan of the city of Schoonhoven dated 1743 (van Berkum 1762) situates the tower on a rampart extending into the canal, one of six such raised fortifications that encircled the island city. Klotz's vantage point is from across the canal, facing the point of the pentagonal rampart, the view foreshortened as it recedes into depth. KS

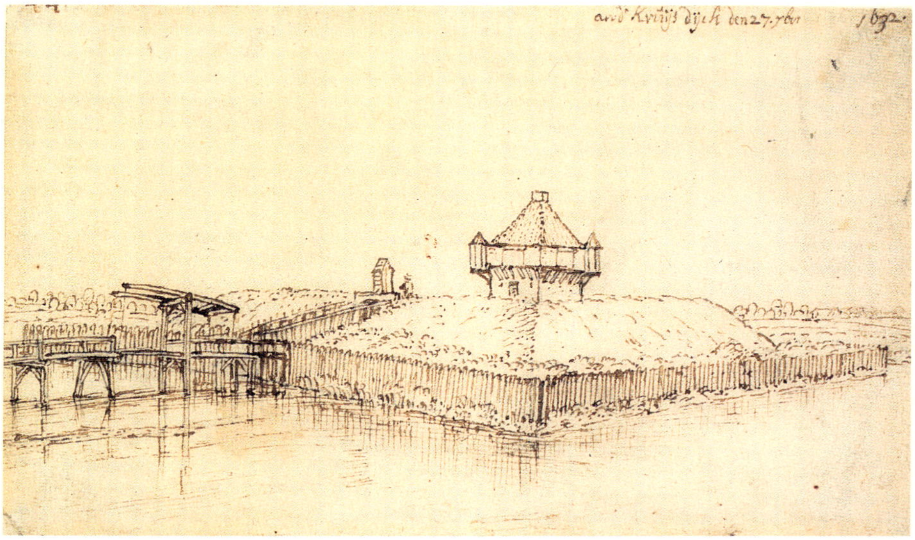

23

ROCHUS VAN VEEN

Dutch, Beverwijk ca. 1640–1708 Haarlem

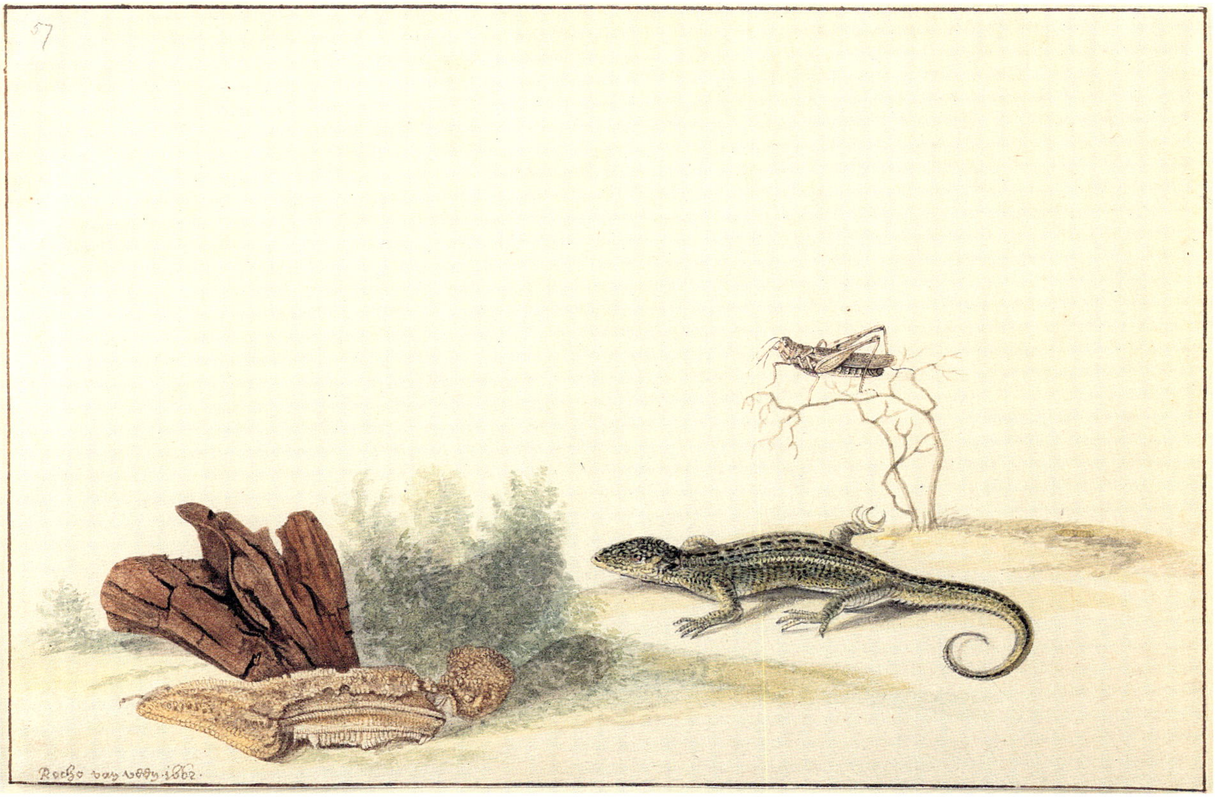

24

24

Lizard and Grasshopper in a Landscape

Watercolor; ruled border in pen and brown ink.

7⅜ x 11⅜ in. (198 x 290 mm).

WATERMARK: Foolscap (Churchill no. 346: seventeenth century).

Signed and dated at lower left, in pen and brown ink, *Rocho van Veen. 1662;* inscribed at upper left, in pencil, *57*.

PROVENANCE: E. Weyhe, Inc., New York.

A naturalist as well as a draftsman, van Veen throughout his life appears to have made drawings of natural history subjects in abbreviated landscape settings. Comparable sheets are *A Dragonfly and a Toadstool* of 1677, in the Abrams collection (Wellesley and elsewhere 1969, no. 39, repr.), and *A Moth on a Branch* of 1681, recently on the art market (sale, Amsterdam, Sotheby's, 10 November 1998, no. 138, repr.). The artist also made drawings of a single subject in isolation on the page—for example, *A Peacock* (sale, Paris, Drouot Richelieu, 16 November 1993, no. 35, repr.). Another drawing of this type, *Buff-Tip Moth, and a Large Yellow Underwing, a Bumble Bee and Another Insect (Nephrotoma Crocata: Linnaeus)*, signed and dated 1665, also was executed on paper with a foolscap watermark (sale, London, Christie's, 25 June 1974, no. 115, repr.).

In recording the creatures of the natural world, van Veen was working in the tradition of Joris Hoefnagel

(1542–1600) and Jacques de Gheyn II (1565–1629), whose drawings melded a high degree of naturalism with sufficient artifice to convey an impression of a faithful representation of their subject (Washington and New York 1986–87, nos. 48, 73, repr.). Van Veen, in this early drawing, has rendered with fidelity the anatomical details of both lizard and grasshopper, but in his placement of them within the landscape—the grasshopper, for example, perches in the tree on its three left legs and only one right leg—indeed, in the landscape itself, has relied perhaps too much on his imagination.

This work once belonged to an album of Dutch drawings of natural history subjects that included the sheet by Willem de Heer and Maria Sibylla Merian and the drawing attributed to Pieter Holsteyn the Elder in the present catalogue (see Nos. 16 and 26). KS

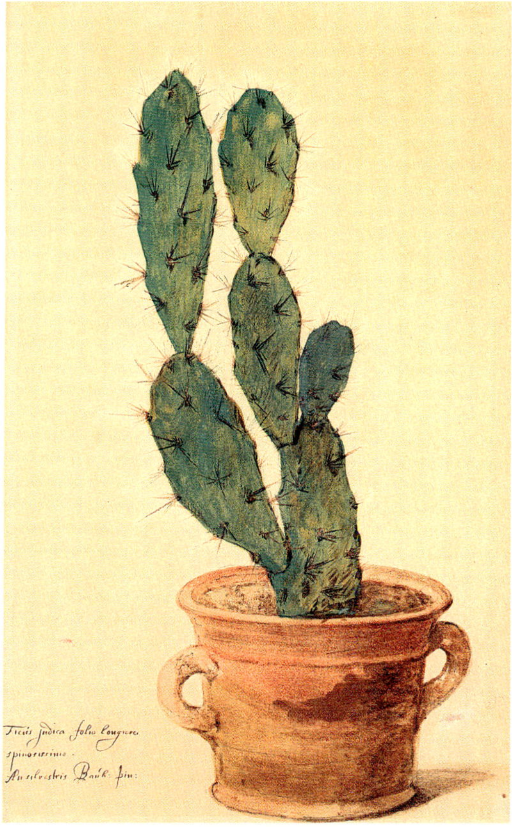

25

ARNOLDUS SYENS

Dutch, Amsterdam 1640–1678 Leiden

25

Cactus in a Pot

Watercolor over black chalk.

13 x 8⅛ in. (330 x 208 mm).

WATERMARK: R[?]B.

Inscribed at lower left, in pen and brown ink, *Ficus judica folio longiore / spinosussimo. / Ansilvestris Ban'h: Pin:.*

PROVENANCE: Professor Alphonse Vorenkamp, Northampton, Massachusetts, 1935; Kate Schaeffer, New York.

EXHIBITION: New York 1948, no. 52.

Syens was professor of medicine and botany at Leiden University, the oldest university in the Netherlands and from the late sixteenth to the mid-eighteenth century the most important institution of higher learning in Europe. Syens took his degree there in 1659 (the subject of his thesis was "De Hydrope"), no doubt working in the university's botanical garden, laid out in 1587 and one of the oldest in Europe.

The subject of this drawing is a member of the species *Cactaceae*, which is native to North and Central America. As Wilfrid Blunt observed, the Dutch colonies in the New World "acted as a great stimulus to botanical draughtsmen" (Blunt and Stearn 1994, p. 131) not only for artists traveling with naturalists recording their findings but also for botanists and artists cultivating and studying species newly imported from the Americas. Such probably was the case for Syens, and his drawing has the straightforward, unadorned character of a working sheet, complete with detailed inscription. Paradoxically its directness has something of a modern quality as well, a style Edouard Manet might have found familiar.

Charles Ryskamp owns a second drawing in watercolor by Syens of a potted plant. KS

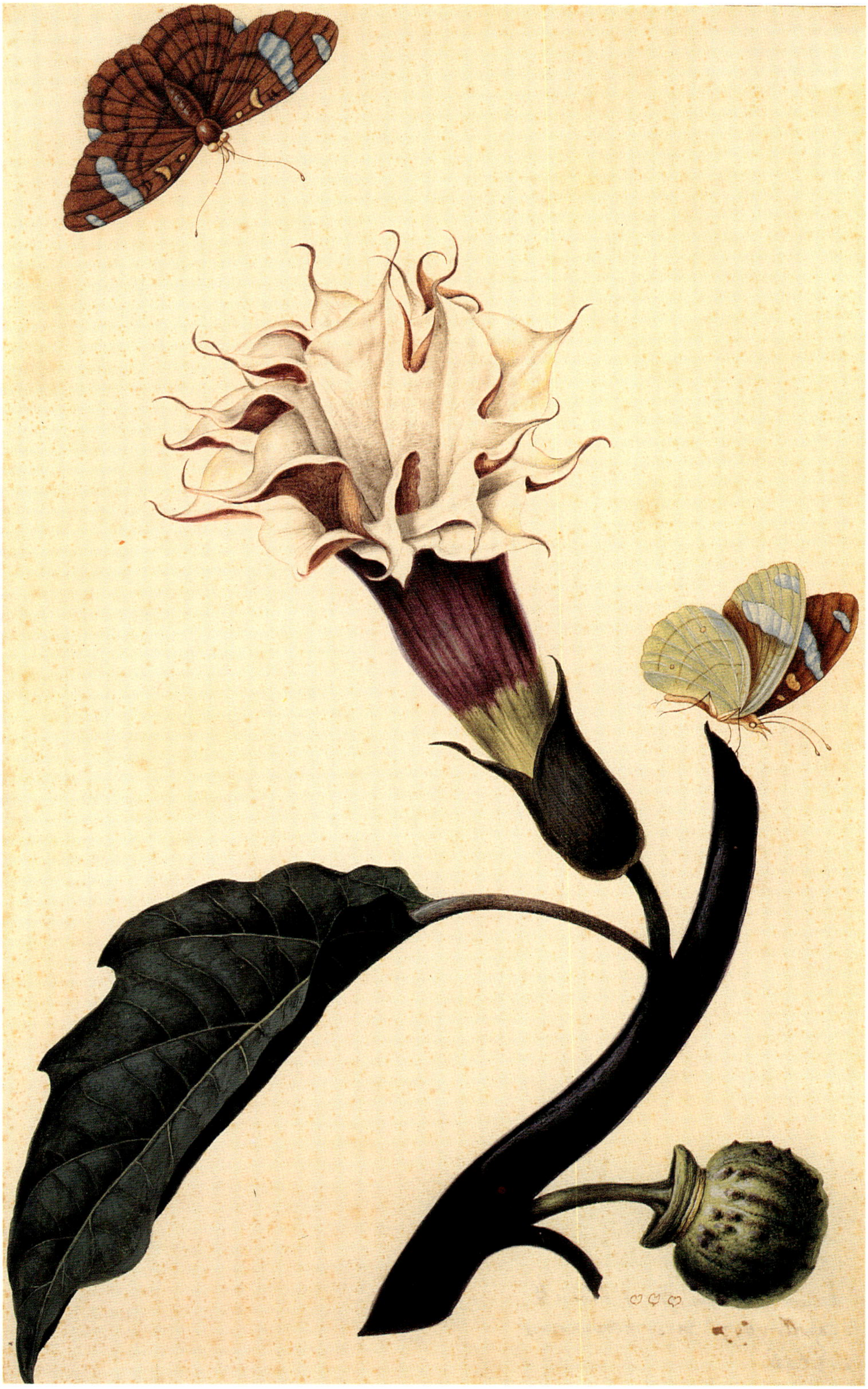

26

WILLEM DE HEER

Dutch, 1638(?)–1681 and

MARIA SIBYLLA MERIAN

Dutch, Frankfurt-am-Main 1647–1717 Amsterdam

26

Datura with Butterflies

Watercolor and bodycolor, traces of gum arabic, over black chalk, heightened with white.

13⅛ x 8¼ in. (333 x 210 mm).

Inscribed at lower right, in pen and brown ink, miscellaneous heart-shaped marks; on verso at lower left, in the hand of Agneta Blok, *datura Contareni. flos et fructus.* [symbol] / *2 capellen by ju.*[r] *m:s: merian. 1695* / *N 628*; at lower center, in black chalk, a paraph [?]; at bottom center, in graphite, *9001* [?].

PROVENANCE: Agneta Blok (1629–1704), Vijverhof, Amsterdam; Valerius Röver (1686–1739), Delft; E. Weyhe, Inc., New York.

According to Dr. Sam Segal (correspondence, 1 October 1985), the present drawing was executed in two stages—the flower in 1679 by the Amsterdam painter Willem de Heer and the butterflies in 1695 by the still-life painter and naturalist Maria Sibylla Merian. The inscription, as Dr. Segal has noted, is written in the hand of Agneta Blok, a passionate collector of exotic plants and flowers, which she cultivated in her famous garden at De Vijverhof, a country house along the River Vecht, about fifteen miles southeast of Amsterdam. Blok's garden contained between 450 and 500 different varieties, many of which she commissioned artists to record in watercolor (Stampfle and Turner, forthcoming). It is not known whether Blok commissioned the flower drawing from de Heer, but Dr. Segal believes it likely that she commissioned the butterflies from Merian. Another drawing executed by both de Heer (flower) and Merian (butterflies) also was formerly in the collections of Agneta Blok and Valerius Röver (whereabouts unknown; Segal correspondence).

While not a true scientific name, *Datura Contareni* refers to the thorn apple, a flowering plant native to India.

KS

ALIDA WITHOOS

Dutch, Amersfoort 1659/60–after 1715 Hoorn

27

Nasturtium

Watercolor and bodycolor, over black chalk.

15⁹⁄₁₆ x 9⅞ in. (396 x 250 mm).

WATERMARK: Fleur-de-lis (close to Heawood no. 1785: 1670).

Signed at lower right, in pen and brown ink, *Alida Withoos;* inscribed at lower left, *Nasturtium Indicum*.

PROVENANCE: William Drummond, London.

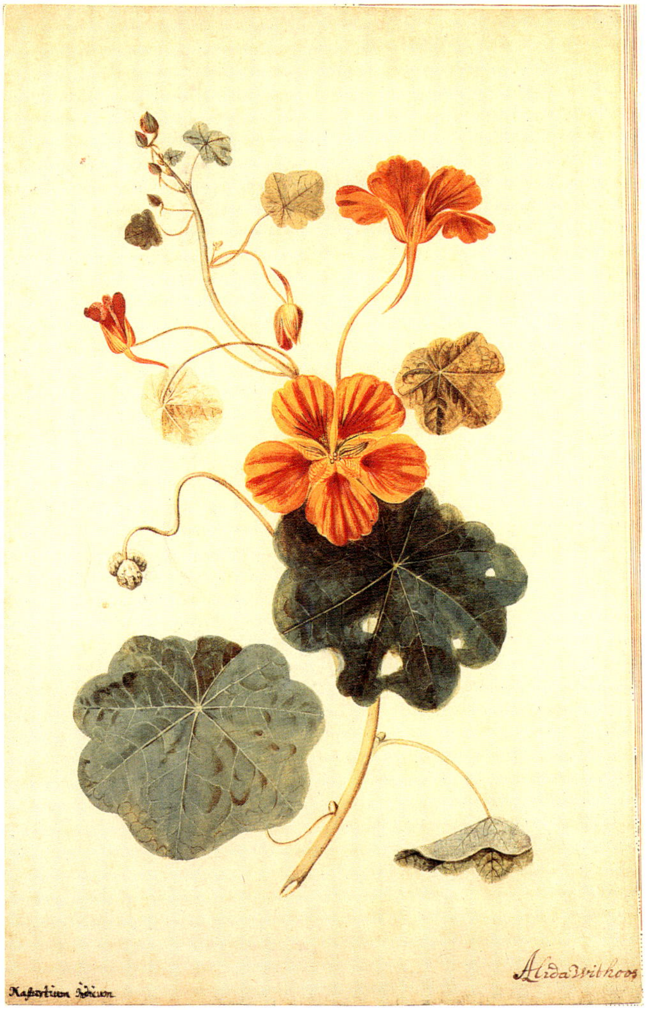

27

Withoos and her brother Pieter are the best known of the children of the still-life painter Matthias Withoos (1627–1703). Likely the pupil of her father, who traveled in Italy and whose patrons included Cardinal Leopoldo de' Medici, she is known for her paintings of still lifes and landscapes, sometimes combined in the same composition. This sheet, a vibrant study of a nasturtium, is exemplary of her botanical drawings in which, aiming to inform as well as to please the eye, she depicted her subject in several stages of growth and from numerous vantage points to show both the upper and lower sides of leaves and blossoms. The nasturtium, a climbing plant native to South America, nonetheless came to be known as "Indian cress," a name to which Withoos's inscription may relate. *An Austrian Briar*, a work comparable to the present sheet, was recently on the art market (sale, Amsterdam, Christie's, 24 November 1992, no. 238, repr.). Withoos probably used such drawings in composing her still-life paintings; see, for example, *A Forest Floor Still Life with Various Flowers* (sale, London, Sotheby's, 9 July 1998, no. 258, repr.). KS

JOHANN ELIAS RIDINGER

German, Ulm 1698–1767 Augsburg

28

Owls

Black chalk.

11½ x 10¼ in. (293 x 257 mm).

WATERMARK: Strasburg bend and lily above initials *C & IH* (Dutch, late seventeenth century).

Inscribed and dated on small strip added at lower center, in black chalk, [illegible], *1748* [illegible]; numbered on verso at lower left, in pen and black ink, *No 1227*.

PROVENANCE: August Laube and Son, Zurich.

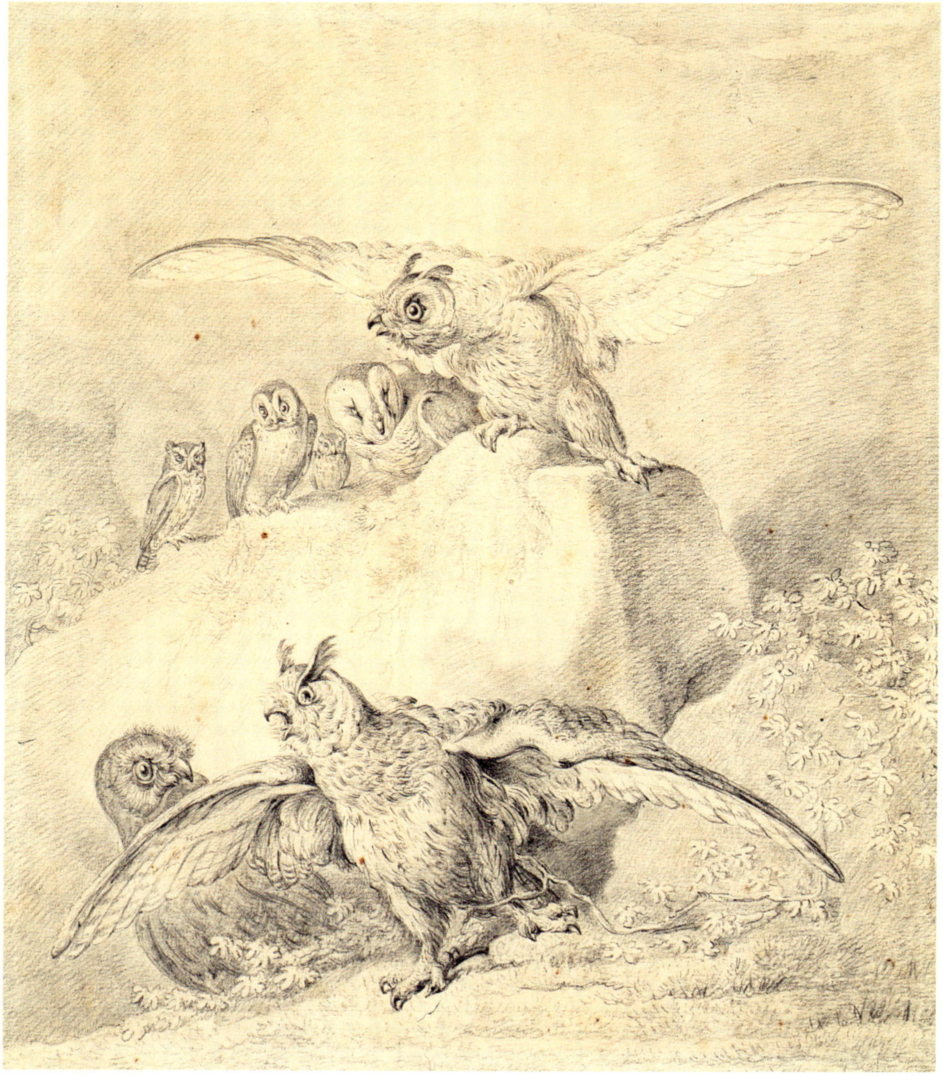

28

The great eighteenth-century German animal artist Johann Elias Ridinger studied with both Johann Falch (1687–1727), the animal and still life painter, and Georg Philipp Rugendas (1666–1742). He founded his own art publishing house in Augsburg shortly after his marriage in 1723 and thereafter was much in demand, executing over 1,200 drawings of animals, mostly preparatory for his own prints.

This lively subject was designed in preparation for a plate in one of Ridinger's animal series. Although some changes were made between the drawing and the print, the drawing was used for the upper portion of the print *Raubvögel und Eulen in Neues Thier Reus Büchl Erster Theil, allerei Art Hunde vorstellend* (Thienemann 1856, nos. 755–62, not repr.). The drawing is in reverse of the print, and the artist made some changes in the placement of the birds and the rocky background. Perhaps a subsequent preparatory drawing is yet to be discovered. The pheasants and peacocks below the owls in the print do not appear in the present drawing. The print, which Ridinger made in 1748, is accompanied by a lengthy inscription in German, which is from Psalm 104:29, *Verbirgst Du Dein Angesicht, so erschrocken sie Du nimmst weg ihren Odem, so vergehen sie, u[nd] werden zu Staub* (Thou hidest thy face, they are troubled; thou takest away their breath, they die and return to their dust). This is followed by a key naming all the types of owls and birds illustrated in the print: *a. der grosse Uhu; b. kleinere Ohr Eule; c. Schleyer Eule; d. Stock Eule; e. Brand Eule; f. grave Eure; g. Schafferchen*[?]; *h. Kautz; i. Gemeine Eshe*[?]; *k. Chine fischer Pfau; l. Kranich; m. Bisam Ente; n. gemeine Tauben; o. Weisse Bisam Ente; p. Diestsicher*[?] *oder Haus*[?]; *q. Keks*[?].

A year later, in 1749, Ridinger executed another series of four plates of birds, including a study of owls. Two preparatory drawings for this series are preserved in Montpellier, and depict owls in their nocturnal habitat and birds of the day (Paris 1974–75, nos. 67, 68, pl. XXXII [*Oiseaux de Nuit*]). Unlike the present work, the Montpellier drawing of owls is horizontal in format (10⅝ x 16⅛ in.; 271 x 409 mm) and is executed in metalpoint and gray wash and heightened with white. CDD

29

Three Hunting Horns (also, counterproof of *Three Hunting Horns*)

Red chalk.

9 x 7 ¼ in. (230 x 183 mm); counterproof, 8 11/16 x 7 3/16 in. (228 x 182 mm).

Numbered on verso of drawing, in black chalk, *H XIX;* inscribed on verso of counterproof, in graphite, *6 Theil pferde / 1 oranien pferd.*

PROVENANCE: Adalbert von Lanna (Lugt 2773); Rudolf von Gutmann (Lugt 2770); Christian M. Nebehay, Vienna.

This drawing appears to be an unused study for one of Ridinger's prints, possibly for one in a series devoted to hunting subjects, since similar horns appear in other prints by the artist. What is unusual here is that its counterproof, which is executed in red chalk, has remained with the drawing for years. To take a counterproof, a piece of damp paper is applied under pressure to the original, resulting in a reverse impression of the drawing. The purpose of such a counterproof is usually to transfer the image to a printmaker's plate. If a print of these particular horns exists, it has yet to be discovered.

At the beginning of the last century, these works passed through two important German collections before entering that of Charles Ryskamp. First, they were owned by Freiherr Adalbert von Lanna, well known for his collection of German Renaissance drawings, and from there it passed into the collection of Rudolf von Gutmann. Gutmann, who purchased the work directly from the von Lanna collection, was one of the most important Austrian collectors of old master prints and books before World War I. CDD

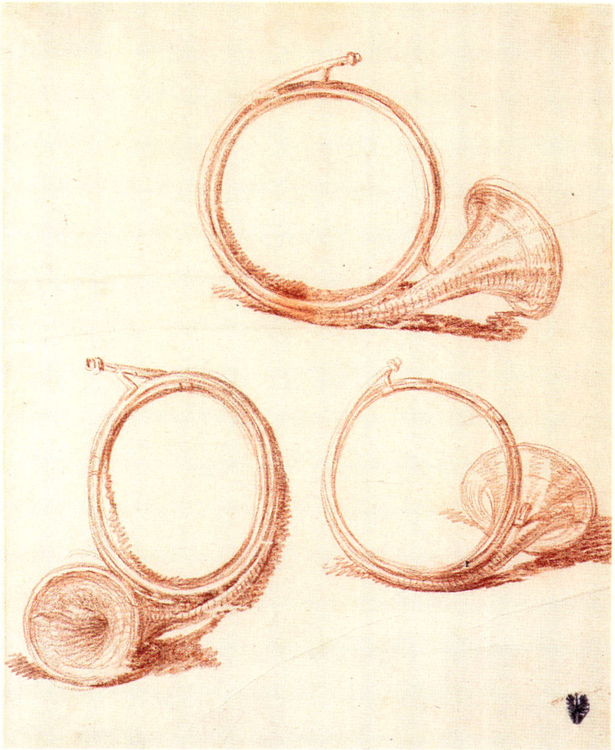

29

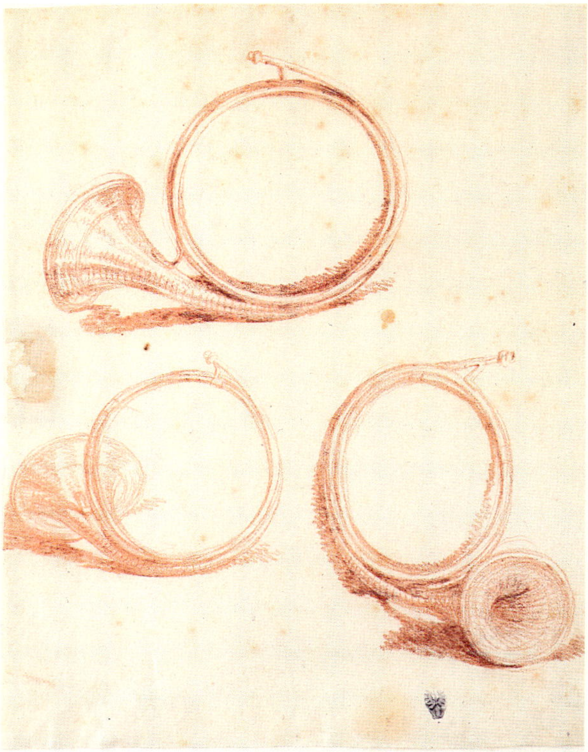

29 COUNTERPROOF

GIOVANNI PAOLO PANINI

Italian, Piacenza 1691–1765 Rome

30

Four Studies for Half-Length Portraits of Men

Red chalk.

8½ x 8½ in. (215 x 217 mm).

PROVENANCE: Flavia Ormond Fine Arts Ltd., London.

EXHIBITION: New York 1998a, no. 18, repr.

Trained in his native Piacenza as a painter of illusionistic architecture, Panini moved to Rome in 1711. There he studied with Benedetto Luti (1666–1724) and Andrea Locatelli (1695–1741) before embarking upon his own, highly successful, career. The real and imaginary views of Rome and its environs for which he is celebrated are populated with numerous small figures, many of which he evidently studied from life. Among Panini's known drawings, a fairly large number depict individual figures, some of which correspond to those in his paintings.

The two most significant groups of such studies are in the Kupferstichkabinett, Berlin, and the British Museum, London, which possesses an album of figure drawings in red and black chalk, occasionally enlivened with touches of watercolor (*Disegni Originali di Gio. Paolo Panini;* acc. no. 197.B.5; some repr. Paris 1992–93, figs. 6–21, 23–26, 59–65). Few of these drawings appear to be portraits, however, and most are more detailed and distinguished by a more feathery handling of the chalk than the present sheet. Nevertheless, the presence of portraits in many paintings by the artist, together with the fact that other drawings plausibly ascribed to Panini vary considerably in style, suggest that the attribution may well be correct. This conclusion is supported by the possibility that the figure represented at the upper left and lower right could be a self-portrait (compare, for example, the self-portrait in Panini's painting *The East Façade of the Castello di Rivoli,* now in the Museo Civico di Arte Antico, Turin; Arisi 1986, pl. 82). WMG

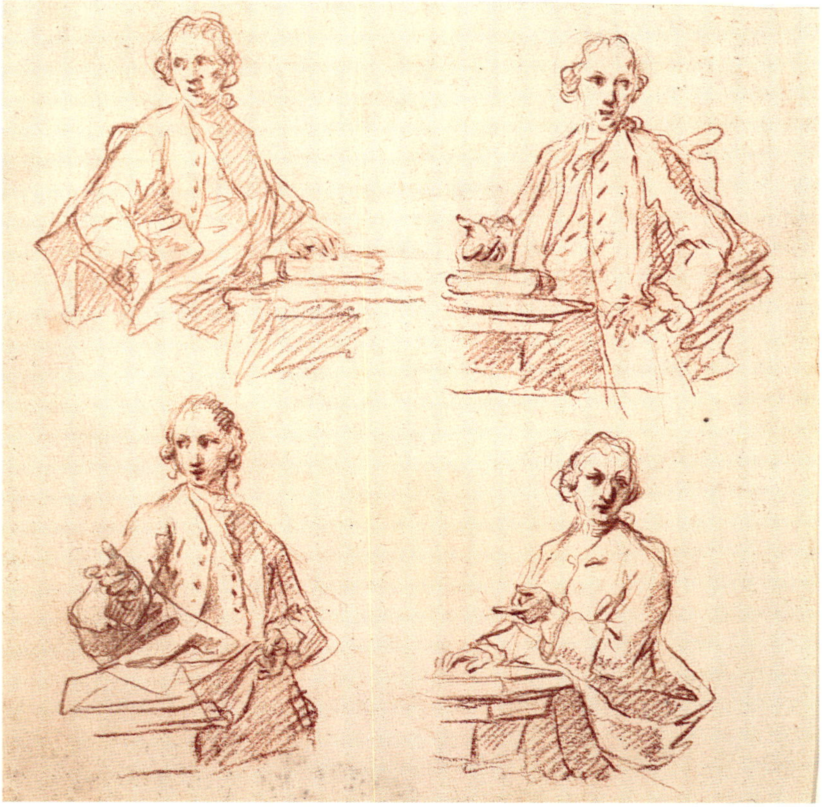

30

LOUIS CARROGIS, CALLED CARMONTELLE

French, Paris 1717–1806 Paris

31

Portrait of the Chevalier de Lézay

Red and black chalk on cream paper.

7⁷⁄₁₆ x 5¾ in. (190 x 146 mm).

WATERMARK: Crown surmounting a shield, fragmentary.

Inscribed on verso, in pen and brown ink, *M^r le chev. de Lézay officier/ du Regt. de dragons de beaufremont / carmontel delin. 1756.*

PROVENANCE: Jean Masson, Amiens (1856–1933; his stamp at lower right; Lugt S. 1494a); his sale, Paris, Galerie Georges Petit, 7–8 May 1923, no. 28, repr.; Richard Owen, Paris; Countess Sala; Charles E. Slatkin Galleries, New York; Stephen Currier; Michael Currier.

EXHIBITION: Paris 1920, no. 182.

Carmontelle began his career as a tutor to aristocratic children in Paris. At the outset of the Seven Years' War (1756–63), however, he abandoned tutoring to work as a topographical artist for Pons de Saint-Maurice. After the war Saint-Maurice introduced Carmontelle to Louis-Philippe, duc d'Orléans, who appointed the artist tutor to his son Philippe, duc de Chartres. Having become an active member of the retinue of Louis-Philippe, Carmontelle organized theatrical productions based upon his own *proverbes* (brief, moralizing plays).

Perhaps Carmontelle's greatest achievement as an artist is a series of watercolor portraits, almost all full-length and in profile, depicting members of the duke's household and courtiers at the Palais Royal and Villers-Cotterets. These drawings provide an unparalleled visual record of pre-Revolutionary Parisian society. Carmontelle carefully mounted and kept the majority of these portraits, which numbered about seven hundred and fifty at his estate sale in 1807, and on occasion he made replicas to give to the sitters. Among his drawings of visitors to the ducal household is a portrait of the young Mozart with his father and sister (British Museum, London).

The present drawing was executed when Carmontelle was working for Pons de Saint-Maurice and made informal, three-quarter-length portrait studies of the soldiers in his regiment, the Dragons de Beaufremont. This sheet, dated 1756, depicts the chevalier de Lézay, an officer of the Dragons. Other studies of soldiers from this period include *Portrait of M. de la Neuville Morfleuri, captain of the Dragons*, 1756 (sale, Paris, Palais Galliera, 11 December 1969, no. 2, repr.); *Portrait of M. de Cawkvonbias of the Beaufremont Regiment*, 1757 (sale, Paris, Hôtel Drouot, 17 December 1900, no. 12); and *Portrait of the duc de Cogni, mestre de campe of the Dragons*, 1757 (sale, New York, Parke-Bernet, 21 October 1970, no. 25). These drawings of soldiers reveal Carmontelle's early propensity for portraiture and prefigure his work for the duc d'Orléans.

JT

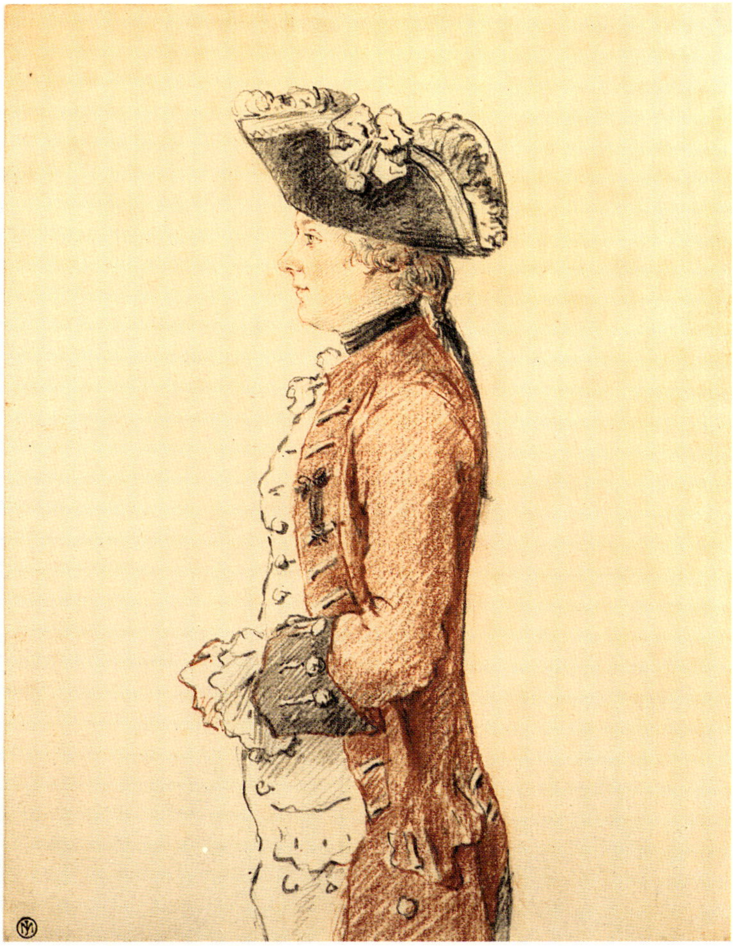

31

FRANÇOIS WATTEAU, CALLED WATTEAU DE LILLE, LE FILS

French, Valenciennes 1758–1823 Lille

32

An Elegant Woman Seated in Profile Holding a Card

Graphite.

10⁹⁄₁₆ x 8¼ in. (268 x 209 mm).

WATERMARK: Shield surmounted by crown.

Signed in pencil, at lower left, *Watteau fils fecit*.

PROVENANCE: G. Mühlbacher (d. 1906), Paris; his sale, Paris, Galerie Georges Petit, 15–18 May 1899, part of no. 314; W. M. Brady and Co., New York.

LITERATURE: Maës 1998, p. 418, under no. FD25.

Watteau, called Watteau de Lille, was a son of the painter Louis Watteau, himself the nephew of the great rococo artist Antoine. François studied under his father at the Lille school of drawing before traveling to Paris on a scholarship in 1775 to study with Louis-Jacques Durameau (1733–1796) and then at the Académie Royale. He returned to Lille and became his father's assistant at the school in 1786, succeeding him as its director in 1798. Eventually he became assistant curator at the Musée des Beaux-Arts, Lille, an institution established in part by his father.

This drawing is a study for an illustration in the *Gallerie des modes et costumes français*, begun in 1778 and published in 1787. The *Gallerie* is considered the first publication devoted exclusively to fashion, illustrated with 445 plates engraved after drawings by artists including Pierre-Thomas Leclerc, Claude-Louis Desrais, and Augustin de Saint-Aubin. Between 1784 and 1787, Watteau contributed 118 illustrations for which fewer than 30 drawings survive. In the *Gallerie* this illustration is entitled *Aussi brillante que Vénus la belle Dorine s'occupe de ce qu'elle a lu dans un billet dicté par l'amour le plus vif; / sa robe est à la Marlborough, et son chapeau à la Charlotte*. The illustration was engraved by Pierre-Charles Baquoy in 1785, which suggests a slightly earlier date for the drawing. JT

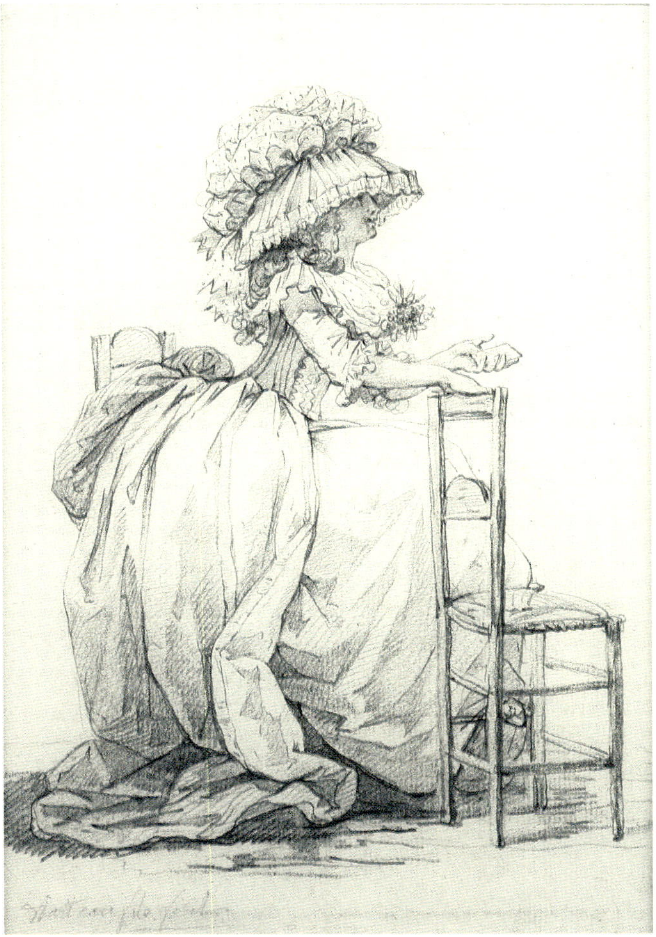

32

PIERRE OZANNE

French, Brest 1737–1813 Brest

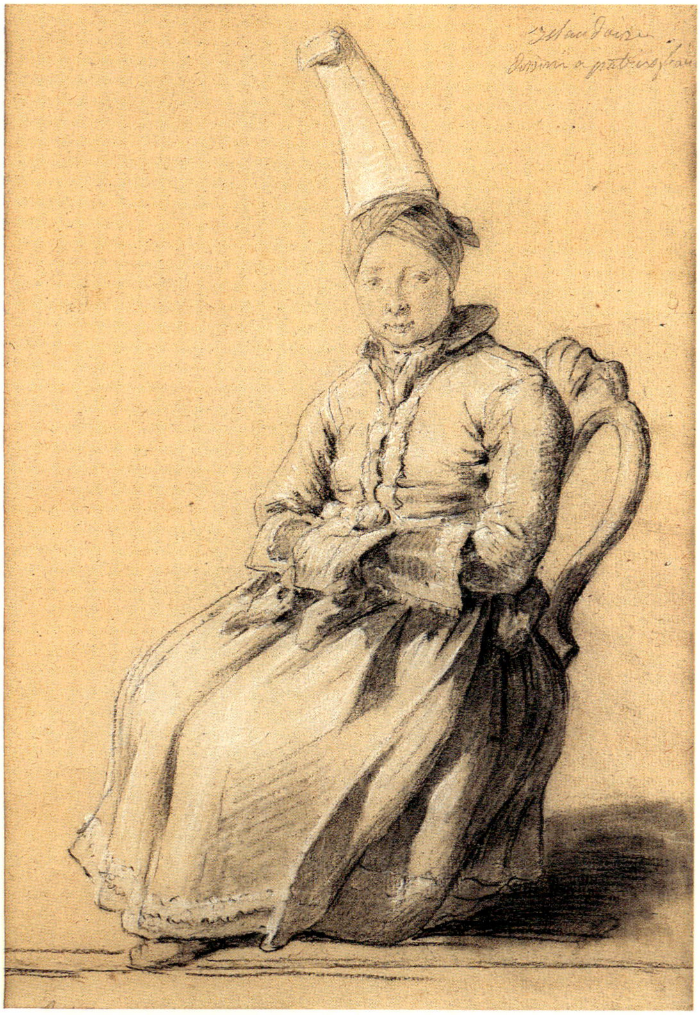

33

33

An Icelandic Woman

Black chalk, stumped, heightened with white chalk, on light brown paper; sheet extended along top and bottom.

11¾ x 7⅞ in. (298 x 201 mm).

Inscribed by the artist at upper right, in graphite, *Islandaise/dessiné à patrix fiord.*

PROVENANCE: Richard Day Ltd., London.

Born to a family of artists in the seaside town of Brest, Ozanne began his career as a pupil of his brother Nicolas, who was later tutor to the dauphin, the future Louis XVI. Pierre succeeded his brother as drawing master of the *Gardes du Pavillon Amiral et Marine* in 1751. He is best known for his depictions of ships, ports, and other aspects of maritime life.

In 1771–72, Ozanne traveled the Atlantic aboard the research frigate *La Flore*, which departed from Brest on 29 October 1771 in order to survey longitude and latitude as well as to create maps of the ocean. The frigate traveled around the Iberian Peninsula, along the coast of Morocco, through the Canary Islands, past the island of Gorée and the Cape Verde Islands, crossing the Atlantic by way of the Antilles and Martinique and heading north to Newfoundland before turning east to Iceland, passing south of the Faroe Islands, continuing to Denmark, and finally returning to Brest on 8 October 1772.

Ozanne executed numerous drawings during the voyage, mostly of ports visited or detailed views of *La Flore*, many of which were subsequently engraved. An *album factice* of pen and wash drawings from the journey that includes a harbor view inscribed *Islande / Patrixfjord vu du mouillage le matin* is preserved in the Louvre (acc. no. 31602). The present drawing also was executed at Patrick's Fjord, located on the northwestern projection of Iceland. The sheet is one of several chalk studies from this voyage of figures in traditional local costume (for two drawings of women from the island of Gorée, see *La revue du Louvre* 1989, repr., unpaginated).

JT

FRENCH SCHOOL, EIGHTEENTH CENTURY

34

Still Life with Kitchen Objects

Black chalk, heightened with white chalk, on light brown paper.

6 7/16 x 9 7/8 in. (164 x 251 mm).

WATERMARK: Indecipherable, perhaps four letters.

Inscribed on verso, at lower left, in graphite, *403;* at right center, *Chardin,* encircled.

PROVENANCE: Eugène Calando (Lugt 837); his sale, Paris, Hôtel Drouot, 11–12 December 1899, no. 25 (attributed to Chardin); Yvonne Tan Bunzl, London.

EXHIBITION: London 1984a, no. 40, repr.

During the latter half of the eighteenth century and well into the nineteenth, a proliferation of artists devoted their careers to depicting still-life subjects inspired by the master of the genre, Jean-Siméon Chardin (1699–1779). An example of Chardin's profound influence, this sheet was executed when studies of such subjects were exceedingly rare, as artists often worked directly on canvas. Following the format of Chardin's early works, this study combines a small number of vessels and a few vegetables placed on a simple ledge. A small, upside-down pot rests next to a larger, lidded pot from which extends the handle of a long spoon; alongside the pot is a wide-lipped cup. A head of garlic is loosely described in front of the cup, and what is perhaps a green onion or a carrot is indicated at left. Although the juxtaposition of elements is derived from Chardin, the upturned pot is unusual. In his still lifes Chardin typically placed a pot on its side in order to depict the interior.

This sheet was attributed to Henri-Horace Roland Delaporte (1724?–1793) by Matthias Polakovits; Yvonne Tan Bunzl noted that an attribution to Anne Vallayer-Coster (1744–1818) had also been proposed. Delaporte, Vallayer-Coster, and such artists as Nicholas Henry Jeurat de Bertry (1728–after 1796) popularized studies of kitchen objects and utensils during the latter half of the eighteenth century. Delaporte may have been a student of Jean-Baptiste Oudry (1686–1755), or at least worked in his atelier. His painted still lifes, however, are closer to those of Chardin, to whom they have often been erroneously attributed. Yet, Delaporte was a rare draftsman, as was Chardin, and the paucity of extant drawings by his hand makes the confirmation of this attribution difficult. Vallayer-Coster, a popular painter of flowers and still-life subjects, was an active draftsman, although this delicate study does not seem to be by her hand (see Roland-Michel 1970). JT

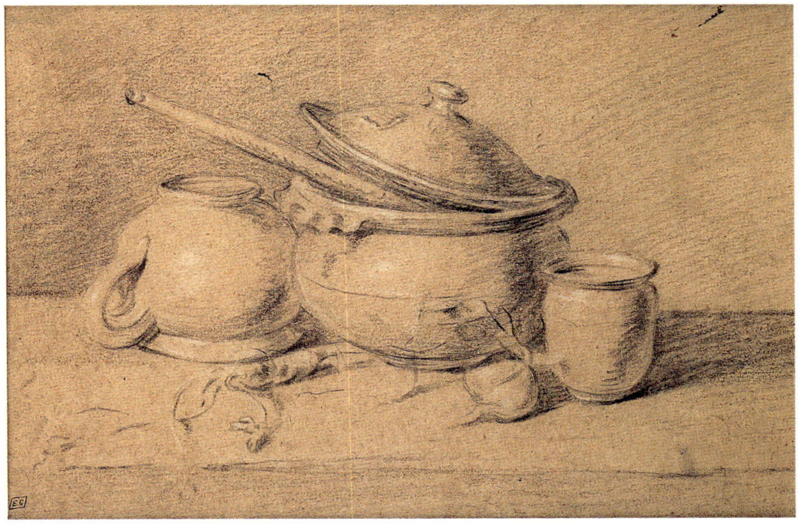

34

JEAN-JOSEPH-XAVIER BIDAULD

French, Carpentras 1758–1846 Montmorency

35

Wall and Smokestack

Watercolor on wove paper; framing lines in brown ink.

4 11/16 x 3 5/16 in. (119 x 84 mm).

PROVENANCE: Jacques Petit-Hory, Paris (his mark, in purple ink, on verso of mount); Hervé Aaron and Alan Salz, New York.

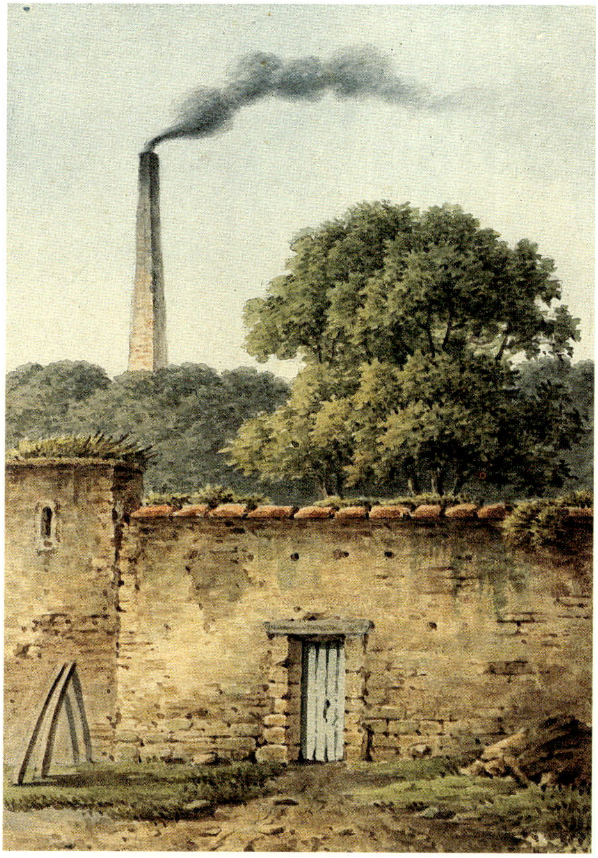

35

Along with Pierre-Henri de Valenciennes (1750–1819), Bidauld was one of the few active proponents of neoclassical landscape painting in the early nineteenth century. He began his career studying with his brother, a painter in Lyons, before moving to Paris in 1783. He journeyed to Rome in 1785 under the sponsorship of the art dealer Antoine-Charles Dulac and traveled throughout Italy before returning to Paris five years later. It was in Italy that Bidauld began working *en plein air,* later finishing the works in his studio. Following his return to France, Bidauld became one of the leading practitioners of historical landscape painting as well as one of the few painters who worked out of doors. He first exhibited at the Salon in 1791 and continued to do so for decades. In 1823 he earned the distinction of being the first landscape painter to be admitted to the Académie des Beaux-Arts.

Bidauld's bucolic scenes are characterized by a vast landscape, structured by architectural elements, and occasionally dotted with diminutive figures. This small-scale study focuses primarily on architecture, through which Bidauld created a seamless transition from the rustic to the industrial: over a garden wall, punctuated by a small doorway, a smokestack emitting a plume of smoke is visible above a cluster of trees. Even in this compact composition, Bidauld strictly ordered the view in terms of verticals and horizontals and managed to evoke a sense of space and light. This vignette exemplifies the artist's watercolor manner, in which small strokes of opaque color are applied with great care. JT

FRENCH SCHOOL, LATE EIGHTEENTH CENTURY

36

Study of a Gourd

Watercolor and some gouache over black chalk.

13 5/16 x 9 3/4 in. (348 x 248 mm).

PROVENANCE: William Drummond, London.

Although this drawing has been attributed to the German school, it seems more French in character and is close to, if not actually by, Jean-Baptiste Huet (1745–1811). This artist is principally known for his pastoral subjects, which are reminiscent of Jean-Baptiste Le Prince (1734–1781) and François Boucher (1703–1771), whose work he emulated. However, a group of very modern-looking plant studies by this master has recently come to light, including a study of two pumpkins in the Ashmolean Museum, Oxford (Rome 1991, no. 85, repr.), and the extraordinary study *Corn Husks and Wheat* that the Morgan Library acquired in 1992 (acc. no. 1992.2; New York 1995a, no. 19, repr.). Since both of these works are executed on the same type of paper and numbered as if part of a sequence, while the present work is on a different paper stock and bears no numbers or inscriptions, it is difficult to say with certainty that it is by Huet as well. Certainly the handling of watercolor and gouache as well as the indication of cast shadows is remarkably similar in all three of these works. CDD

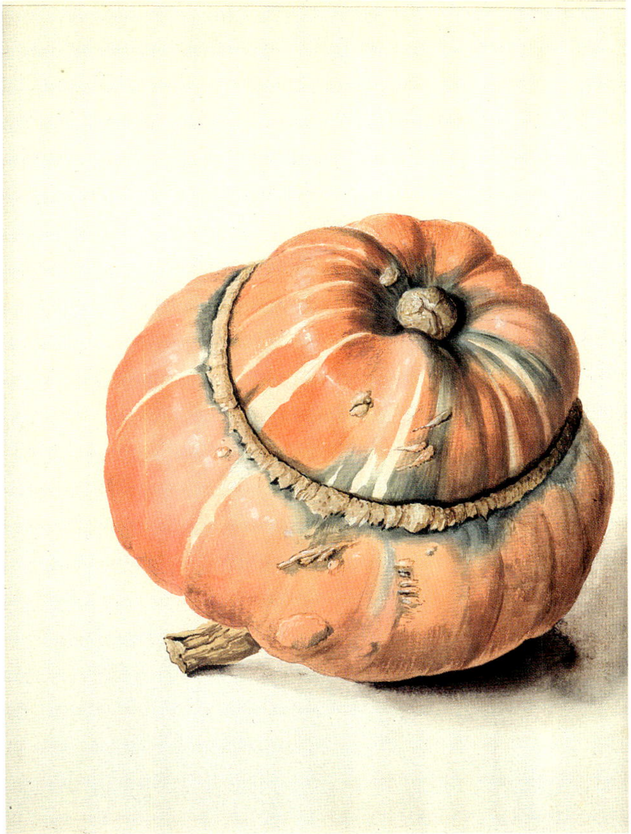

36

PIERRE-JOSEPH REDOUTÉ

French, Saint-Hubert, Belgium, 1759–1840 Paris

37

Plum Branches Intertwined

Watercolor on vellum.

12⅝ x 10⅜ in. (322 x 263 mm).

Signed, *P. J. Redouté.*

PROVENANCE: Richard Day Ltd, London.

EXHIBITION: New York 1984, no. 94.

Unquestionably the best-known botanical illustrator, Redouté received his early training from his father, who was also an artist. At the age of thirteen he left home and traveled in Belgium and the Netherlands, where he learned to paint flowers, becoming a great admirer of the work of Jan van Huysum (1682–1749). In 1782 he moved to Paris to work with his elder brother, a successful stage designer. In his leisure time he learned engraving and painted flowers in the royal botanical garden. His engravings of flowers brought him to the attention of Gérard van Spaendonck (1746–1822) as well as the bibliophile and botanist Charles-Louis L'Héritier de Brutelle, who recognized the young artist's talent and aptitude for botanical illustration. L'Héritier taught him how to render botanical detail, employed him as illustrator, and took him to London, where he learned the art of stipple engraving. Redouté was appointed draftsman to Marie-Antoinette, and after the Revolution he joined van Spaendonck on the staff of the Muséum nationale d'Histoire naturelle. In 1805 the empress Joséphine appointed him her flower painter, and under her patronage he illustrated, among other things, both volumes of the botanist Pierre Ventenat's *Jardin de la Malmaison* (1802–4) and all eight volumes of *Les Liliacées* (1802–17), and began *Les Roses* (1817–24). Eventually he succeeded van Spaendonck as official painter of *vélins.* Redouté's technique was modeled on that of van Spaendonck: pure watercolor, gradated with infinite subtlety and very occasionally touched with gouache to suggest sheen. The extreme delicacy of handling gives Redouté's work a fragile, almost poetic beauty.

In this work Redouté artfully combined two different plum trees to enrich an otherwise blue and green palette with a variety of golden plum that he may have seen at Malmaison. In 1802 and 1804 he published *Jardin de la Malmaison,* and it is possible that the present drawing was made in connection with this work. A similar drawing by the artist that was sold at auction in 1999, depicting the branch of a fruit-bearing plum tree with a wasp drinking water on a leaf and measuring 13⅜ x 10¼ in. (340 x 260 mm; sale, New York, Christie's, 28 January 1999, no. 169, repr.), has much in common with the present work and was probably executed for the same project.

CDD

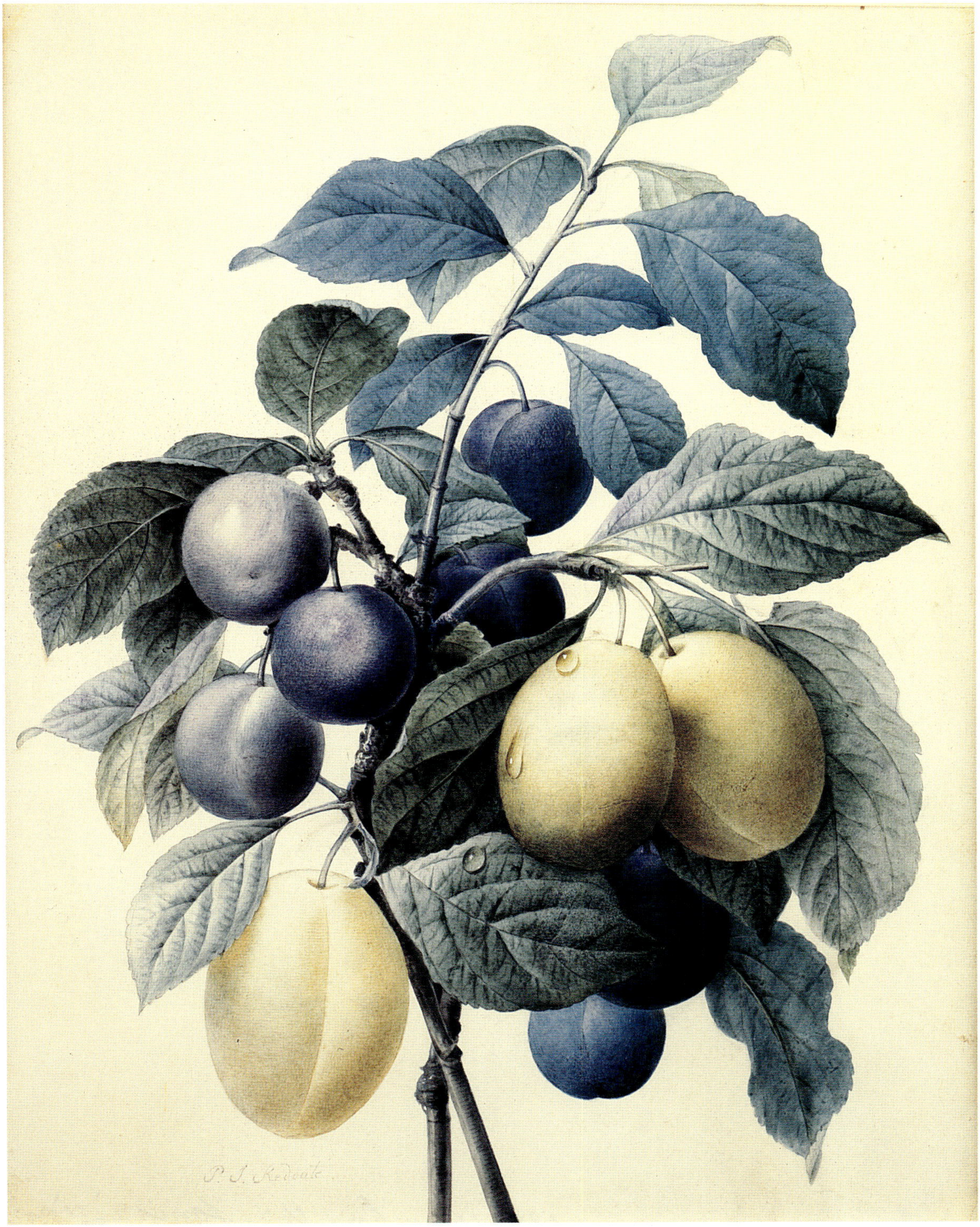

37

PANCRACE BESSA

French, Paris 1772–1846 Ecouen

38

Peaches

Watercolor and gum arabic, over graphite, heightened with gold, on vellum.

8¹¹⁄₁₆ x 10⅜ in. (221 x 264 mm).

PROVENANCE: Galerie Michel Meyer, Paris, 1991.

EXHIBITION: Paris 1991, no. 27, repr.

An important painter of flowers and fruits, Bessa is said to have studied with Gérard van Spaendonck (1746–1822), professor of flower painting at the Jardin des Plantes and master of Pierre-Joseph Redouté (see No. 37). Bessa also was one of the few male pupils of Redouté, the most celebrated flower painter of his day, with whom he collaborated on *Description des plantes rares cultivées à Malmaison et à Navarre* (1812–17), a monument of botanical illustration produced for the empress Joséphine, and in 1823 he was named (jointly with

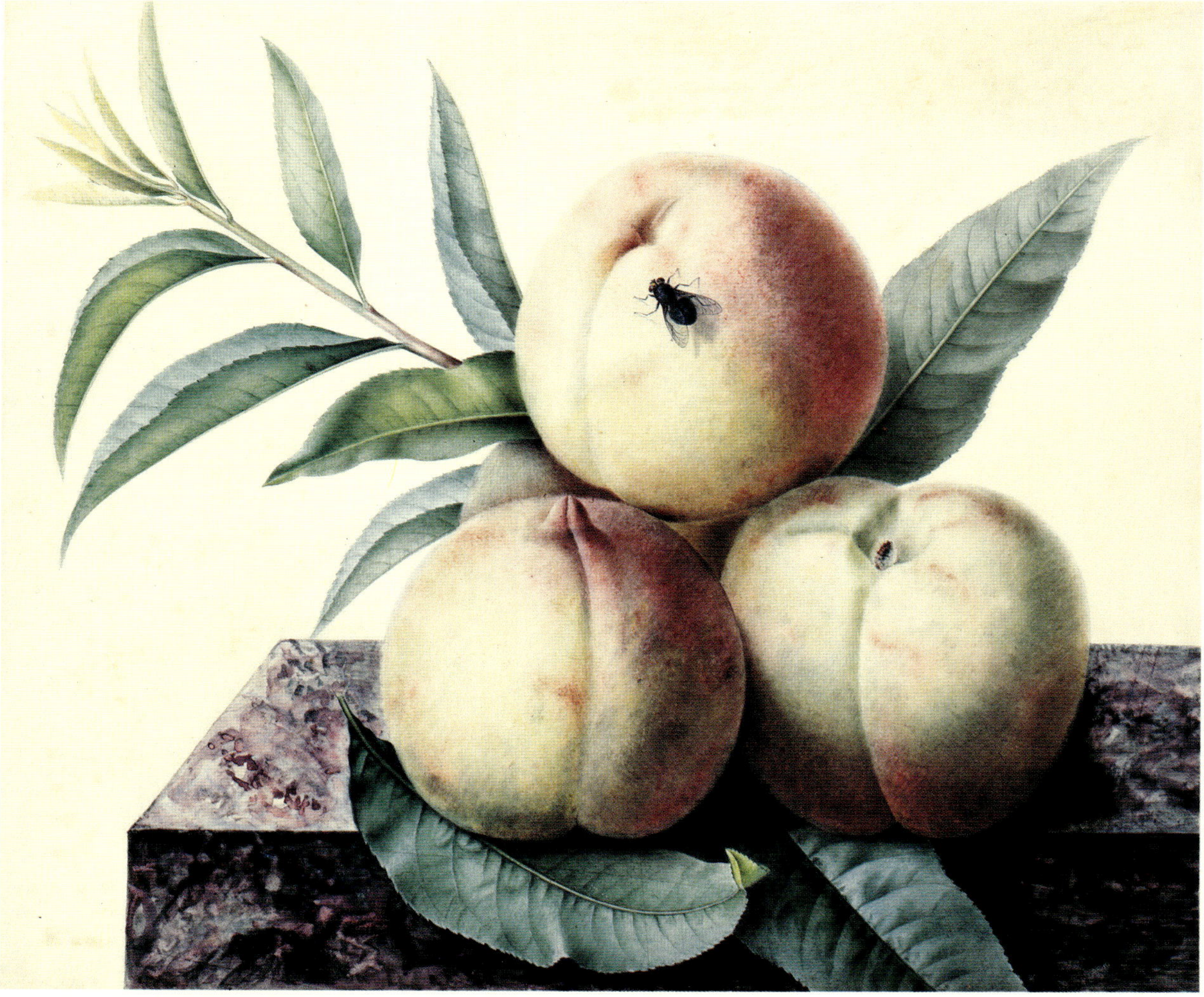

38

Redouté) painter on vellum to the Muséum nationale d'Histoire naturelle in Paris.

The present drawing may be compared with another of Bessa's works, *Potted Auricula,* in the Fitzwilliam Museum, Cambridge (Scrase 1997, no. 48, repr.), signed and dated 1817, in which a terra-cotta pot holding a flowering plant is set at the near edge of a marble surface, almost directly against the picture plane, the leaves extending over the edge of the pot, seeming to push into the viewer's space. By contrast, in *Peaches and Grapes*, recently on the art market (sale, New York, Sotheby's, 9 January 1996, no. 94, repr.), signed and dated 1838, the assemblage has been moved back from the picture plane, with some flowers and blackberries disposed beneath the peaches, serving to separate the main subject from the viewer and creating an effect that is more decorative and less daring than that of the present sheet or the Cambridge example. Based on the similarity in the treatment of space between these two works, the present drawing may be dated about 1820. KS

HENDRIK REEKERS

Dutch, Haarlem 1815–1854 Haarlem

39

Apples and a Walnut

Watercolor over pencil, with touches of gum arabic; ruled border in pen and black ink.

13¼ x 9^{13}/16 in. (337 x 248 mm).

Signed and dated at lower right, in pen and black ink, *H R.eekers. 1836*.

PROVENANCE: Baskett and Day, London.

EXHIBITION: London 1976, no. 50.

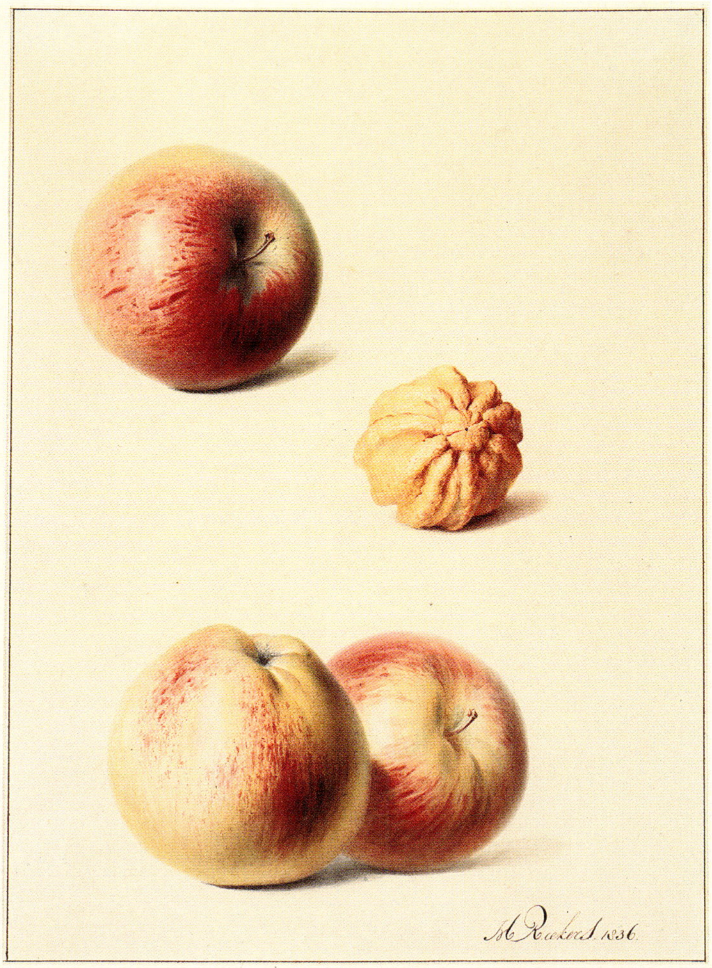

39

A still-life painter and lithographer, Reekers was a pupil of his father, Johannes Reekers (1790–1858). Comparison of the present drawing with one by the elder Reekers, *Studies of Plums, a Peach, and Rosehips*, formerly in the collection of Hans van Leeuwen (sale, Amsterdam, Christie's, 10 November 1999, no. 203, repr.), reveals both the close connection between father and son and the subtle ways in which the younger artist achieved a distinctly modern sensibility. Working in the same media used in the present drawing and on a similar size sheet, the elder artist arranged his subjects in two orderly rows across the surface of the sheet, the upper row receding slightly into depth. The younger artist, using a vertical orientation, positioned the fruits and nut in the same plane, giving the impression that the objects are floating in space. He also achieved a naturalism that verges on trompe l'oeil, whereas the older artist depicted his subject with a touch that was decidedly more blunt. Forms are built up in layers of feathery strokes of the brush, a technique the younger artist evidently learned from his father but handled more expertly, achieving greater naturalism.

A similar work is *Papaver somniferum (Opium Poppy with a Moth)* in the Fitzwilliam Museum, Cambridge (Palm Beach and elsewhere 1983–84, no. 85, repr.), in which the subject, isolated on the page, is positioned close to the picture plane and appears to float in space. While a work such as this may have been done in preparation for a print, the present drawing more likely was executed for later use in a more elaborate composition, such as *Fruit* in the Musées Royaux des Beaux-Arts, Brussels (acc. no. 4060/3014; Nève 1913, no. 3014). KS

BENJAMIN WEST

American, Springfield (now Swarthmore), Pennsylvania, 1738–1820 London

40

A Stunted Tree

Brush and gray wash.
12⅝ x 13½ in. (321 x 342 mm).
PROVENANCE: John Baskett Ltd., London.
EXHIBITION: London 1970, no. 7.

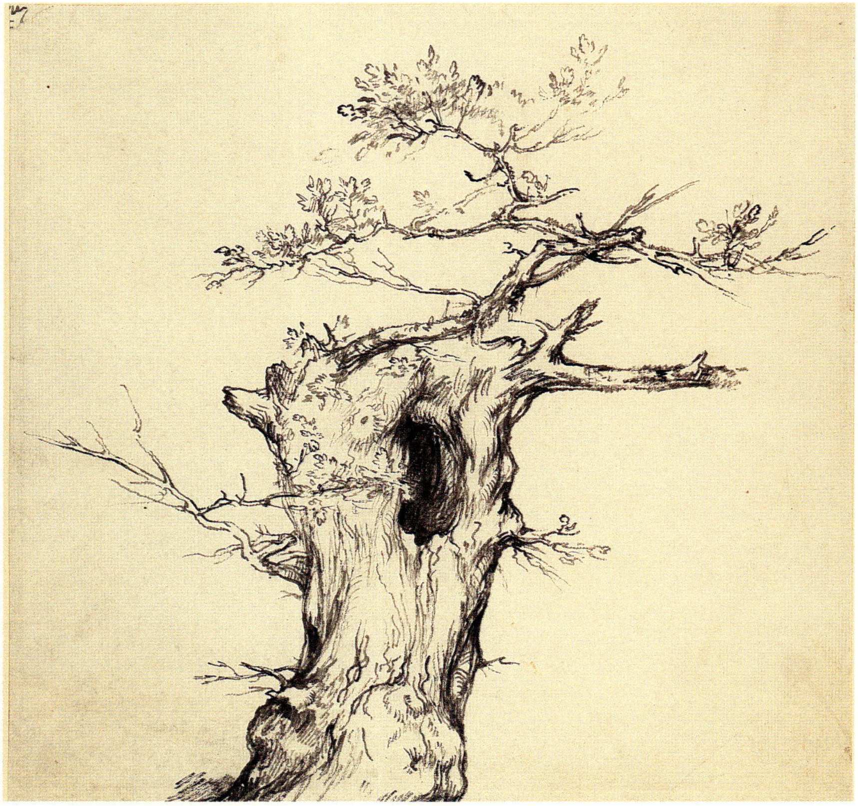

40

Born just outside Philadelphia, West cultivated his natural talent at an early age by painting portraits before moving to the city and receiving formal training. With the support of generous benefactors, he traveled to Italy in 1760. As the first American history painter working abroad, West caused a sensation upon his debut in Italy. Success followed him to England in 1763, where he intended to stay briefly but settled permanently. His achievements were considerable: he was appointed history painter to King George III in 1769 and became president of the Royal Academy in 1792. Although he devoted his career to history painting in the neoclassical mode, West is often considered a precursor of romanticism as a result of his practice of drawing directly from life and exploring dramatic themes of heroism and death. His studio became a destination for the next generation of American artists, and his influence changed the course of American painting.

Throughout his career West enjoyed drawing from nature and produced a number of landscape and topographical drawings. Gnarled, weather-beaten trees were a favorite subject; he made numerous studies after such trees, often as highly finished sheets. This drawing may be related to a group of tree studies executed by West at Windsor Park in 1784. Ruth Kraemer has noted that although the motif of the gnarled tree also appears in works by his son Raphael Lamar West (1769–1850), the careful execution of this sheet confirms its execution by the father. JT

WILLIAM BARTRAM

American, Philadelphia 1739–1823 Philadelphia

41

"The Soft Shell'd Tortoise . . ."

Brush and gray and black wash, over graphite.

$3\frac{3}{8}$ x $4\frac{15}{16}$ in. (86 x 126 mm).

WATERMARK: None visible through lining.

Inscribed at lower edge, in pen and black ink, *The soft shell'd Tortoise got in Savanah River Georgia.*

PROVENANCE: Sir Lewis Alexander Ogilvie Grant, fifth earl of Seafield (1767–1840); Sabin Galleries Ltd., London.

Son of the naturalist John Bartram (1699–1777), who served as botanist to King George III, William Bartram developed an interest in the natural world accompanying his father on trips throughout eastern North America to collect and draw plants for his patrons in Europe. His earliest drawings were executed in the 1750s as illustrations for his father's natural history collections. The elder Bartram circulated them among British and European naturalists, one of whom—Dr. John Fothergill (1712–1780), a leading botanist—became William's first and most important patron. Fothergill financed Bartram's four-year, 2,400-mile expedition through southeastern North America, begun in 1773, on which he collected specimens, made drawings, and recorded his findings, the text of which became the basis for his most famous work, *Travels through North and South Carolina, Georgia, East and West Florida, the Cherokee Country, the Extensive Territories of the Muscogulges, or Creek Confederacy, and the Country of the Chactaws*, published in Philadelphia in 1791.

According to Dr. John Edmondson, this drawing, which represents the Spiny soft-shell turtle (*Apalone spinifera* Le Sueur), likely was made in May 1773, when Bartram traveled upriver from Savannah a month after beginning his southern expedition (correspondence, 23 July 1999). Drawings by the artist of five other types of

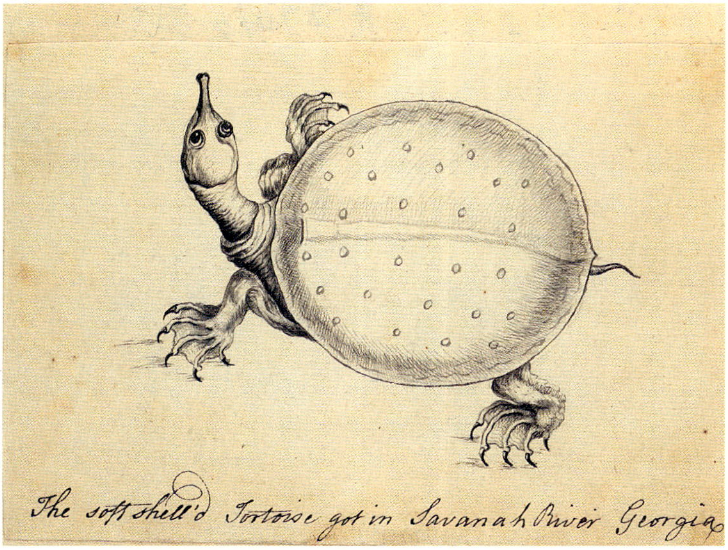

41

turtles are known: three done in the 1750s for his father's patron Peter Collinson (collection of Lord Derby, Knowsley Hall) and two done in the 1770s for his patron John Fothergill (British Museum; Ewan 1968, pp. 22–23, pls. 24 and 58). Bartram's *Travels* (pls. IX and X) reproduces engravings after his drawings of two other types of soft-shell turtles.

Dr. Edmondson notes that the present drawing, probably a preliminary study, is closer in style to the sketches that Bartram sent to Collinson (*Gentleman's Magazine* 1758, plate opposite p. 478, fig. 3) than to the more finished works he executed as a professional artist (Ewan 1968, pl. 21). Despite its somewhat schematic quality, the present drawing displays Bartram's characteristically delicate handling of the brush with which he defined form with extremely fine strokes, using parallel hatching for pale shadow and crosshatching and wash for deeper shadow. KS

JAMES SEYMOUR

British, London 1702–1752 London

42

A Racehorse with Jockey Up

Graphite.

6½ x 8 in. (165 x 203 mm).

WATERMARK: Initials *LVG*.

PROVENANCE: William Drummond, London; Jacqueline Kennedy Onassis, New York; her sale, New York, Sotheby's, 23 April 1996, no. 720, repr.

EXHIBITION: London 1978, no. 13.

A self-taught artist and one of the first English painters to specialize in sporting scenes, Seymour produced a considerable quantity of pencil drawings with sporting subjects, a number of which were in the collection of the late Paul Mellon. As country house life flourished in the early eighteenth century, and sports such as hunting, racing, and riding became increasingly common rural pastimes, artists were called upon to document particular sporting events and to create portraits of prize animals and their owners. A contemporary and rival of John Wootton (1682–1764), Seymour worked in a naive but meticulous style and was popular with the affluent patrons whose commissions established the English sporting genre.

This drawing is one of a number by the artist depicting jockeys guiding their horses through stock moves

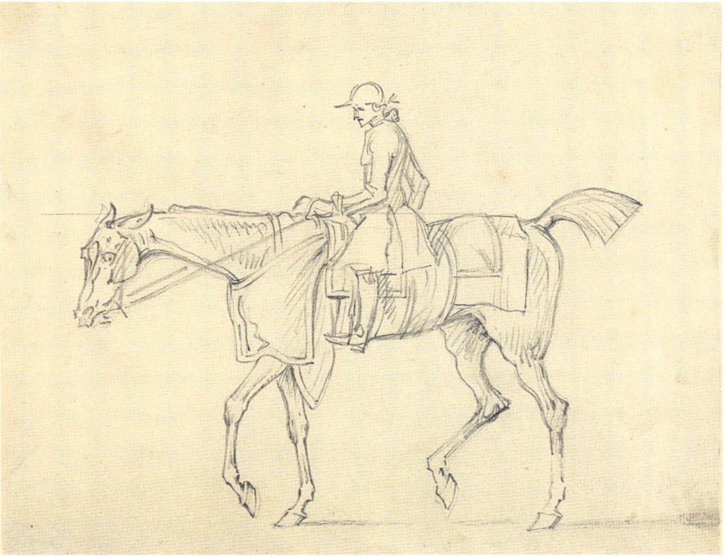

42

and poses. The jockey is shown upright, astride his horse and grasping the reins, a pose characteristic of Seymour's representations of equestrians in such paintings as *Mr. Peter Delmé's Hounds on the Hampshire Downs* of 1738 (collection of Mrs. Paul Mellon). The profile is particularly suited to Seymour's simplistic style of describing horseflesh as well as to his less developed skill at drawing figures.

This is one of five drawings of similar subjects that Mrs. Onassis bought in the company of Charles Ryskamp. His collection also includes another study by Seymour of a horse with grooms, and in 1998 he gave the Morgan Library the artist's *Duke of Buccleuch on Horseback*. JT

GEORGE STUBBS

British, Liverpool 1724–1806 London

43

A Bust-Length Portrait of Warren Hastings, Wearing a Blue Coat, Red Waistcoat, and Top Hat

Watercolor over pencil; cut to an oval.

5 7/16 x 4 5/16 in. (138 x 109 mm).

PROVENANCE: Hall and Knight Ltd., New York.

EXHIBITION: New York 2000a, no. 3, repr.

Rightly regarded as the quintessential painter of horses, hounds, and the hunt, Stubbs also was a gifted printmaker and made a number of ambitious history pictures, small-scale enamel paintings on copper, and portraits. His drawings are scarce, and this fine example, among Charles Ryskamp's most recent acquisitions, is one of very few sheets in this country outside the important group of drawings by the artist at the Yale Center for British Art, New Haven.

Warren Hastings (1732–1818) spent much of his life in India, where he was closely associated with the East India Company, and in 1774, he became governor-general of Bengal. His political adversaries in England soon became critical of his conduct in office, however, and in 1787, he was impeached for "high crimes and misdemeanours." The ensuing trial was to last until 1795, when Hastings, finally acquitted of all charges, was able to retire to his family's estate at Daylesford in Warwickshire.

Stubbs painted a portrait of Hastings in 1791 (perhaps the picture formerly in the collection of the earl of Rosebery; see London and New Haven 1984–85, p. 173, under no. 130). He thereafter made two versions

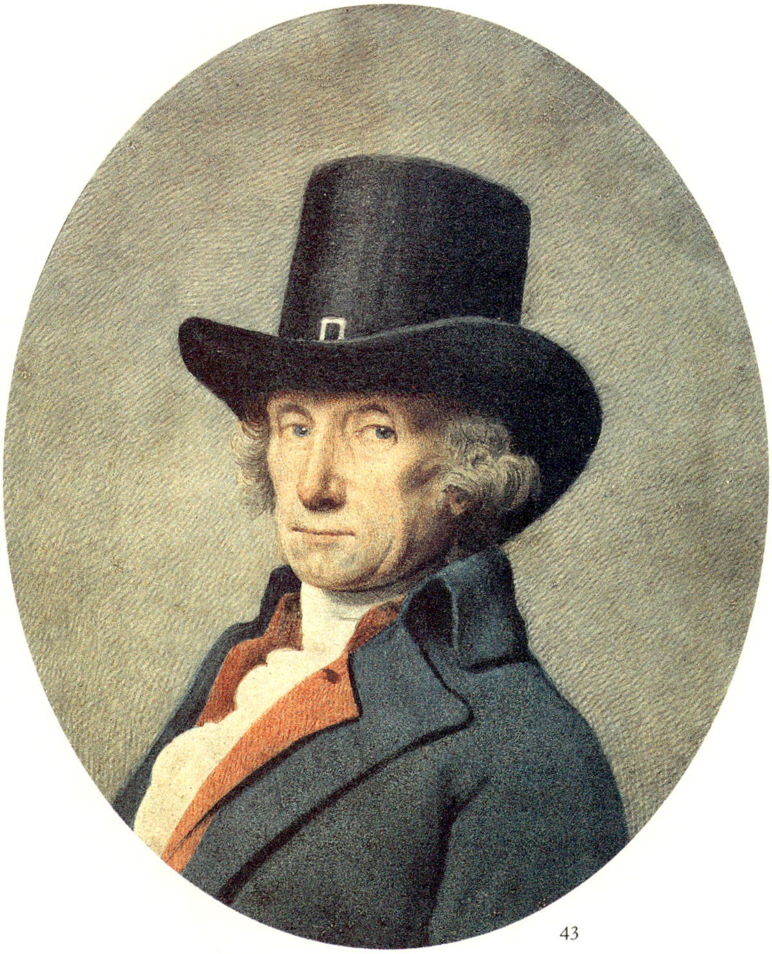

43

in enamel, one in a private collection (London and New Haven 1984–85, no. 130, repr.) and the other in the Victoria Memorial Hall, Calcutta. These were followed by a print, published by his son, the engraver George Townley Stubbs (ca. 1756–ca. 1815), in which the pose and features of the sitter correspond very closely not only to the painted portrait but also to the present watercolor. As Nicholas Hall has suggested (New York 2000a, pp. 59–60), both the omission of the small button on Hastings's lapel in the print and the rather free underdrawing in pencil imply that the present work may have been executed by Stubbs to serve as a model for the engraving. WMG

PAUL SANDBY

British, Nottingham 1731–1809 London

44

Stoke Poges Church with Mr. Gray's Tombstone in the Foreground

Graphite, gray and brown ink, with touches of watercolor.

8¼ x 11⅜ in. (210 x 289 mm).

PROVENANCE: W. M. (according to old label inscribed, *The Parish Church of Stoke Poges Coun: Berks with Mr. Grays Tombstone Drawn by Paul Sandby. Given by him to W. M. . . .*); Spink and Son Ltd., London.

EXHIBITION: London 1987b, no. 5.

A founding member of the Royal Academy, Sandby was important in establishing watercolor painting as an independent artistic medium rather than just for the tinting of topographical drawings. Although Sandby produced many finished watercolors, the medium would have to wait for the advent of Turner and Girtin to realize its full expressive potential.

This work is topographical in character since the artist was concerned with describing St. Giles's Church in Stoke Poges, where in 1751 the poet Thomas Gray (1716–1771) wrote his famous *Elegy in a Country Churchyard*. Using pencil and pen and ink, Sandby carefully recorded the appearance of the church and completed the work in watercolor. He greatly admired the works of Gray, who was buried in the family vault at Stoke Poges in 1771. Gray also inspired Sandby's painting *Snowdon* at the time of the publication of *The Bard* in 1757. In 1833 John Constable drew the same church from a different viewpoint (No. 64). CDD

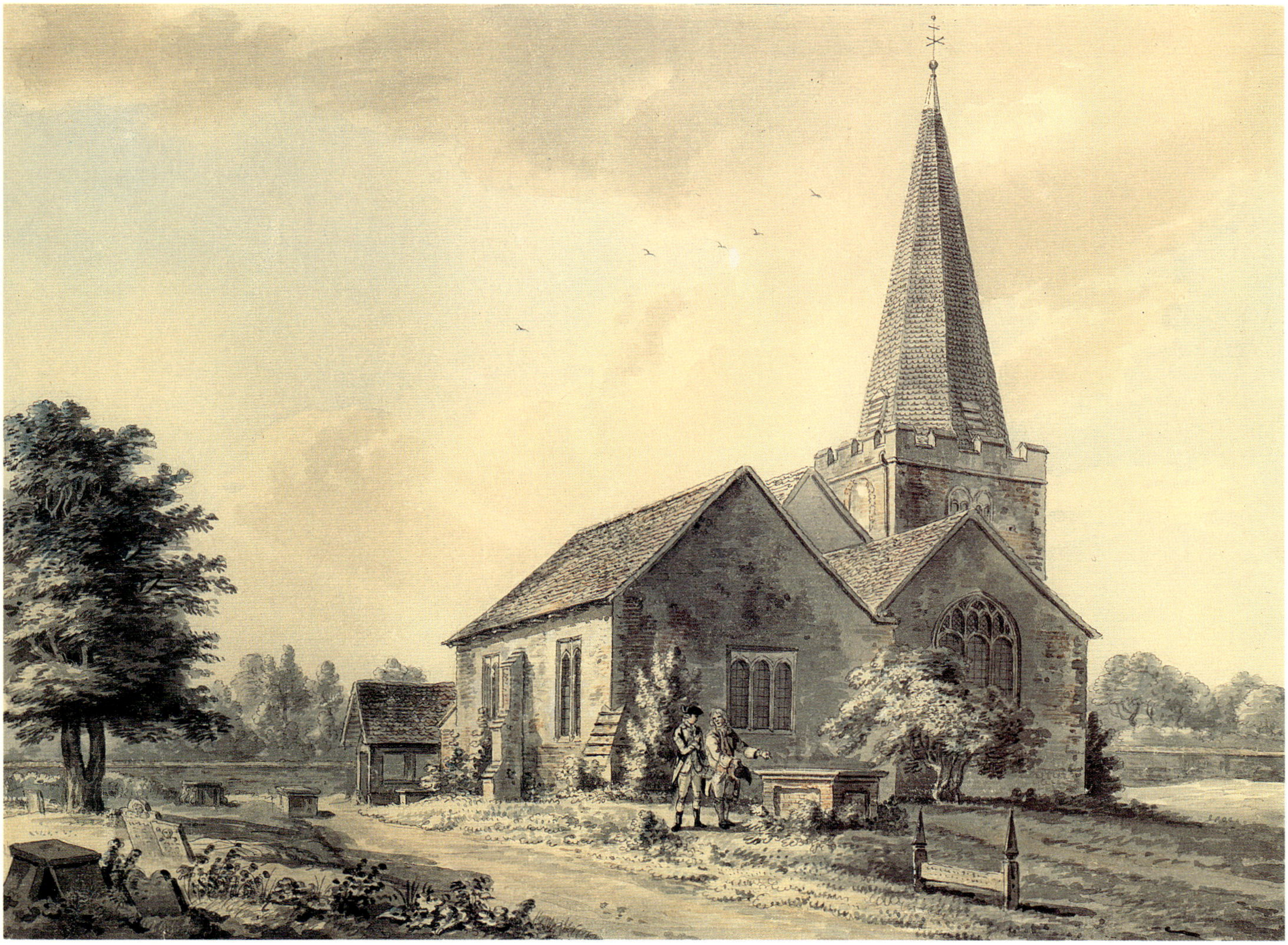

44

HENRY FUSELI

British, Zurich 1741–1825 Putney Hill, near London

45

A Sibyl

Pencil; verso rubbed with red chalk.

4½ x 5⁷⁄₁₆ in. (114 x 139 mm).

WATERMARK: Partial letter *W*.

Initialed at lower right of image, in pencil, *H. F.*

PROVENANCE: William Drummond, London.

EXHIBITION: London 1980, no. 87, repr.

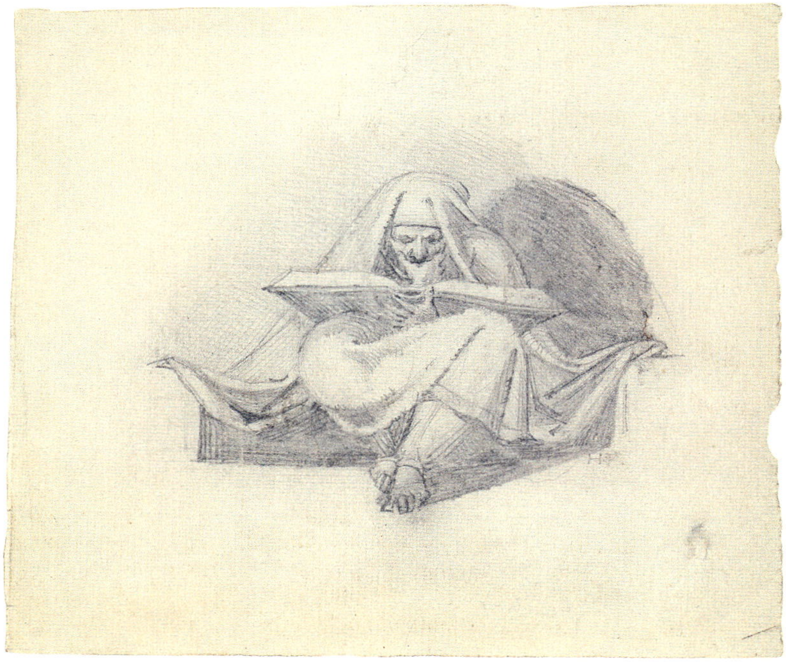

45

This compact design is preparatory for the tailpiece of the 1792 edition of *Essays on Physiognomy* (originally published as *Physiognomische Fragmente zur Beförderung der Menschenkenntnis und Menschenliebe*, 1775–78), written by Fuseli's close friend, the Swiss physiognomist, theologian, and poet Johann Caspar Lavater (1741–1801). During his student days in Zurich, Fuseli formed a long-lived relationship with Lavater, whose *Essays* are considered his most significant contribution as an author and who is best remembered for the invention of physiognomy, the study of facial features and expressions as outward manifestations of character.

Fuseli's interest in physiognomy was genuine, even if he did not accept Lavater's theories in their entirety. The artist oversaw the illustration of the 1792 edition, for which his drawings were engraved by Thomas Holloway (1800–1883), the same artist who had engraved Fuseli's designs for the 1781–83 French edition. The verso of this drawing has been rubbed with red chalk, while the sharp pencil incisions on the recto indicate that it was traced for transfer in preparation for the engraving. Two proof impressions of this figure are also in the Ryskamp collection. This image of a sibyl pondering an open book has become a popular, widely reproduced publishing logo.

Peter Tomory has suggested that Fuseli based this figure upon an engraving of a seated carpenter by Albrecht Altdorfer (1480–1538), *A Thinking Man* (B.55). If this is true, the drawing may be seen as a reflection of Fuseli's interest in early German prints. JT

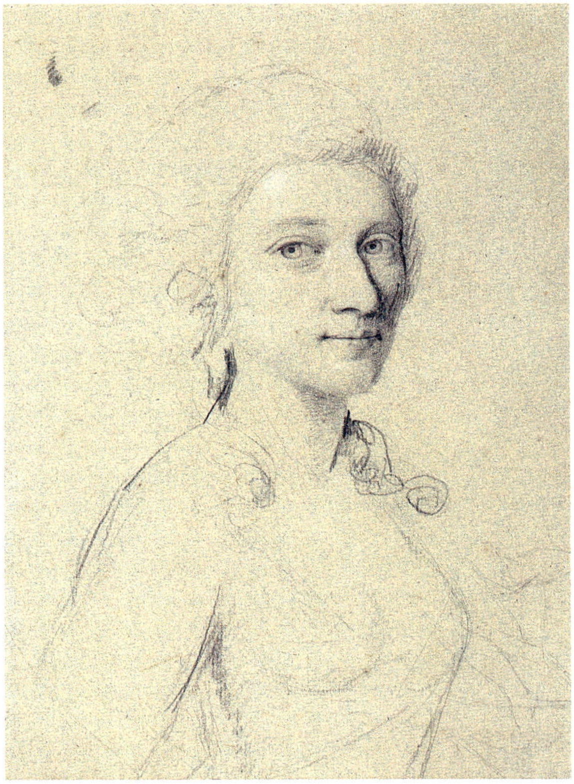

46

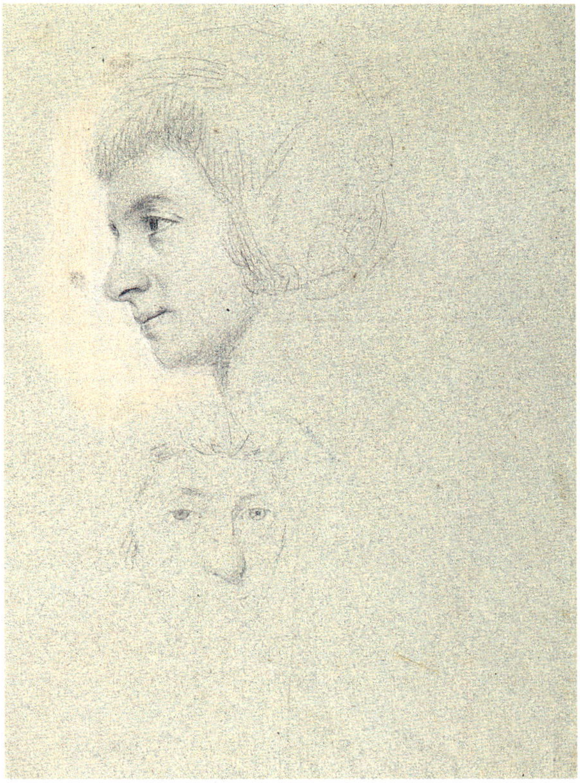

46v

JENS JUEL

Danish, Balslev, Fünen, 1745–1802 Copenhagen

46

Bust-Length Portrait of a Woman

VERSO: *Two Studies of the Head of a Woman*

Black chalk, heightened with white chalk, on blue paper faded to gray; the head of a woman in profile on verso silhouetted in pink chalk.

11⅝ x 8½ in. (296 x 215 mm).

WATERMARK: Coat of arms.

PROVENANCE: Thomas le Claire, Hamburg.

Juel studied first in Hamburg and then at the Kunstakademi, Copenhagen, where he was influenced by the work of the Swedish-born Carl Gustaf Pilo (1712–92/93), professor there from 1748 and for more than two decades the foremost portraitist in Denmark. After a seven-year sojourn in Hamburg, Dresden, Rome, Paris, and Geneva, Juel returned to Copenhagen and was appointed court painter in 1780. During the next forty years, he produced a very large number of elegant yet remarkably unidealized portraits of royal, aristocratic, and bourgeois sitters as well as a smaller group of highly influential pure landscapes.

Clearly drawn from life, the sketches on this sheet presumably are preparatory for a commissioned painting. While the pose and features of the sitter bear comparison with those in many of Juel's extant portraits, none of the artist's paintings seems to represent the same figure as the drawing (see Poulsen 1991). WMG

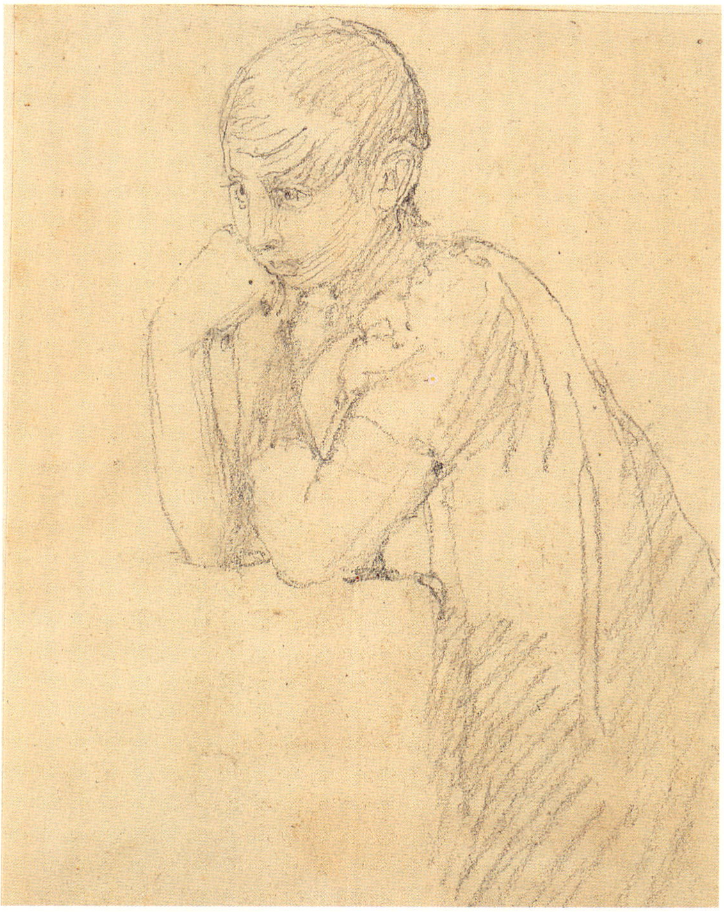

47

JOHN FLAXMAN

British, York 1755–1826 London

47

Portrait of Delvalle Lowry

Graphite, fixed, on dark cream wove paper.

6¾ x 5¼ in. (170 x 132 mm).

Inscribed and signed by the artist on the original mount at lower left, in pencil, *Delvalle Lowry;* at lower right, *Flaxman;* inscribed (in a later hand) on verso of mount, in pencil, *Delvalle Elizabeth Rebecca VARLEY (1800–1860) / (Daughter of the Engraver Wilson Lowry / & 2nd Wife of John Varley).*

PROVENANCE: Wilson Lowry, London; by descent; Spink and Son Ltd., London; W. M. Brady and Co., New York.

Flaxman began his career as a sculptor, supplementing his income by providing Josiah Wedgwood with neoclassical silhouette designs for his jasperware reliefs. He saved enough money to travel to Italy in 1787, where he studied antique marbles. It was during his stay there that he received his most important early commissions, including those for his starkly linear illustrations to Dante's *Divine Comedy* and Homer's *Iliad* and *Odyssey*. After returning to England in about 1795, Flaxman established himself as a monumental sculptor with the tomb he created for William Murray, first earl of Mansfield, in Westminster Abbey. Despite his heightened reputation and devotion to religious sculpture, Flaxman found time to draw intimate and spontaneous portraits of his family and friends. These portraits are characterized by their free and casual rendering, a striking contrast to the hard-edged style of his illustrations.

The present sheet is from an album of drawings that included portraits of Wilson Lowry's (1762–1824) family by Flaxman, John Varley (1778–1842), Mathilda Lowry Heming (1808–1855), and other artists. Lowry, a mechanical and architectural engraver, was elected to the Royal Society in 1812. The subject of this drawing is Delvalle, his daughter from his second marriage, to Rebecca Delvalle (1761–1848), a mineralogist. Delvalle Lowry published *Conversations on Mineralogy* in 1822, a discussion of mineralogy intended for a popular audience of students and amateurs. Later, as Delvalle Varley, she published *Rudimentary Treatise on Mineralogy* (1849).

Flaxman inscribed the original mount *Delvalle Lowry,* indicating that the portrait was drawn before 1825,when the twenty-five-year-old Delvalle married the forty-seven-year-old Varley (his second marriage; Varley's first wife had died in 1824). A drawing of Delvalle by Varley in the Victoria and Albert Museum, London (Kauffman 1984, p. 58, no. 34, repr.), can be dated roughly to 1815, when the sitter was fifteen years old. In the present portrait she appears even younger than she does in the London sheet, suggesting that Flaxman's portrait may have been executed between 1810 and 1815. JT

WILLIAM BLAKE

British, London 1757–1827 London

48

Sketches for America *and Other Books*

VERSO: *The Lion Lying Down with the Ox*

Pencil.
8 x 10⅝ in. (205 x 270 mm).
Inscribed (in a later hand) at upper right and on arm at lower right, *C-2*; at upper left, *2*.
PROVENANCE: W. A. White, 1905; Rosenbach, New York, 1939; Mrs. Gerard B. Lambert, Princeton, New Jersey.
LITERATURE: Keynes 1970, no. 5, repr. (recto), and no. 16, repr. (verso); Bindman 1977, p. 47; Butlin 1981, pp. 117–18, no. 226, pls. 259–60.
EXHIBITIONS: New York 1905, no. 106; Philadelphia 1939, no. 194; Princeton 1969–70, no. 24; New York 1974 (unnumbered); New York 1992, no. 27, repr. (recto), no. 32, repr. (verso).

After attending a drawing academy in London, Blake trained as an engraver, which provided him with the necessary skills to illustrate and publish his own work. This is best revealed in his illustrated books of the 1780s and 1790s, which were printed and colored by hand and combine text and image in an innovative, complex manner. The present double-sided sheet contains studies related to at least two of Blake's early writings.

The studies of limbs on the recto are typical of Blake's work. The figures of a running woman and a man with broken chains dangling from his arms relate to the first plate of Blake's book *America, A Prophecy*, of 1793–94. Butlin and Hamlyn (New York 1992) also relate this sheet to *The Marriage of Heaven and Hell* and suggest that Blake may have used these studies as a source for illustrations in other prophetic books of the early 1790s.

The verso, which may predate the recto, contains a sketch for an illustration accompanying Blake's first symbolic poem, *Tiriel,* of about 1789. There are twelve known illustrations for the poem (Yale Center for British Art, New Haven), although none is a literal depiction of the verse. This scene may be related to the lion lying with the patient ox as the blind tyrant Tiriel stands by, holding his whip. Keynes suggests that the two figures may be Har and Heva, Tiriel's parents, depicted as children—an allusion to their senility. He dates this side of the sheet as early as 1788, although Butlin and Hamlyn suggest a later date, about 1790–95. JT

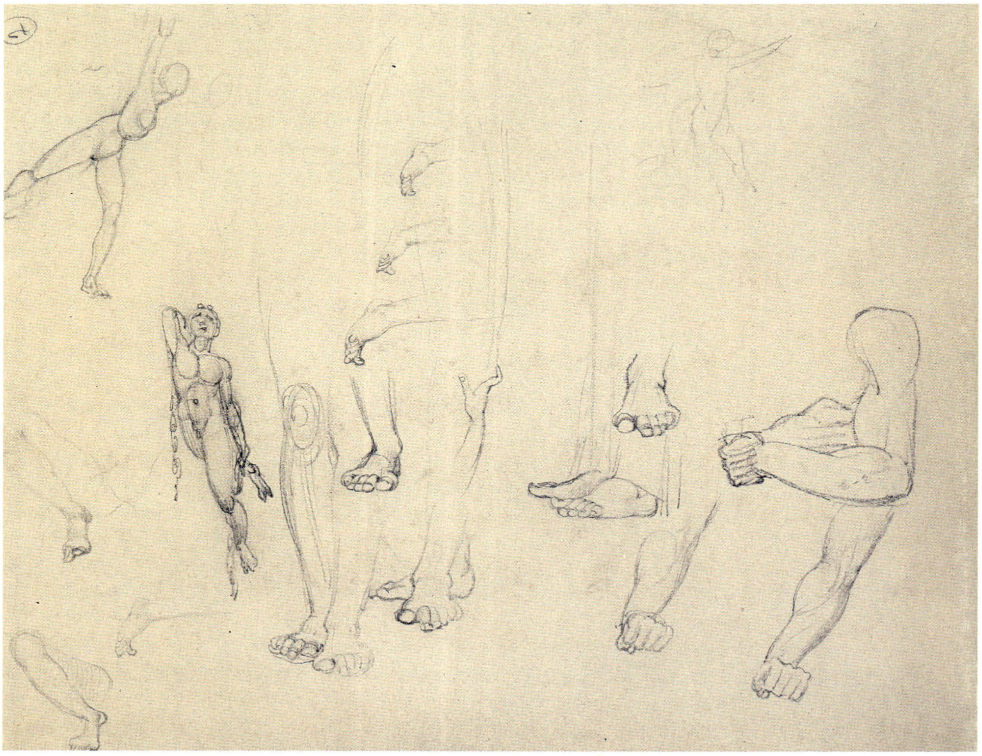

48

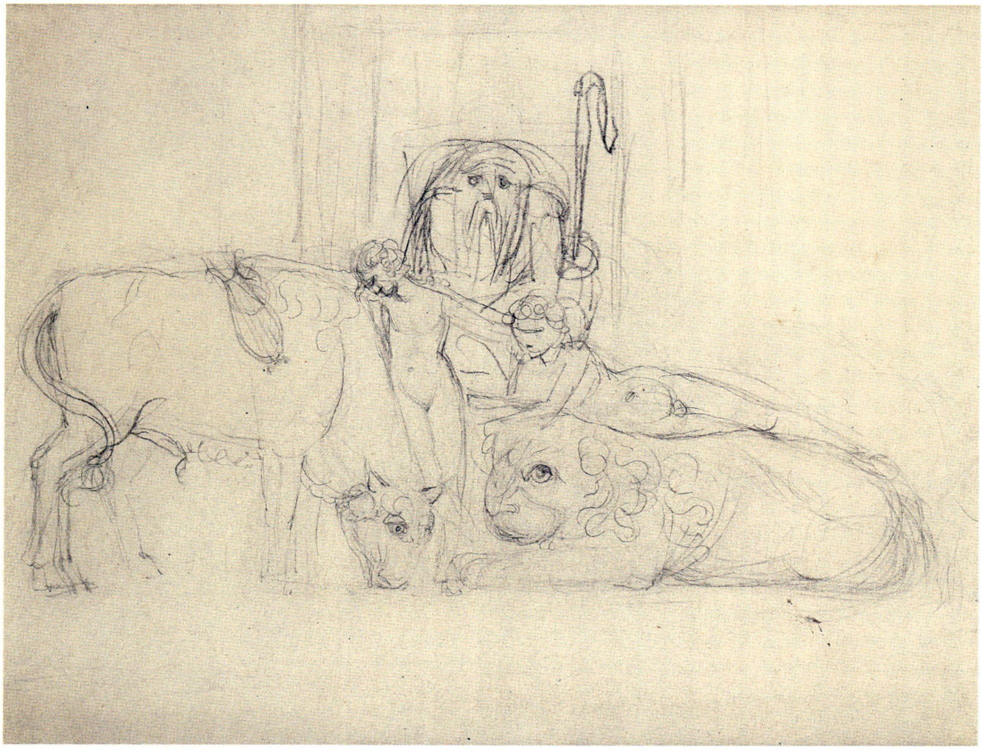

48v

49

Owen Glendower

Pencil.

9⅛ x 7⅛ in. (232 x 181 mm).

Inscribed at right of center, in pencil, *Owen Glendower*, over previously erased inscription.

PROVENANCE: Tyler Blake; sale, New York, Urquhart and Marckwald, 13 December 1942; Mrs. Gerard B. Lambert, Princeton, New Jersey.

LITERATURE: (?) Rossetti 1863, p. 245, list 2, no. 54; (?) Rossetti 1880, p. 261, list 2, no. 59; *Blake* 1927, no. 48; Butlin 1981, no. 744, pl. 955.

EXHIBITION: (?) Cambridge, Massachusetts, 1930.

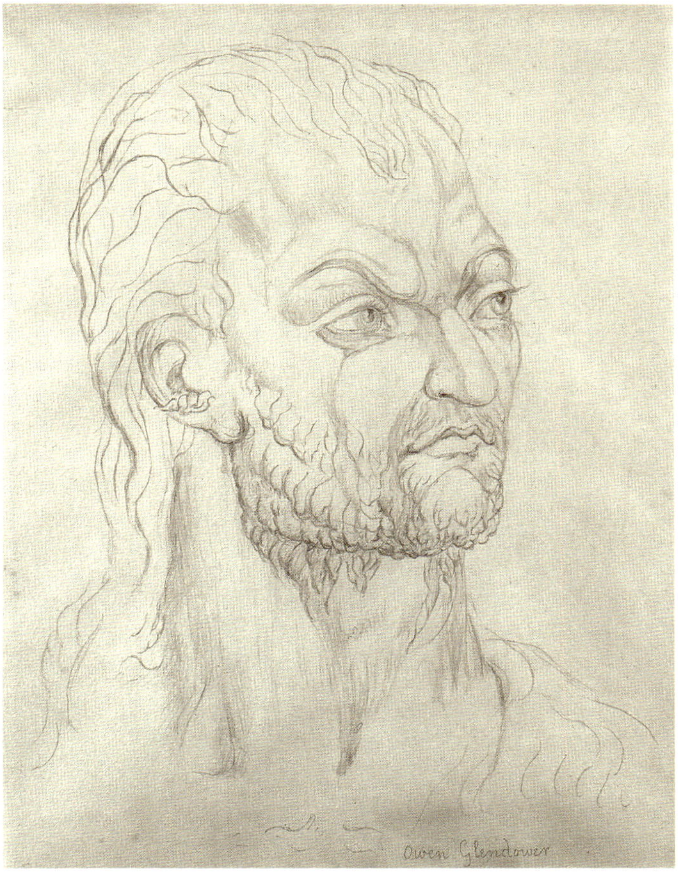

49

This sheet belongs to Blake's series of imaginary portraits of historic figures that he executed for his friend, the landscape painter John Varley (1778–1842), mostly during evenings spent at Varley's home from 1819 to 1825. Some of these portraits were drawn in a sketchbook used by Varley, while others were done on separate sheets; many exist in several versions. A few were engraved by John Linnell (Nos. 89–91) for the only volume of Varley's projected four-part *Treatise on Zodiacal Physiognomy,* published in 1828.

The present sheet is one of two, almost identical, visionary portraits of Owen Glendower; the other is in the National Gallery of Canada, Ottawa. Glendower (ca. 1359–1416), or Owain ab Gruffydd, lord of Glyndwr and Sycharth, was a Welshman who led a rebellion against Henry IV on his ascension to the throne and proclaimed himself Prince of Wales. He also appears in Part I of Shakespeare's *Henry IV*. This drawing is slightly larger than the Ottawa sheet, and its inscription has been effaced and rewritten, possibly by Linnell or Varley. The similarity of the two sheets and their shared provenance has led to confusion in their documentation. In fact, many of Blake's visionary heads were copied or traced by Linnell and Varley, perhaps to aid in their engraving, and are considered near-contemporary replicas.

Charles Ryskamp has given the Morgan Library Blake's imaginary portrait of the fourteenth-century British rebel Wat Tyler. That sheet, roughly the same size as this one and executed in pencil, was inscribed and dated by Linnell, *October 30, 1819, 1 a.m.* JT

THOMAS ROWLANDSON

British, London 1756/57–1827 London

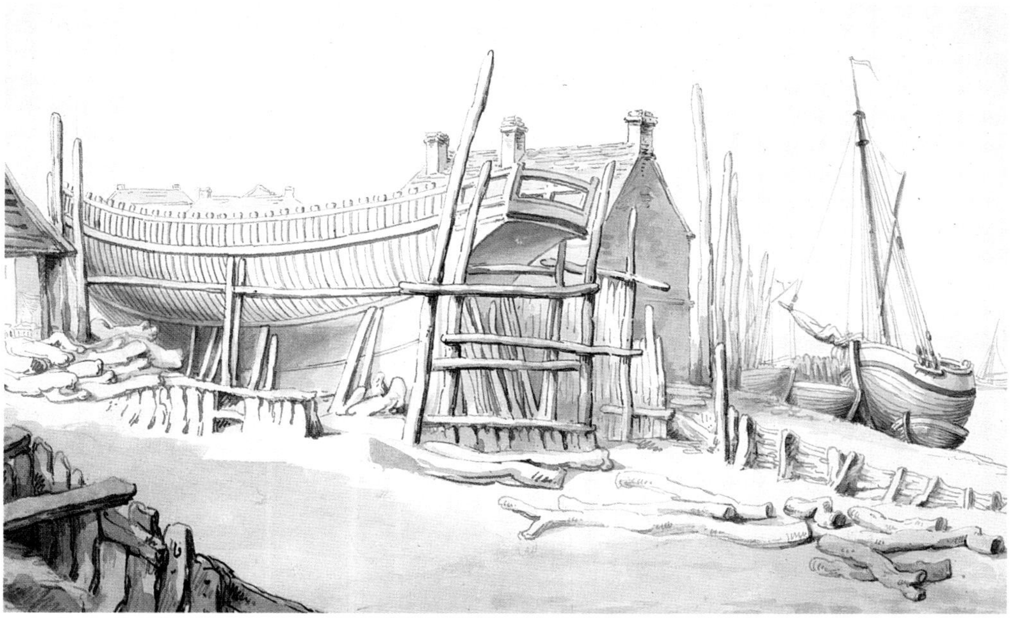

50

50

Shipbuilding at Ringmore on the River Avon, Devon

Pen and black ink, gray wash, with traces of graphite.

6⁹⁄₁₆ x 10⅞ in. (166 x 276 mm).

PROVENANCE: Sale, London, Sotheby's, 7 July 1983, no. 15a, repr.; Spink and Son Ltd., London.

The Pierpont Morgan Library, Gift of Charles Ryskamp, in memory of J. Richardson Dilworth, 1997.95

Rowlandson is perhaps the most prolific British draftsman; it has been suggested that his oeuvre numbers more than ten thousand sheets (Wark 1975, p. 1). Although he is best remembered for his unrivaled talent for comical subjects, Rowlandson's thematic range was broad and varied and also encompassed rustic genre scenes, landscapes, and figure drawings. As a humorist, the artist's keen observation of people informed his work; he was an equally close observer of nature in his landscapes and depictions of London and the surrounding urban milieu.

Throughout his career, Rowlandson was interested in the city's docks and boatyards. He turned to the banks of the Thames to observe the activity aboard the ships and ferries and make accurate and detailed drawings of the vessels. The present sheet is one of numerous studies of boats executed by the artist on his travels outside London. Here Rowlandson has depicted a shipyard at Ringmore, a town on the Avon River in Devon. Using gray wash on white paper to simulate the dazzling effects of sunlight, the artist has depicted the partially constructed hull of a sailboat, which dwarfs the surrounding buildings in the yard. We know that Rowlandson was in Devon in 1804; he executed a drawing of the November 15th launching of H.M.S. *Hibernia* from nearby Devonport (Baskett and Snelgrove 1978, no. 269). The present sheet may date from this trip. JT

FRANZ KOBELL

German, Mannheim 1749–1822 Munich

51

Landscape

Brush and brown wash over black chalk; ruled border in chalk gone over with brown ink.

7 x 8¾ in. (177 x 220 mm).

PROVENANCE: Unknown collector, initials AOCN; Arturo Cuellar, Zurich.

This small, vivid drawing was probably executed *en plein air* around 1800, as was the group of seven similar landscapes now in the collection of the Harvard University Art Museums (Cambridge 1998, pp. 6–7, repr.). In these broad, rather quick studies, Kobell depicted landscape motifs in a structured arrangement and emphasized the effects of light on the land and sky. A member of an artistically inclined family, Franz was the younger brother of Ferdinand Kobell (1740–1799), primarily a landscape painter, whose major influences were seventeenth-century Dutch painting and Claude Lorrain (1600–1682). Like his brother, Franz also was influenced by the landscapes of Claude. Although he was a painter, Franz seemed to prefer *plein air* drawing to painting in oils, executing more watercolor sketches and ink drawings than paintings. He lived in Rome between 1779 and 1784 before returning to Munich. His elder brother's sons Wilhelm von Kobell (1766–1855) and Egid von Kobell (1772–1847) also were artists. CDD

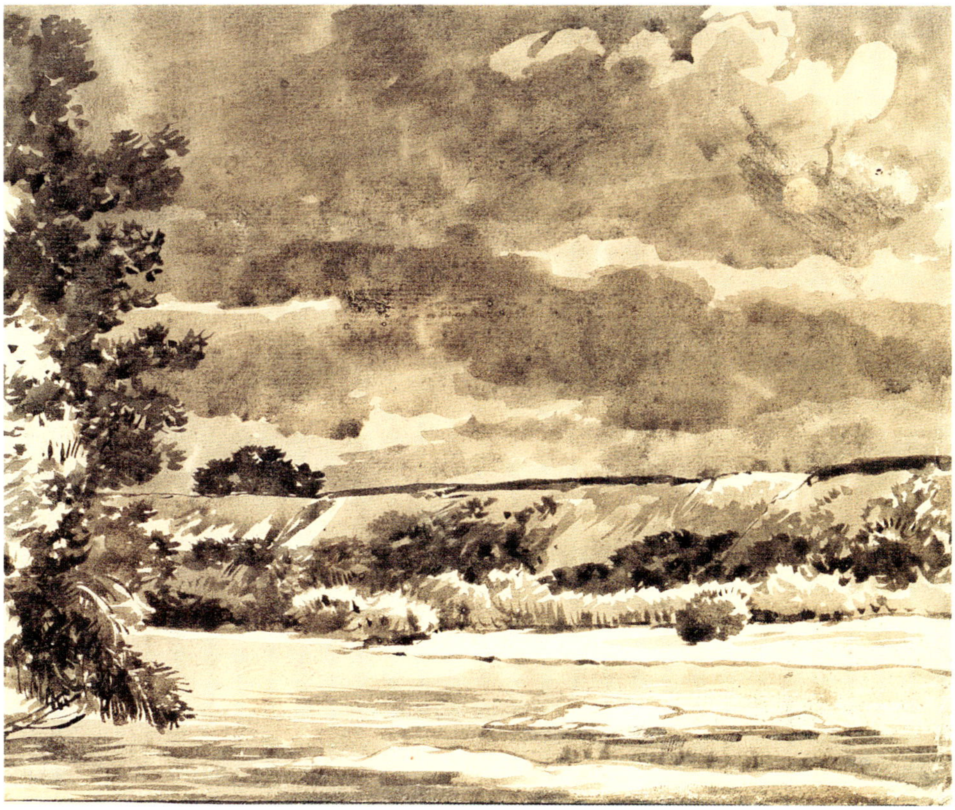

51

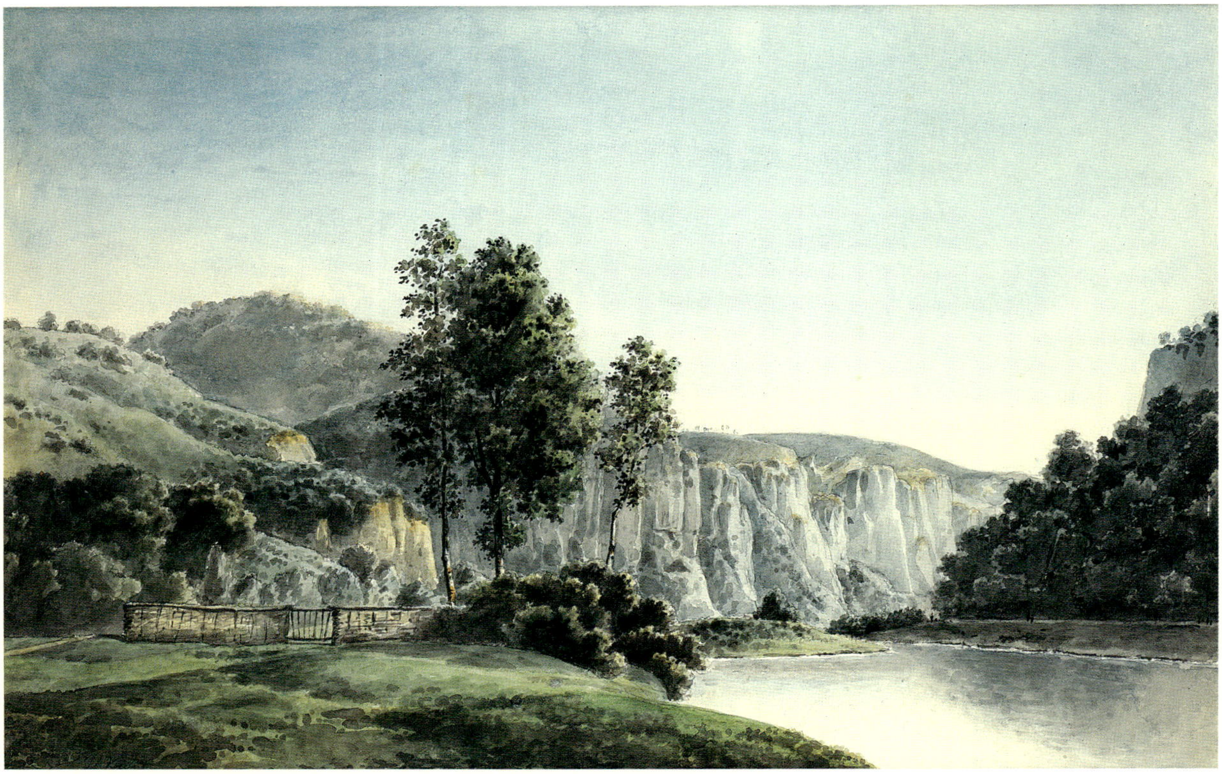

52

JOSEPHUS AUGUSTUS KNIP

Dutch, Tilburg 1777–1847 Berlicum

52

River Landscape with Distant Cliffs

Watercolor over graphite; double framing lines in watercolor, left and right margins trimmed.

10⅛ x 14 15/16 in. (262 x 384 mm).

WATERMARK: J. Whatman, partially cut off (similar to Heawood no. 117).

Signed at lower left, *JA Knip*, the surname gone over in a darker shade.

PROVENANCE: Sale, Amsterdam, Sotheby's, 15 November 1995, no. 208, repr.; sale, Amsterdam, Sotheby's, 10 November 1998, no. 99, repr.

Josephus Augustus Knip was the most celebrated member of a family of Dutch artists active from about 1770 to the turn of the twentieth century. After training in the studio of his father, Nicolaas Frederick Knip (1741–1808), he established himself in Paris in 1801. In 1808, supported by Jacques-Louis David, Knip applied for and won the Prix de Rome, departing the following year. When he returned to the Netherlands in 1812, he brought with him a portfolio of some five hundred and seventy drawings of landscapes, ancient ruins, and figure studies that he used in compositions throughout his career.

Before leaving for Italy in 1809, Knip traveled through present-day southern Belgium, visiting the city of Namur on the Meuse River. It was there that he likely made this drawing, whose landscape of rocky cliffs bears a strong resemblance to that found in two other watercolor views, one in the Boijmans Van Beuningen Museum, Rotterdam, and one recently on the art market, both signed by the artist and bearing inscriptions that identify the location as Namur (Hertogenbosch 1977, no. 77, repr., and sale, Amsterdam, Sotheby's, 15 November 1995, no. 128, repr.).

Knip made working studies during his travels that he incorporated into larger, more finished views. The present drawing may have been undertaken as such a study, for the steep cliffs and forested hills of this picturesque landscape are the sort of subject that appealed to him. Yet, unlike so many of his other studies that he left unfinished—for example, the empty foreground in *Ruins of a Cloister at Namen*, 1809 (Hertogenbosch 1977, no. 25, repr.)—this drawing has a finished quality, suggesting that Knip (or his brother Mattheus Derk Knip [1785–1845], according to Fransje Kuyvenhoven in a letter of 1 September 1999) subsequently may have added to the composition. KS

53
Studies of Farm Implements

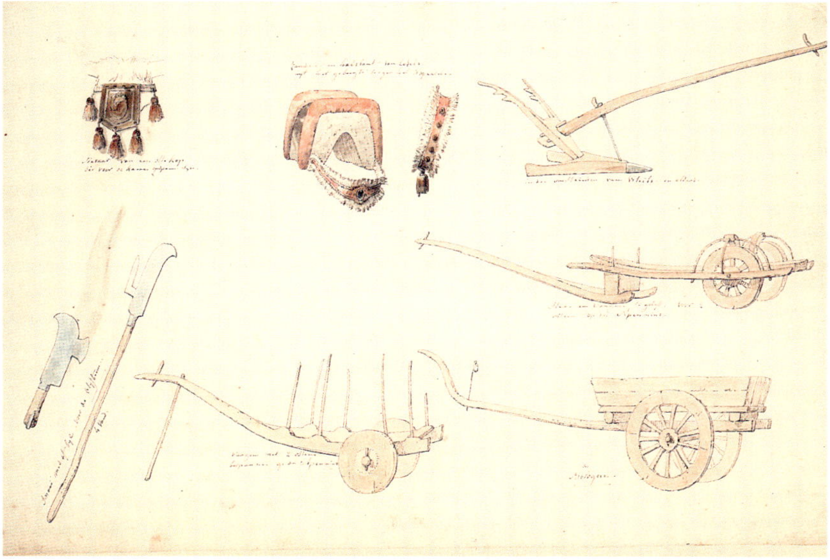

53

Pen and black ink and watercolor over preliminary indications in graphite.

9 x 14$\frac{3}{16}$ in. (235 x 365 mm).

WATERMARK: JW, partially cut off.

Inscribed at upper left, in pen and black ink, *Sieraat van een Ossekop / di[e] voor de karren gespannen Syn*; at upper center, *Zaadel en halsbant van Eezels / uÿt het gebergte teegen het Napelsche.*; at upper right, *in de omstreecken van Viterbo en elders*; at right center, *Slee en Waagen te gelÿk, voor 2 / ossem op de Apennins.*; at lower left, *Snoei mas of bÿl, voor de Olyfboom . . . / 4 voed*; at lower center, *Waagen met 2 ossens / bespannen op de Apennins*; at lower right *a / Bologne*; on verso, at right, in pencil, *BM [B11?] 359*.

PROVENANCE: Private collection, New York; Bob P. Haboldt and Co., New York.

During his three-year sojourn (1809–12) as a pensionnaire of Louis Napoléon, Knip made several hundred drawings of the Italian landscape, its buildings, and ruins, as well as studies of staffage, costume, plants, animals, and farm implements. The present sheet, with inscriptions *Napelsche, Viterbo, Apennins,* and *Bologne* attesting to the places he visited, can be dated to this period. A similar sheet, depicting a range of implements different from those pictured here, is preserved in the Boijmans Van Beuningen Museum, Rotterdam (Hertogenbosch 1977, no. 69, repr.). Knip recorded subjects such as these for later use in his fully worked-up drawings in watercolor and gouache. A horse-drawn wagon similar to that in the lower right corner of this drawing appears in a work attributed to Knip in the Boijmans Van Beuningen Museum, *Landscape with Covered Wagon, Near Boxtel* (Rotterdam 1994–95, no. 36, repr.). KS

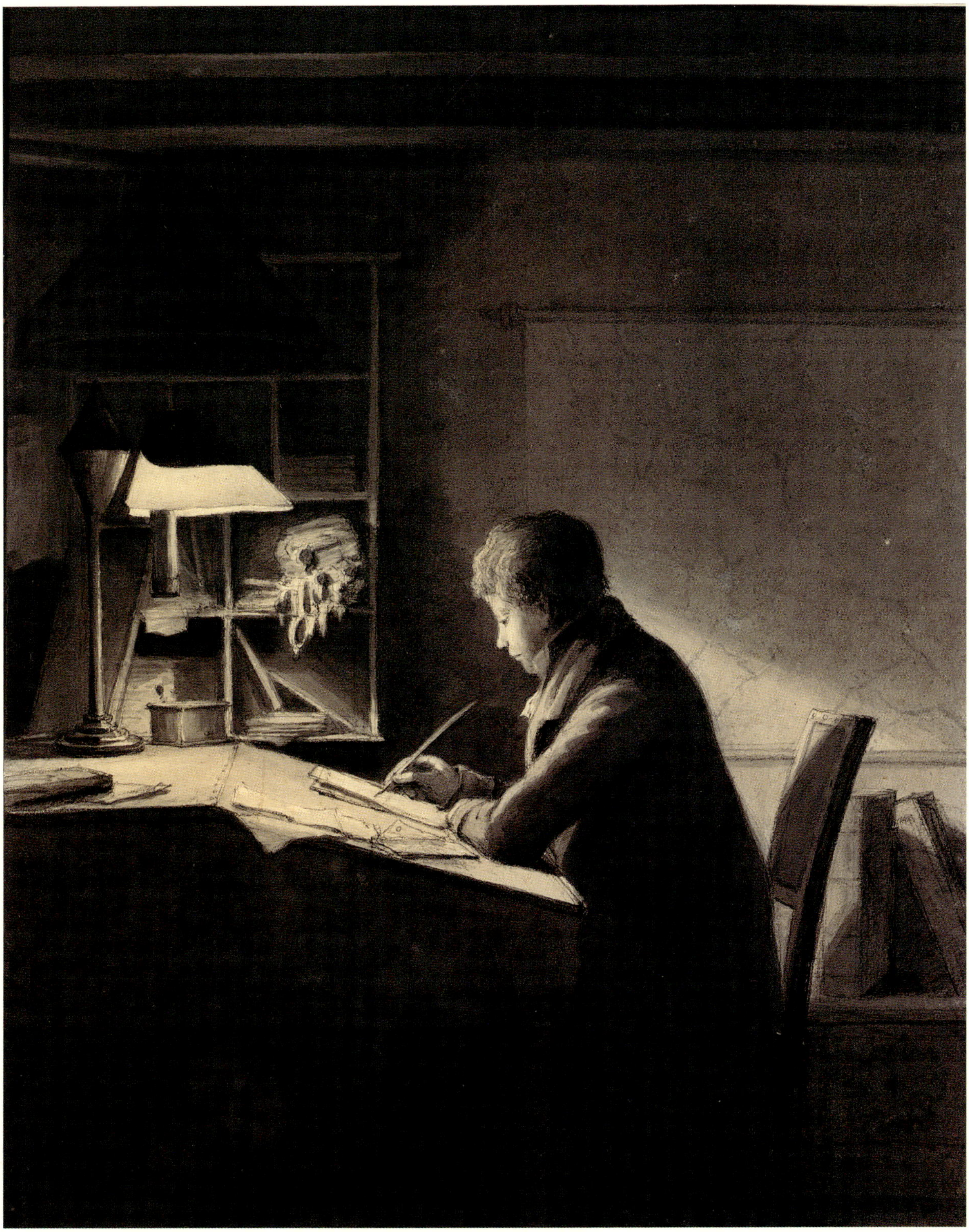

54

JOHANNES JELGERHUIS

Dutch, Leeuwarden 1770–1836 Amsterdam

54

A Young Man Seated at a Writing Desk

Black chalk, gray wash.

14⅜ x 11 7/16 in. (364 x 290 mm).

WATERMARK: None visible through lining.

Formerly signed on original mount, in pencil, *J. Jelgerhuis* (since cut by framer).

PROVENANCE: Galerie Fischer-Kiener, Paris, ca. 1975; Douglas Druick, Chicago; W. M. Brady and Co., New York.

Known as an actor as well as an artist, Jelgerhuis studied painting and drawing with his father, the portrait painter Rienk Jelgerhuis (1729–1806), and Pieter Barbiers Pieterszn (1749–1842), a painter of landscapes and set designs for theater. Following Pieterszn, Jelgerhuis began his career painting sets and soon took up acting as well. He designed costumes and wrote and published theoretical tracts on drama illustrated with prints after his own designs. Numerous examples of these costume drawings survive, executed most often in watercolor or pen and ink and wash, such as *Studies of Actors and Actresses* in the Boijmans Van Beuningen Museum, Rotterdam (Rotterdam 1994–95, no. 14, repr.).

Jelgerhuis was prolific, and his subject matter was wide-ranging, including landscapes, genre scenes, and church interiors. So numerous were his church interiors, in particular, that among his contemporaries he began to be known as the new Pieter Saenredam (1597–1665). Works by other artists of the Dutch golden age were also of special interest to Jelgerhuis, and in a notebook he kept while on tour with a theater company in 1816 he recorded his thoughts on how the Dutch countryside compared with the works of the old masters.

This drawing with its quiet simplicity recalls the intimate interiors of Johannes Vermeer; indeed, the map hanging on the wall behind the sitter may be seen as a quotation of the older artist. A similarly contemplative mood is evoked in a painting by Jelgerhuis of 1825 entitled *Interior of a Kitchen* (Nijmegen and elsewhere 1969–70, no. 17-227, repr.). Despite the businesslike setting of the present drawing, which Robert-Jan te Rijdt dates to ca. 1805–15 (correspondence, 16 February 2000)—the map on the wall, the large volumes on a low chest behind the sitter, and the pile of documents affixed with seals at the side of the desk suggest an office, not a study—the feeling is intimate and personal. The artist is positioned at almost eye level with his subject, expressing a certain sympathy with the young man.

KS

JOHANNES CHRISTIANUS SCHOTEL

Dutch, Dordrecht 1787–1838 Dordrecht

55

Seated Woman

Black chalk, some stumping, on heavy wove paper; ruled border in graphite.

10⅝ x 9¾ in. (270 x 247 mm).

WATERMARK: Fragment.

Inscribed on verso, at lower left, in pencil, *J. G. Schotel*; on old mount, in pen and brown ink, *J. G. Schotel*.

PROVENANCE: Martin Moeller, Hamburg.

Schotel was a passionate draftsman. After studying briefly as a child with Adriaan Meulemans (1753–1835), he took up the family business of silk and cotton manufacture, spending all his free time drawing. In 1805 he enrolled in the drawing society Pictura, where he attended biweekly figure study sessions. Around 1808 he sought out Dordrecht's foremost marine painter, Martinus Schouman (1770–1848), but he quickly surpassed his master in both oil painting and draftsmanship. Schotel was so successful that when his textile business foundered in 1809, he was able to support himself with commissions for his artwork.

Schotel is known today for his marine paintings and the virtuosic preparatory drawings in pen and wash that he made for them, their energetic line reminiscent of Willem van de Velde the Elder (1611–1693). The rare figures that appear in these works are small in scale and subordinated to ships, sea, and sky. In type they resemble the figures that Schotel sketched during the life drawing classes he attended as a young man, a number of which, dated 1805/10, are preserved in the Rijksmuseum, Amsterdam, and the Teyler Museum, Haarlem.

The present drawing, by contrast, is an intimate study, even though the sitter, whose identity is not known, is represented from the back. The figure is positioned close to the picture plane and set in a limited but well-defined environment, unlike those in Schotel's life drawing studies, which are isolated and often set further back (see, for example, *Kneeling Man*, Rijksmuseum, Amsterdam, acc. no. 1953:91, and *Study of a Kneeling Woman*, Teyler Museum, Haarlem, acc. no. Z45). The drawing also may date from later in Schotel's career than the life drawing figures, for his handling of the chalk is freer and more expressive. Here he varied the intensity of his strokes to model form, suggest texture, and convey a range of tonalities—from the fineness of the sitter's hair to the deeply creased folds of fabric gathered about her—letting the white of the paper suggest highlights across the crown of her head and down her right arm. The searching strokes along the edge of the sitter's right shoulder show a mature artist, in complete control of his medium, thinking on paper. KS

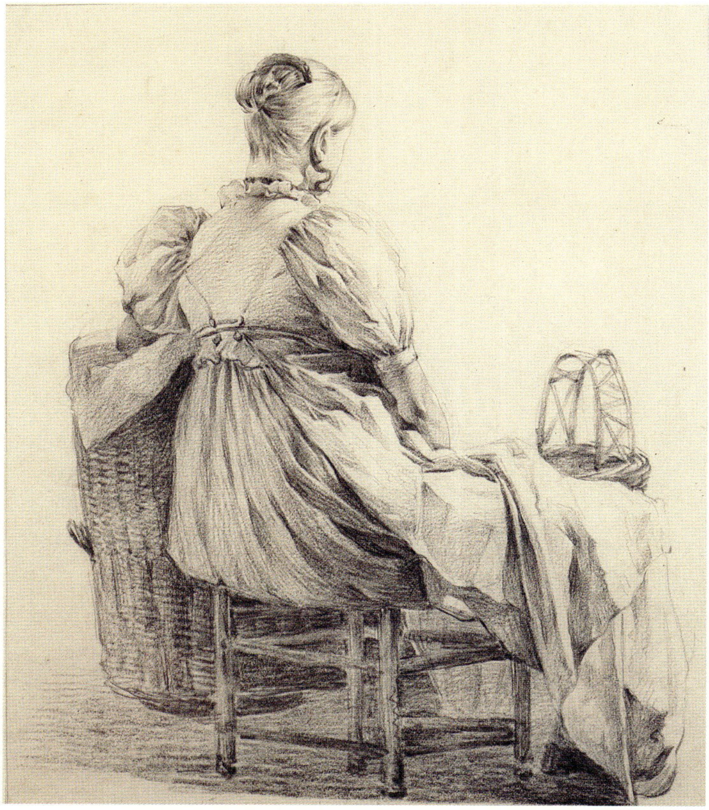

55

LUIGI SABATELLI

Italian, Florence 1772–1850 Milan

56

Heads of Two Young Men in Profile

Pen and black ink.

9 x 6⅜ in. (230 x 163 mm).

Inscribed in pen and ink, *Bozzetto di Luigi Sabatelli do: il gnomino 1795 e comae prosperi,* and, *Giuseppe Bazzuoli di anni 10 e mesi 10.*

PROVENANCE: Bezzuoli-Macciò-Parri; Flavia Ormond Fine Arts Ltd., London.

EXHIBITION: New York 1998b, no. 22, repr.

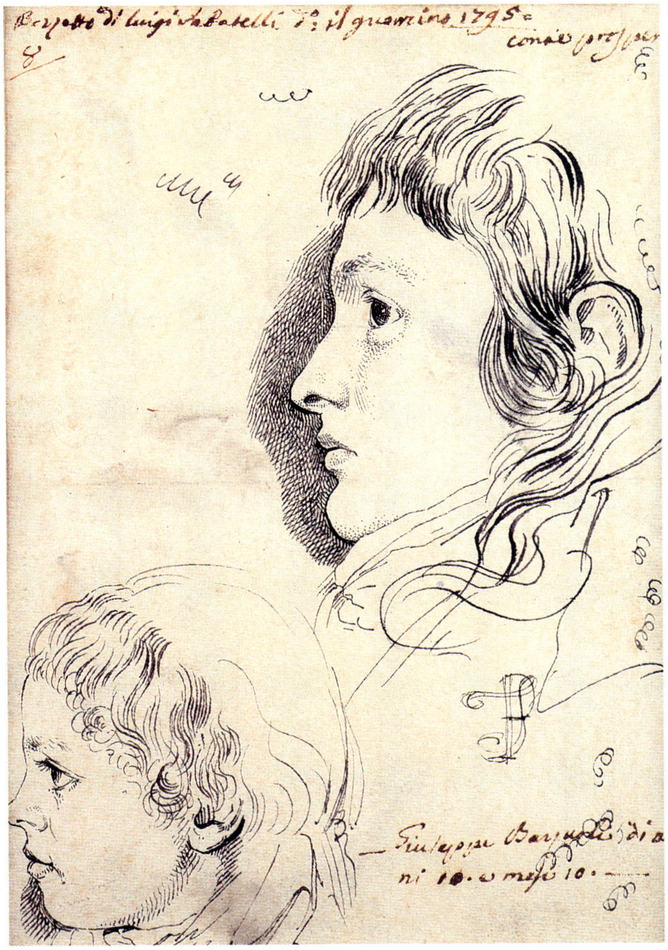

56

Active principally in Florence and Milan, Sabatelli was a prolific painter and a significant figure in the neoclassical and early romantic movements in Italy. The sketch at the upper right is a youthful self-portrait, while the one at the lower left represents the artist's friend Giuseppe Bezzuoli (or Bazzuoli; 1784–1855), who eventually was to become another of Italy's leading painters. Inscribed and dated 1795, the drawing probably was made in Florence, where Bezzuoli was Sabatelli's neighbor.

Sabatelli evidently taught his young friend the principles of drawing, and Flavia Ormond has suggested that the sheet may be related to Bezzuoli's artistic education, proposing that the inscription *comae prosperi* might be translated, "you will do well like me." At any rate, the drawing seems to have been a gift from Sabatelli to Bezzuoli, in whose family it remained until the mid-1990s. WMG

FRANÇOIS PASCAL SIMON, BARON GÉRARD

French, Rome 1770–1837 Paris

57

Study for The Tenth of August 1792

Black chalk.

8½ x 6¾ in. (215 x 171 mm).

PROVENANCE: Baron Gérard d'Harcourt, Paris; by descent through the artist's family; Colnaghi, New York.

EXHIBITIONS: New York 1982, no. 26, pl. XI; New York 1989, no. 31b, repr.; New York 1999, no. 99, repr.

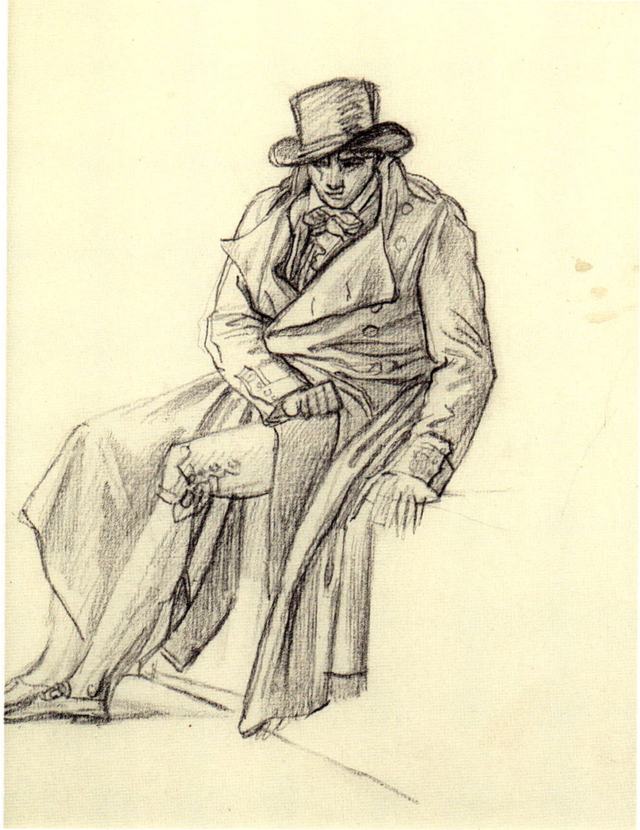

57

Gérard entered the studio of the neoclassical painter Jacques-Louis David (1748–1825) in 1786 and remained under his direction throughout the Revolution, eventually emerging as one of his most talented students. To protect his favored pupil during the Terror, David arranged for Gérard's nomination to the Revolutionary Tribunal in 1793. Although Gérard began exhibiting at the Salon as early as 1791, his career did not flourish until after 1798, when he began receiving imperial commissions. Following the Restoration, Gérard became *peintre du roi* to Louis XVIII, and was elected a member of the Académie des Beaux-Arts.

This drawing is one of several figure studies for *Le 10 Aôut 1792*, a *modello* for which is in the Louvre (acc. no. 26725). The painting was never completed; a large unfinished canvas, squared for transfer, is in a private collection in London. An oil study for the composition was exhibited in 1992 (on paper mounted to panel; Munich and New York 1992, p. 14, repr.), and several studies for individual figures are extant. The present sheet is a study for the seated male deputy at the lower right of the composition. Although he is depicted as a youth in this drawing, the corresponding figure in the study at the Louvre is in the same pose and attire but has the features of an older man.

Gérard submitted the composition in 1794 to a contest sponsored by the Committee of Public Safety (Comité de salut publique). He shared first prize with François-André Vincent (1746–1816) and received a commission for a full-scale painting of the subject formally titled *Le Moment où le Peuple, pénétrant dans le lieu des séances du Corps Législatif, demande à grands cris la destitution du tyran*. This was Gérard's first official commission and marked his public debut as an artist. The scene depicts a moment from the eventful day of 10 August 1792, when a group of agitated revolutionaries interrupted the Assembly and confronted the secretaries of the Séance, revealing precious objects stolen from the royal apartments of the Tuileries as they demanded the deposition of the monarchy.

JT

JEAN-BAPTISTE ISABEY

French, Nancy 1767–1855 Paris

58

Portrait of a Young Man

Black chalk, stumped, heightened with white gouache, on light pinkish brown paper.
7⅛ x 5¾ in. (180 x 145 mm).
Signed and dated at left, in black chalk, *Isabey / 1810*.
PROVENANCE: Richard Day Ltd., London.
EXHIBITION: New York 1990, unnumbered handlist.

This 1810 portrait exemplifies what a young man of the time would have considered fashionable. His coat is trimmed in black velvet, and he wears a partly unbuttoned waistcoat. His windswept hair is brushed forward in a Brutus style and extended along the jawline by close-cropped whiskers. In format and technique the drawing resembles another portrait by Isabey, which is in the Morgan Library and represents the composer André Grétry (1747–1813; Paris and New York 1993–94, no. 98, repr.). The portrait of Grétry is also oval; however, the identity of the pleasant, intelligent-looking subject of the present work is not known.

Isabey was a friend of Napoléon and Joséphine. He was appointed first painter to the empress in 1805. In this capacity he not only painted their likenesses but also was in charge of organizing fetes at the Tuileries and Malmaison and was named *peintre des rois*. He was the most brilliant miniature painter of his time and continued in this capacity with Louis XVIII, Charles X, Louis Philippe, and Napoléon III. Working in black chalk, he achieved a great range of effect, alternating between finely pointed and broad applications of the chalk, effectively heightened with white gouache.

CDD

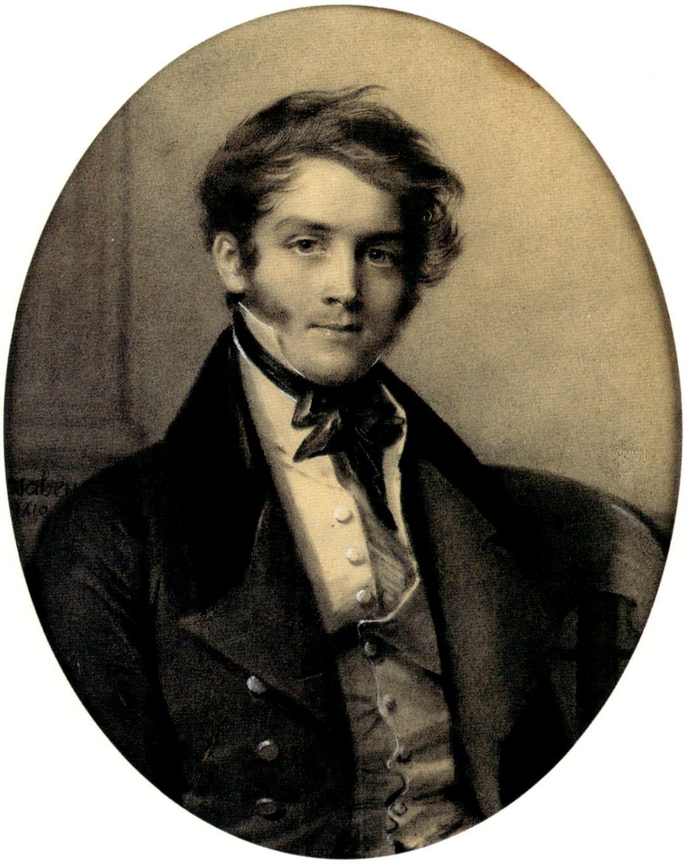

58

PIERRE-ATHANASE CHAUVIN

French, Paris 1774–1832 Rome

59

Two Figures Sketching by a Tree Near a Winding Road, a Castle in the Distance

Black chalk and graphite; framing lines in brown ink.

10⅞ x 8¾ in. (278 x 222 mm).

Inscribed on the original mount at lower right, in pen and black ink, *Pierre Chauvin an VI;* at lower left, in pen and brown ink, *N° 64*.

PROVENANCE: Marie-Madeleine Aubrun, Paris; W. M. Brady and Co., New York.

LITERATURE: Aubrun 1977, p. 215, no. D92, fig. 25.

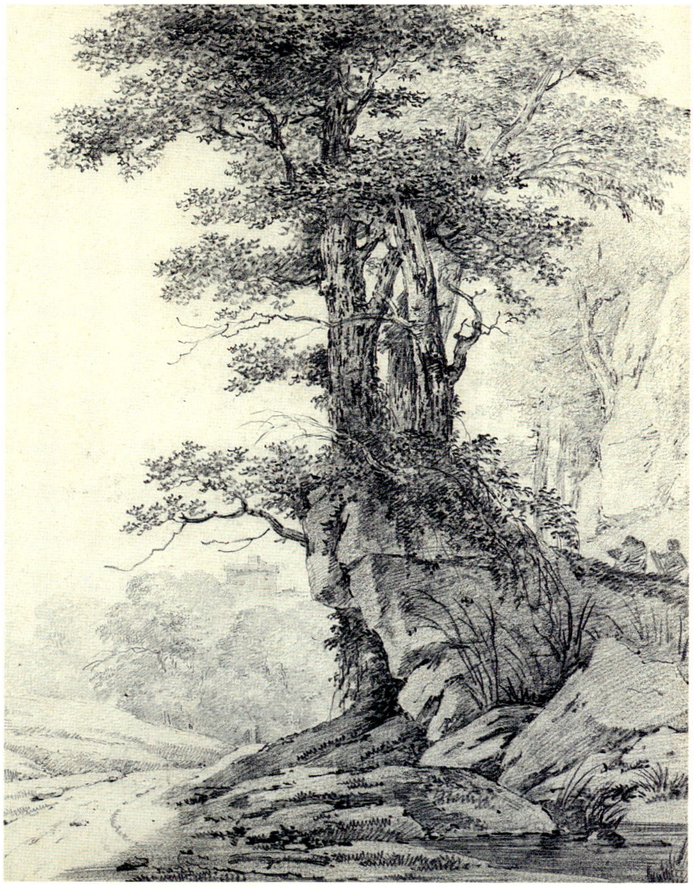

59

A student of the neoclassical landscape painter Pierre-Henri de Valenciennes (1750–1819), Chauvin spent the majority of his career in Rome. In 1802 the statesman Talleyrand became Chauvin's patron. The artist traveled to Italy the same year, settling there permanently in 1804. Although little known today, Chauvin routinely exhibited at the Salon from 1793 until 1831 and was a highly honored and decorated artist. A member of the community of French artists in Rome during the early years of the nineteenth century, Chauvin was friendly with Ingres, for whom he and his wife sat in 1814 (portraits in the Musée Léon-Bonnat, Bayonne).

The present sheet was formerly in the collection of Marie-Madeleine Aubrun, the scholar who compiled the first catalogue of Chauvin's works in a 1977 article (Aubrun 1977). This sheet was one of only five that Aubrun reproduced with the article. In this rare example of Chauvin's draftsmanship, the two figures sketching suggest that the artist may have worked directly from nature, an approach strongly advocated by Valenciennes. In fact the foreground, executed in black chalk, may have been drawn *en plein air*, while the background, executed in graphite, was likely added later. JT

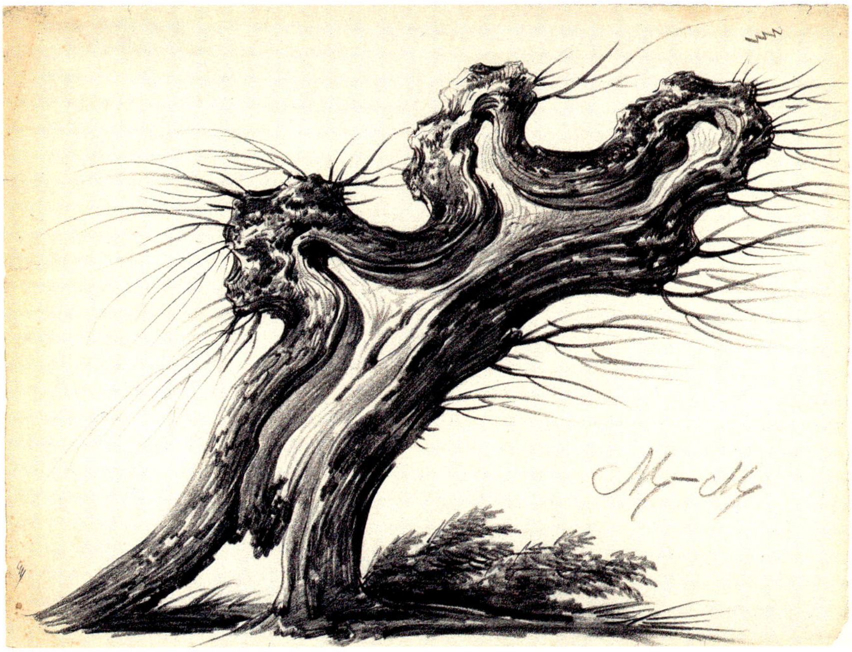

60

ALPHONSE NICOLAS-MICHEL MANDEVARE

French, ca. 1770–ca. 1848

60

Study of a Pollarded Tree

Black chalk.

18$\frac{3}{16}$ x 24$\frac{1}{4}$ in. (460 x 610 mm).

Initialed at lower right, *M—M.*

PROVENANCE: Sale, London, Phillips, 11 December 1991, no. 61, repr.; W. M. Brady and Co., New York.

EXHIBITION: New York 1992a, no. 12, repr.

This lively and highly decorative pollarded tree doubled back on itself in a graceful arc is a characteristic work by Mandevare. Executed in an unusually rich black chalk, it probably was intended as a preparation for a lithograph in one of the artist's books. He published a book in 1804, *Principes Raisonnés du Paysage à l'usage des écoles des Départemens de l'Empire Français,* which was intended to be a landscape painting manual for the amateur artist. The study of a pollarded willow, however, along with many other drawings sold at two sales at Phillips, London (11 December 1991, nos. 61–112, 114, 116, 118, 188–90, and 309, repr., and 8 July 1992, nos. 46–51, 114–21, 280–83, repr.), was probably made in 1829 for another, much later publication. As Marianne Joannides observed (Joannides 1992, pp. 6–7), Mandevare remained a marginal presence on the artistic scene, mentioned little by biographers and critics alike. Since this considerable cache of his drawings has now come to light, however, it is apparent that his work anticipates the oil sketches of rocks and trees produced by such Barbizon artists as Camille Corot (1796–1875) and Théodore Rousseau (1812–1867). CDD

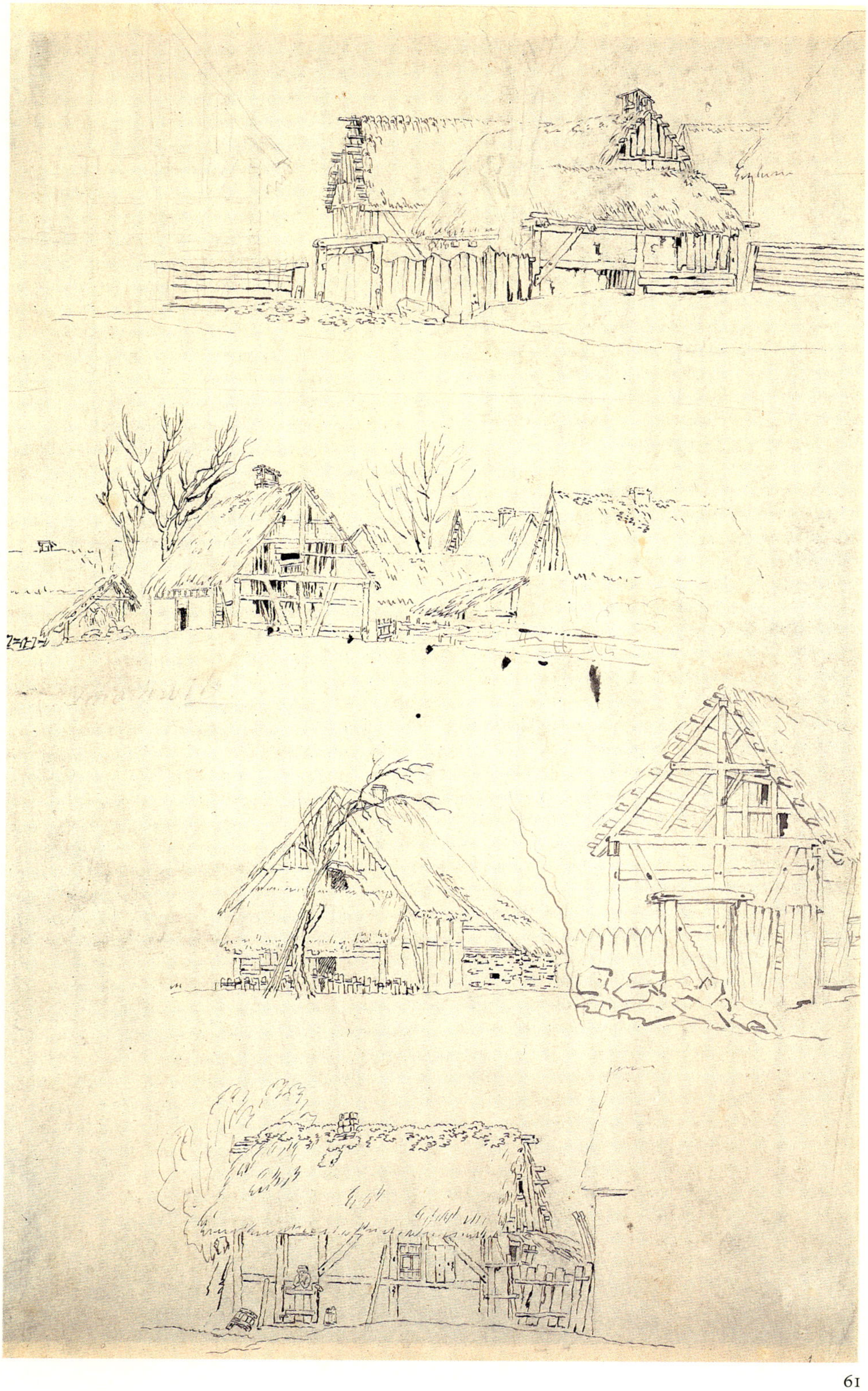

61

CASPAR DAVID FRIEDRICH

German, Greifswald 1774–1840 Dresden

61

Sheet of Studies

Pen and black-brown ink, over graphite (recto and verso).

13⅜ x 8½ in. (340 x 216 mm).

Inscribed by the artist at left, *30 April.*

PROVENANCE: Kurt Meissner, Zurich.

LITERATURE: Zurich 1984, no. 12, repr.

Friedrich studied drawing and etching in his native Greifswald before completing his studies at the Akademi for de Skønne Kunster in Copenhagen. The Danish artists Jens Juel (see No. 46) and Nicolai Abraham Abildgaard (1743–1809) were to exert a strong influence on Friedrich. After a short stay in Berlin, he settled in Dresden, where he received additional training in life drawing. He would become the preeminent German romantic artist, known especially for atmospheric landscapes charged with feeling and religious symbolism. Friedrich traveled within his immediate environs; however, he did not venture beyond central Germany and Bohemia. Even though he loved mountains, he never made the requisite trip to the Alps, which was such a fundamental experience for generations of Northern artists. The mountains, however, were no less important for Friedrich, who held highly personalized views on nature and religion. For him, the mountains were charged with emotive content and symbolized Christian aspiration and hope.

This double-sided leaf from a sketchbook was, as we know from Friedrich's inscription, executed on 30 April, most probably in 1799. The artist's style in this drawing closely resembles that in two sketchbooks of this date in the Nationalgalerie, Berlin (Hofstätter 1974, figs. 99–146, 147–79). Composed of a series of mountain sketches, including a number of farm buildings and a thatched cottage, it also includes a study of two figures on a rock, which the artist was eventually to use in a painting of 1807, *Das Morgen in Gebirge,* now in the Gemäldegalerie, Dresden. He traveled frequently in the Riesengebirge, the mountains bordering Silesia and Bohemia, first in 1799 and then in 1806–7. In 1810 he traveled there with Georg Friedrich Kersting (1785–1847). He also visited the Harz Mountains in 1811. CDD

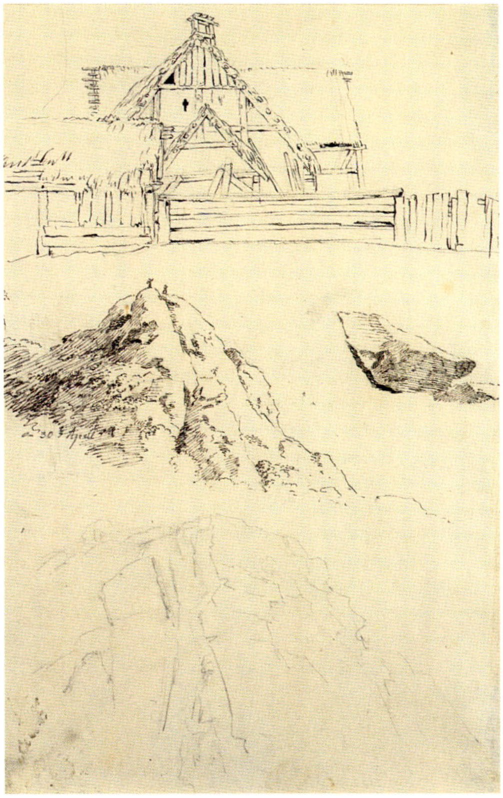

61v

JOSEPH MALLORD WILLIAM TURNER

British, London 1775–1851 London

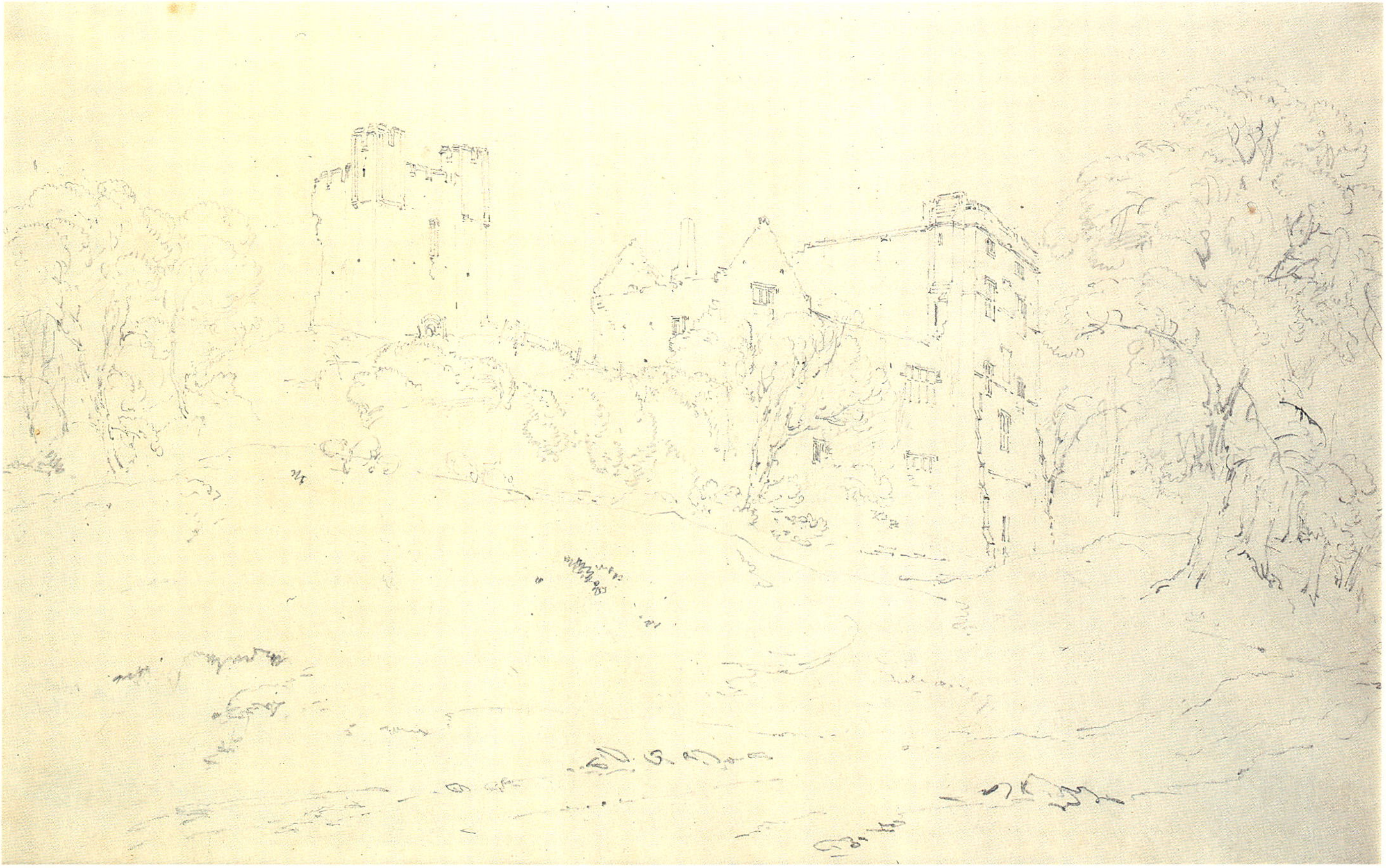

62

62

A Page from the Smaller Fonthill Sketchbook

Pencil on cream paper.

10¼ x 16⅛ in. (260 x 410 mm).

WATERMARK: J. Whatman, 1794.

Inscribed on verso, in pencil, *(another page in Princeton Museum / By J. Ruskin Charles Eliot Norton); From the Smaller Fonthill Sketch Book. 16¼ x 10½ / British Museum, Turner Bequest. Finberg 1.p 123 XLVIII / Northern Tour 1800–1*; in another hand, *J. M. W. Turner RA.*

PROVENANCE: Sale, London, Sotheby's, 19 December 1962, part of no. 241 or 243; J. S. Maas and Co., Ltd., London (The Maas Gallery; as "part of Fonthill House").

EXHIBITION: Princeton 1967.

Turner developed an interest in architectural drawing at a young age, having worked for an architect, Thomas Hardwick, and an architectural draftsman, Thomas Malton (1726–1801). An avid draftsman, Turner filled sketchbooks on his travels with topographical views and line drawings of architecture. He made and exhibited architectural watercolors at the outset of his career. His interest encompassed both historic edifices and contemporary constructions, such as Fonthill Abbey.

According to the inscription on the verso, the present sheet originates from Turner's Smaller Fonthill Sketchbook (1799–1802), now dismembered and the majority of which is in the British Museum. The sheet is the same size and bears the same watermark as other pages from the sketchbook.

The artist spent three weeks at Fonthill in 1799, at age twenty-four, making preparatory sketches for commissioned watercolors. He used the same sketchbook for the next four years on his travels to the north of England and to Scotland. Many of the studies are in the early style of his topographic pencil drawings, characterized by a graphite contour, drawn with a slightly agitated line. For Turner, these sketches were a form of rapid notation and served as a guide for later, more finished drawings. In the course of his travels, he was often attracted to the architecture of castles, abbeys, and cathedrals, and his sketchbooks are filled with such studies. The present sheet reveals a new freedom in Turner's pencil manner, with its energetically drawn foliage and greater attention to composition, using the reserve of the paper as a compositional element. It is far more evocative than some of Turner's straightforward, purely topographical renderings of architecture, perhaps because it is a study of ruins.

The subject of this drawing has been identified variously as part of Fonthill House and Dumblane, or Dunblane, Castle. Neither identification can be confirmed. There are several drawings by Turner of Fonthill Abbey, which is easily identifiable, and this depiction of ruins is not related. Numerous drawings relating to the site of Dumblane or Dumblain in Scotland include a sheet from the same sketchbook in the Ashmolean Museum, Oxford, described by Finberg as depicting "Dumblane Abbey" but presently identified as "Dunblane Cathedral," a drawing of *Dumblane* in Turner's Scotch Lakes sketchbook, and a view of a *Dumblain Abbey, Scotland,* included among the one hundred etchings in his *Liber Studiorum*. He also makes reference to a "Dumblaine" and a "Dunblaine" in his notebook related to the subjects in the *Liber*. This drawing does not, however, represent the same edifice as that of the Ashmolean sheet nor the etching. It is likely that the building depicted here, already in ruins when Turner sketched it about 1800, is no longer extant. JT

CORNELIUS VARLEY

British, London 1781–1873 London

63

Talsarnau, North Wales

Brush and brown wash, over pencil.

9 x 13 in. (229 x 330 mm).

PROVENANCE: Lord Clwyd; Manning Galleries, London; Davis Galleries, New York.

LITERATURE: Thomas and Bennett 1971, p. 307, repr.

EXHIBITION: New York 1969, no. 47, repr.

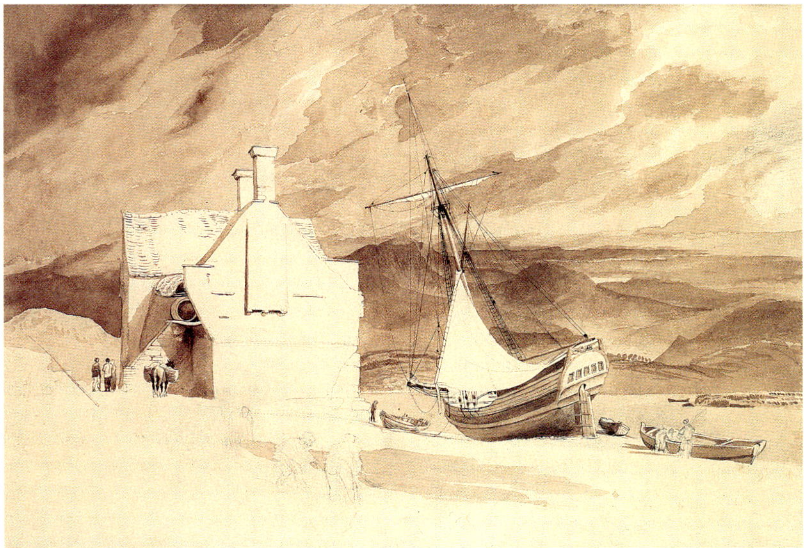

63

Until recently, Cornelius Varley was less well known than his brother John. The elder Varley was highly influential as a painter in watercolors, while Cornelius was known primarily as a scientist, the inventor of a number of lenses and scientific instruments. Of particular interest was a type of camera lucida he patented in 1811 that could reflect a reduced image on paper, allowing the outlines to be traced. But about thirty years ago a cache of Cornelius's drawings and watercolors came to light, making it apparent that he was also a precursor of the British naturalistic landscape movement.

As did many British artists of his generation, Varley made several trips to Wales, from which a number of individual sheets and at least two sketchbooks have survived, including one in the Morgan Library (acc. no. 1973.7; see Ryskamp 1990, pp. 344–59). This drawing of Talsarnau, a small town on a river, near Harlech in north Wales, may have been executed in 1805 when the artist drew scenes of the area around Snowdon. In connection with this drawing, it is interesting to note that Cornelius and his brother John collaborated on *Etchings of Shipping, Barges, Fishing Boats.* Published in 1809, it contains some of the earliest examples of independent lithography in England. CDD

JOHN CONSTABLE

British, East Bergholt, Suffolk, 1776–1837 Hampstead

64

Stoke Poges Church

Brush and brown wash.

3 x 6⅛ in. (86 x 162 mm).

Dated by the artist in black chalk at upper right, *July 6;* signed, inscribed, and dated on verso, in pen and brown ink, *Church of Stoke Poges near Windsor/ in which Gray wrote the Elegy—J. Constable RA to August 23*[?] / *Mr Colvile 183* [cut off]; numbered in pencil at lower left, *63*.

PROVENANCE: Given by the artist to Master Colvile; Hazlitt, Gooden and Fox, London; E. V. Thaw and Co., New York.

LITERATURE: London 1976a, p. 110, fig. 81; Reynolds 1984, p. 248, no. 33.14, pl. 871.

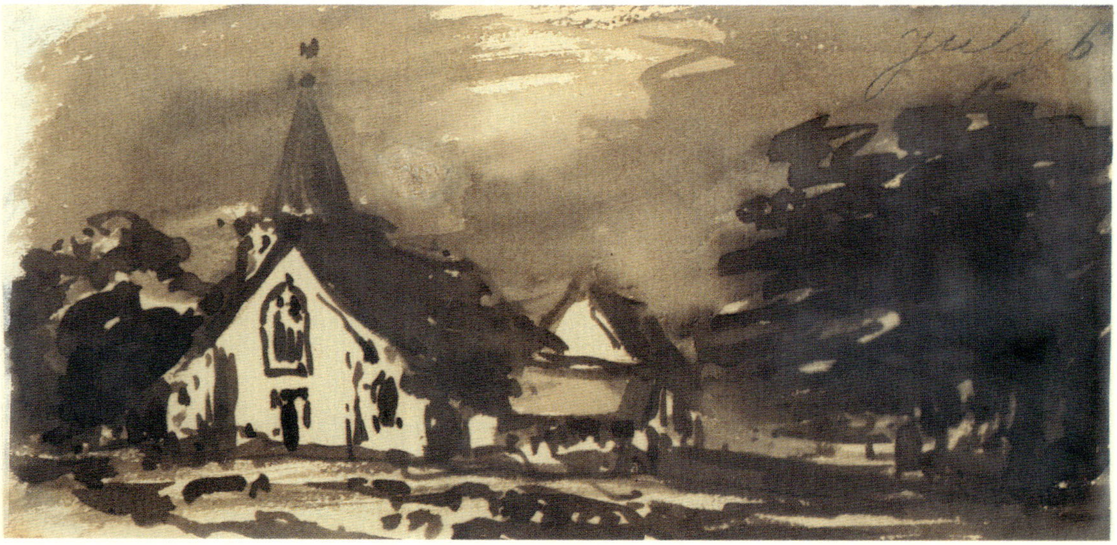

64

Constable's depiction of the church at Stoke Poges was executed perhaps forty years after that of Paul Sandby (No. 44). Set in the evening, Constable's quick sketch is moody and impressionistic and was probably done from memory. In 1833 he made some finished watercolors of the church at Stoke Poges to be engraved in connection with John Martin's edition of Gray's *Elegy* in 1834. In addition to three designs by Constable, the edition contained designs by William Mulready (1786–1863) and other artists. A vignette of the church at Stoke Poges based on a similar drawing, now in the Victoria and Albert Museum, London, was added to the title page of the second edition, published in 1836.

According to the inscriptions, Constable made the sketch on 6 July and gave it to one of his son's school friends, a Master Colvile, on 23 August 1833. Executed in his late, very inky, blot manner, it is by no means as complete a view of Stoke Poges as the watercolor in the Victoria and Albert Museum, London (Reynolds 1984, no. 33.13, pl. 869). This work is small, too, and Constable depicted the church from a deeper perspective that includes the graveyard and more of the surrounding countryside. Another five drawings, including four watercolors, are connected with the project (Reynolds 1984, nos. 33.15–33.19, pls. 872–76). CDD

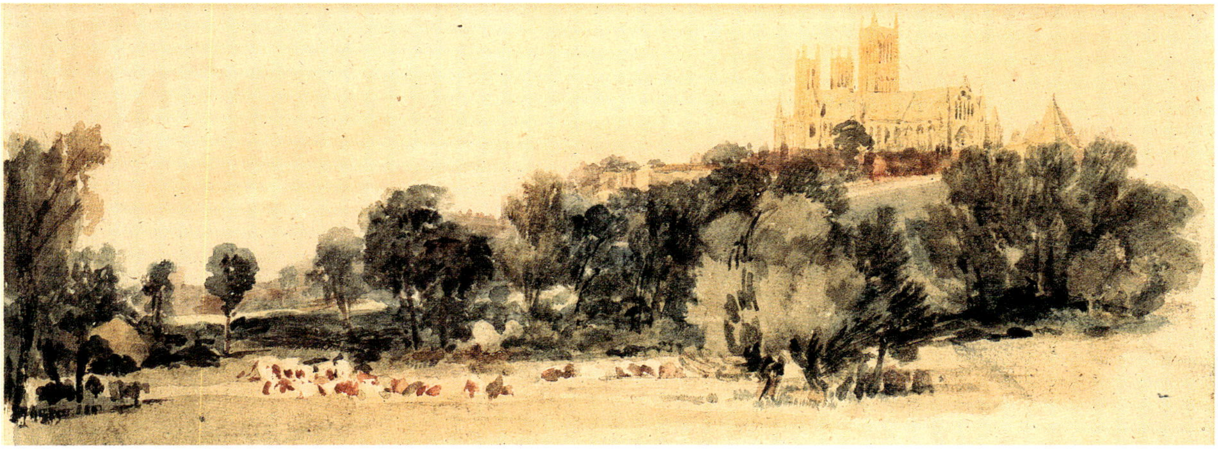

65

PETER DE WINT

British, Hanley 1784–1849 London

65

Lincoln from the Southeast

Watercolor.

$4\frac{1}{8}$ x $11\frac{1}{8}$ in. (108 x 285 mm).

PROVENANCE: Dr. Thomas Monro; Mr. Tiffin; Rev. William Houldsworth; Andrew Wyld, London; Davis and Long, New York.

LITERATURE: Thomas 1982, p. 71, repr.; Smith 1982, p. 14, repr. p. 3.

EXHIBITIONS: London 1979a, no. 17, repr.; New York 1992b, no. 35; Brussels 1994–95, no. 31, repr.

Under the influence of John Varley (1778–1842), de Wint worked *en plein air,* creating a sense of immediacy in his watercolors. His best work is often arranged horizontally on the sheet to allow him to paint sweeping panoramic views. It is difficult to date his works because his watercolor style changed little over the course of his career, and his watercolors share similar characteristics. They are usually rendered in simplified forms; the artist customarily used a warm, dark-toned palette of olive green, Indian red, and ocher. Fortunately, this work can be securely dated, since it is from a book of sketches dated 1816 by the artist; they depict the area around Lincoln, the childhood home of his wife and brother-in-law, where he frequently spent his summers. The present work demonstrates the influence of Thomas Girtin (1775–1802), whose watercolors were familiar to de Wint as a fellow member of the circle of Dr. Thomas Monro.

Even on a relatively small sketchbook page, de Wint realized a sweeping view of Lincoln cathedral that encompasses a gentle pastoral landscape with grazing herds. CDD

DAVID WILKIE

British, Cults, Fife, 1785–1841 off Malta

66

Studies for The Duke of Wellington, Representing His Grace Writing to the King of France on the Night Before the Battle of Waterloo

VERSO: *Studies for* The Duke of Wellington, Representing His Grace Writing to the King of France on the Night Before the Battle of Waterloo

Black chalk, watercolor, and touches of white gouache, on cream wove paper.

Verso: black chalk.

9⅜ x 10 15/16 in. (239 x 277 mm).

PROVENANCE: William Drummond, London.

Perhaps the best known Scottish painter of the nineteenth century, Wilkie trained in Edinburgh and began his career as a portraitist. After traveling to London in 1805 and enrolling in the Royal Academy, he discovered his talent as a painter of genre scenes, for which he received great acclaim. In 1823 he was appointed the king's limner for Scotland, which required him to paint portraits of royalty and courtiers. Although he did not consider portraiture his true métier, Wilkie returned to it throughout his career.

This double-sided sheet of studies is related to a painting by Wilkie in the Aberdeen Art Gallery that was exhibited at the Royal Academy in 1836 as *The Duke of Wellington, Representing His Grace Writing to the King of France on the Night Before the Battle of Waterloo* (DB 482-09). Commissioned by Sir Willoughby Gordon as a companion to Wilkie's portrait of the duke of York (1818–22; National Portrait Gallery, London), the painting was probably begun in 1830 but put aside until 1835, when the duke sat for his portrait. The painting is often erroneously referred to as *Wellington Writing the Dispatch,* a more dramatic subject (correspondence, 18 July 1999, Hamish Miles to William Drummond).

In addition to the present sheet, there are three other known preparatory drawings for the Aberdeen painting: a chalk and watercolor compositional study in Aberdeen, a pen and wash compositional study in Nottingham Castle, and a study in colored chalks for the figure of the duke in the Scottish National Portrait

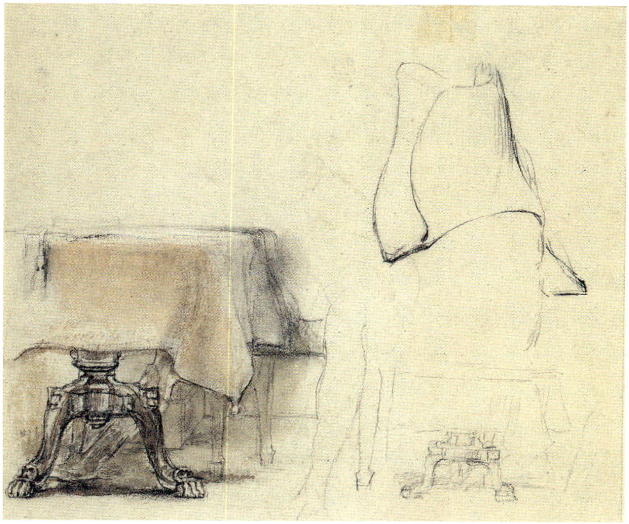

66

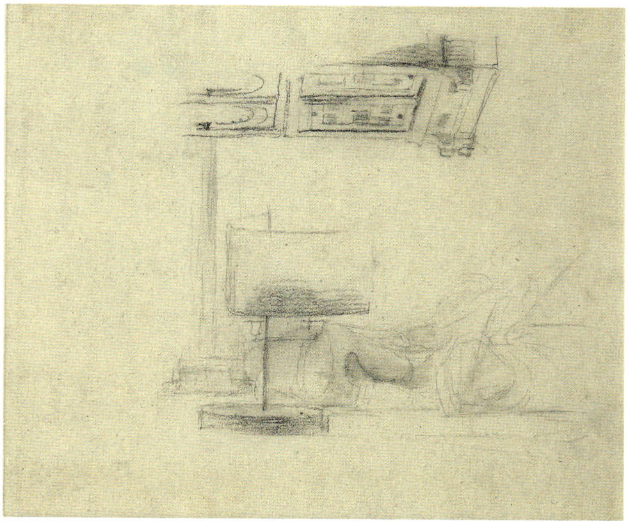

66v

Gallery. The painting depicts Wellington seated at a table, writing a letter by lamplight, while behind him to the right stands a uniformed attendant.

This drawing is part of the preparatory work undertaken by Wilkie before the duke sat for him in 1835. The artist worked out details of the composition, including the seated pose of the duke. The recto contains two studies for the table, a partial study of the duke seated, and a study for his hat, which he does not wear in the final work. On the verso is a study for the tabletop that includes the duke's hand holding a quill, the desk lamp, and an object possibly identifiable as the duke's hat or a satchel. The verso also contains a study for a piece of furniture, perhaps a cabinet, not found in the Aberdeen painting. JT

67
A Study of Two Figures for The Burial of the Scottish Regalia

Black chalk, some red chalk, brown wash, touches of blue, pink, peach, and white gouache, on brown paper.

14 7/16 x 18 7/16 in. (367 x 468 mm).

PROVENANCE: J. S. Maas and Co. Ltd., London (The Maas Gallery).

LITERATURE: New York 1993, under no. 14.

EXHIBITION: New Haven and Raleigh 1987, no. 73, repr.

A master of historical anecdote, Wilkie became widely known through his genre paintings of episodes from British and Scottish history. The story of the Scottish regalia is of immense national importance. The regalia had been removed from Edinburgh Castle to Dunnottar Castle, Grampian, in 1652 by those loyal to the crown to protect it from seizure by Oliver Cromwell and his followers. When the castle was besieged, the regalia was smuggled out and buried under the pulpit of nearby Kinneff Church. Half a century later, in 1707, the regalia was unearthed and returned to Edinburgh under an act of the Scottish and English parliaments (the Act of Union) and placed in an oak chest in the crown room of the castle following the dissolution of the Scottish parliament. Eventually, the public doubted the safety of the regalia and suspected that it had been secretly

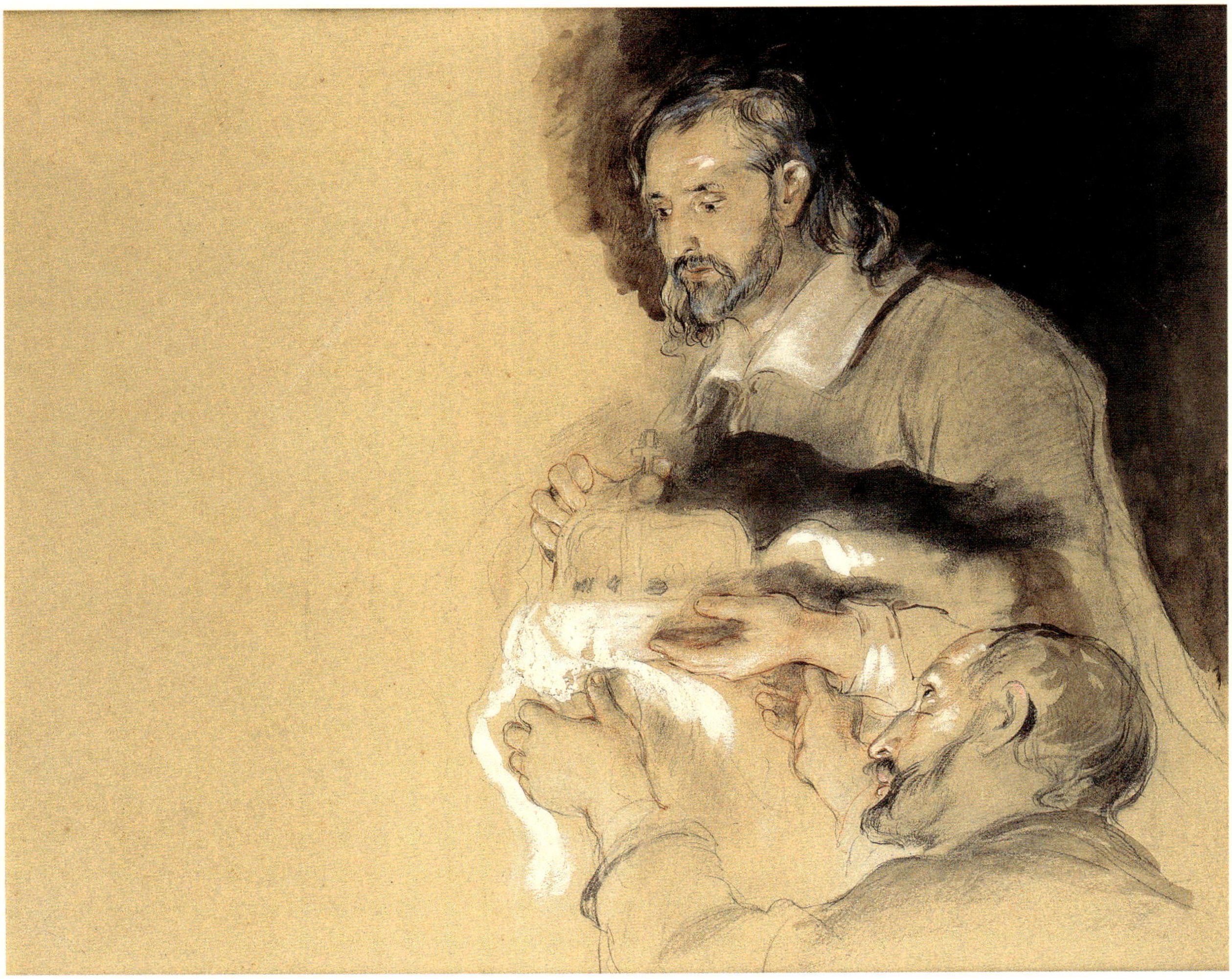

67

taken to London. In 1794 the sealed crown room was opened by the castle's lieutenant governor, who feared the treasure was missing after shaking the chest and hearing nothing. Following a lapse of twenty years, during which the regalia was presumed missing, Sir Walter Scott initiated a national search in 1815. Eventually the crown room was unsealed, and the chest was pried open on 4 February 1818. The regalia was discovered inside, carefully wrapped in linen.

As a posthumous tribute to Scott in 1832, Wilkie began studies for a painting of the original burial of the regalia. Although he never completed the canvas, Wilkie executed a preparatory oil sketch (Fitzwilliam Museum, Cambridge) and two compositional drawings: one in the National Gallery of Scotland, the other in the Hunterian Art Gallery, University of Glasgow. The present sheet, masterfully executed in colored chalks, is preparatory for the two principal figures in the composition. JT

HEINRICH OLIVIER

German, Dessau 1783–1848 Berlin

68

Portrait of Friedrich Olivier (1791–1859) as a Boy

Pencil on light brown wove paper.
$6^{11}/_{16}$ x $4^{5}/_{8}$ in. (170 x 117 mm).
PROVENANCE: William H. Schab, New York.
EXHIBITION: New York 1989a, no. 56, repr.

The young Olivier depicted his brother, who was eight years his junior, half length with his arms folded in front of him. The boy wears a fur-trimmed hat typical of the period. This portrait is generally thought to date around 1805, when Friedrich would have been only fourteen years old. Both brothers studied in Dresden, where they met Philipp Otto Runge (1777–1810) and Caspar David Friedrich (1774–1840). In 1811 the brothers went to the Vienna academy and became friendly with Joseph Anton Koch (1768–1839) and Friedrich Schlegel (1772–1829). In 1816 Julius Schnorr von Carolsfeld (1794–1872) drew a beautiful likeness of the twenty-four-year-old Friedrich; two years later Friedrich and Heinrich accompanied Schnorr to Rome, where they became active in the Brotherhood of St. Luke, the Protestant equivalent of the Nazarenes. Under Schnorr's influence, Friedrich also became interested in portraiture. In this connection it should be mentioned that Charles Ryskamp has recently purchased a drawing executed by Friedrich in 1817 of a young Italian shepherd, Pepe (Munich 1999, no. 7, repr.).

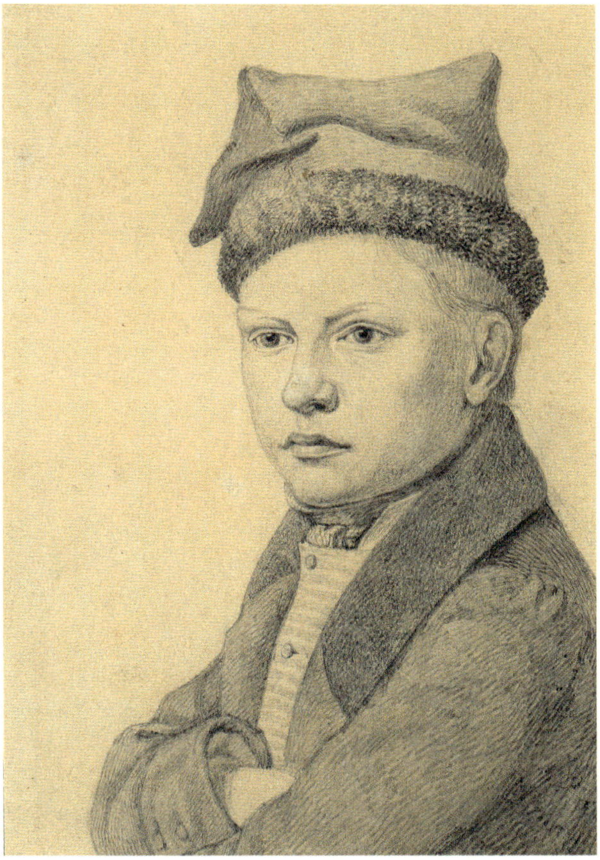

68

While both Olivier brothers were talented portraitists, the remarkable sharpness and clarity of their graphic technique is almost better suited to landscape draftsmanship. Friedrich returned to Vienna in 1823 and also worked with Schnorr on the Nebelunglied frescoes for the Residenz in Munich. Heinrich Olivier joined his brother and Schnorr in Munich somewhat later, becoming a professor of art history at the academy. Drawings by these artists are rare outside Dresden and Berlin, where there are large holdings of their works. CDD

THEODOR MARKUS REHBENITZ

German, Borstel 1791–1861 Kiel

69

Fantastic Landscape with Monk Crossing a Bridge

Pen and black, gray, and brown ink.

6⅝ x 5⅞ in. (169 x 150 mm).

Inscribed on verso, *Ramboux*.

PROVENANCE: Baron Carl Friedrich von Rumohr; August Grahl; C. Henmann; possibly Paul Arndt-München; sale, Leipzig, C. G. Boerner, 16 May 1934, no. 295, pl. XIII; Baskett and Day Ltd., London.

EXHIBITION: London 1987, no. 59, repr. (attributed to Ramboux).

Rehbenitz became acquainted with Friedrich (No. 68) and Ferdinand Olivier (1785–1841), as well as Julius Schnorr von Carolsfeld (1794–1872), when he attended the Vienna academy between 1813 and 1816. He joined the Capitolines, a group of German artists, Protestant in distinction to the Catholic Nazarenes, with whom they shared an admiration for early German art. By 1816 Rehbenitz was living with Schnorr and Friedrich Olivier in Rome. He was also influenced by the Nazarene artists Peter Cornelius and Friedrich Overbeck, whose sister he later married. By 1818 he was in Florence working as a copyist. Between 1827 and 1829 he was German teacher to Marchesa Florenzi in Perugia. Eventually, he returned to Germany and settled in Kiel, where he taught drawing at the university.

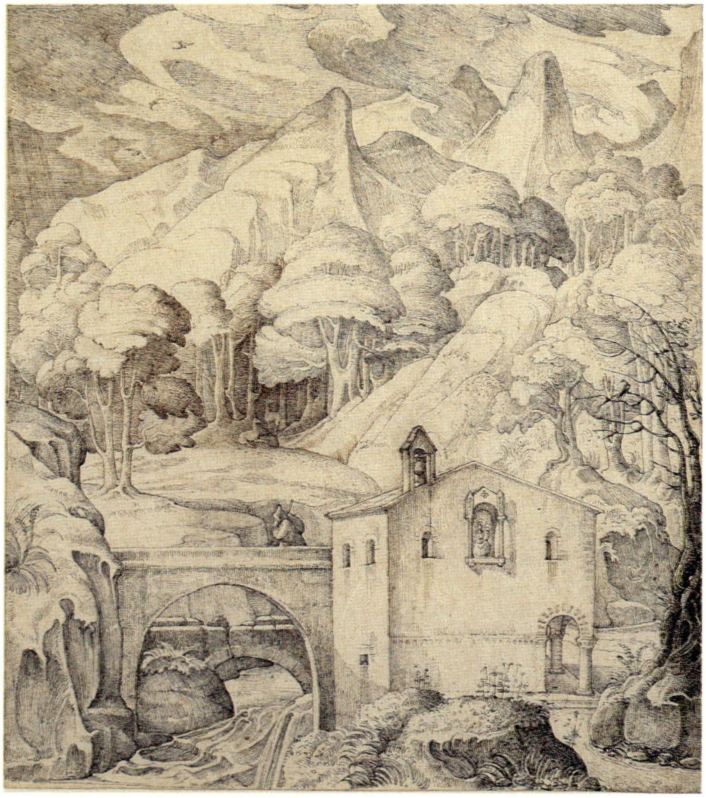

69

The delicacy of Rehbenitz's technique in this fairytale landscape, rendered with a very sharp pencil, suggests silverpoint drawing. It also allowed the artist a profusion of detail, such as the stream rushing under the bridge and the curious, archaizing range of mountains in the background. This work has been ascribed to Johan Anton Alban Ramboux (1790–1866), a close contemporary of Rehbenitz. He, too, practiced a "Gothic" style, but his drawings are more painterly than those of Rehbenitz. CDD

FRIEDRICH SALATHÉ

Swiss, Binningen, near Basel, 1793–1858 Paris

70

View of Trees

VERSO: Various pencil sketches in another direction, including some trees

Pen and brown ink, brown wash, over pencil.

12 x 15 in. (319 x 415 mm).

PROVENANCE: Kurt Meissner, Zurich.

EXHIBITIONS: Zurich 1984, no. 48, repr.; Basel and elsewhere 1988, no. 48, pl. 17; New York 1997–98.

When he studied in Rome between 1815 and 1821, the Swiss-born Salathé became closely associated with the German artistic community. His drawing technique greatly improved during this Italian sojourn as may be seen in landscapes such as this work. His pen line gained strength and verve and was considerably enriched by generous applications of brown and gray wash. It was Salathé's stay in Italy that determined his course as a landscape painter.

While it is not possible to identify whether the location of this rather generalized landscape is Olevano or a site in the environs of Naples, the artist was greatly inspired by the landscapes of both these areas. He obviously made his study *en plein air,* beginning with pencil sketches in the opposite direction on the verso, before turning it over and producing the fully worked pen and wash study on the recto. Back in Switzerland by 1823, he was already beginning to work as an engraver of aquatints, which was to become the main source of his livelihood.

CDD

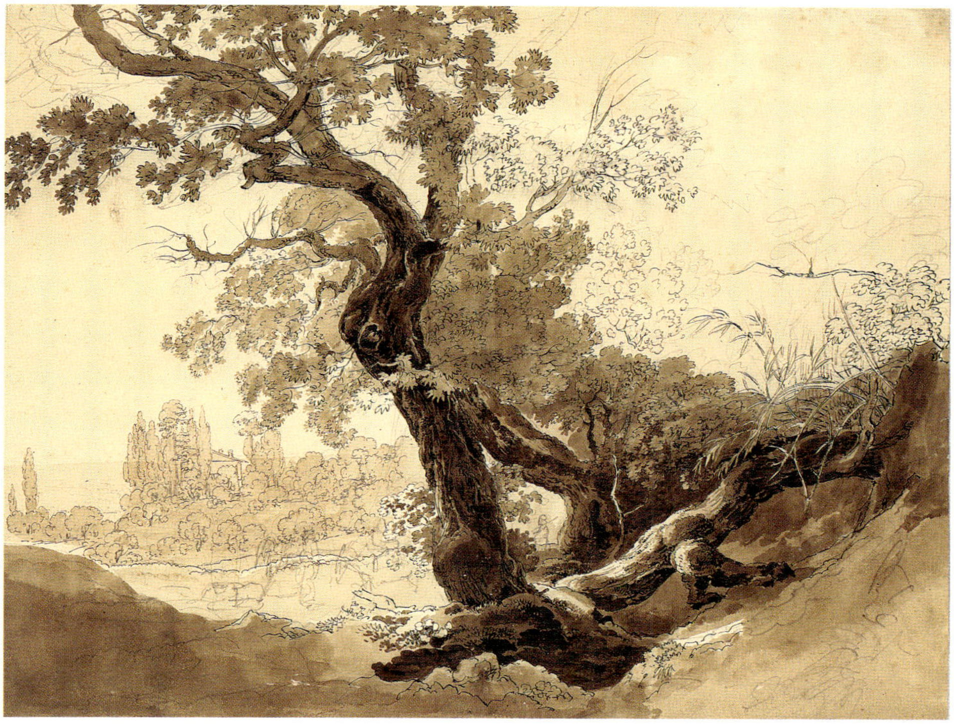

70

FRANZ KRÜGER

German, Grossbadegast 1797–1857 Berlin

71

Portrait of Arzte Funfhausen

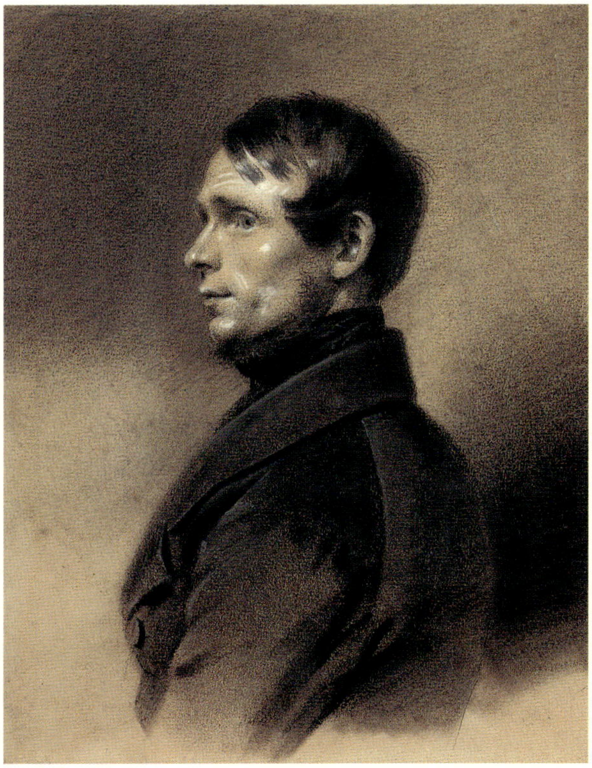

71

Black chalk, heightened with white, on light brown paper.

9 15/16 x 7 11/16 in. (251 x 191 mm).

Inscribed on verso, *Die von Herrn Horwitz erworbene Zeichnung ist von Herrn Professor Franz Krüger gezeichnet und ist der Corps* [?] *Stabsarzt Fünfhausen. —E. Fünfhausen.*

PROVENANCE: The artist's family; Thomas le Claire, Hamburg.

EXHIBITION: Hamburg 1989, no. 52, repr.

Trained in the Berlin academy, Krüger began his career as a painter of military and hunting subjects. He came into prominence with his large painting of the Prussian cavalry in the Napoleonic Wars. As an artist, he was also a frequent traveler to St. Petersburg and executed a number of commissions for Czar Nicholas I. He is known especially for his accurate portrait studies of contemporary subjects. Many of these are now in the Nationalgalerie, Berlin, and the Staatlichen Kunstsammlungen, Dresden. These portraits, which depict his sitters without pretense and with a good deal of insight, were often reproduced as lithographs.

Arzte Funfhausen, a sympathetic and highly intelligent man, as seen by Krüger in this subtly insightful portrait, was a staff medical officer in the Prussian army, according to the inscription on the verso of the present work. The artist often made informal but detailed portrait drawings; see, for example, his portrait of Prince Sergei Alexeievitch Dolgorovsky (1809–1891), who was attached to the Russian mission in Frankfurt in 1829 and was sent to the chancellery at Berlin a year later. In 1832, when Funfhausen sat for this portrait, he was twenty-three years old (Baruch 1994, pp. 106–7, repr.). Three other examples of his draftsmanship—two watercolors and a self-portrait—were exhibited at the Morgan Library in 1988 (New York 1988, nos. 112–14, repr.).

CDD

FRIEDRICH WASMANN

German, Hamburg 1805–1886 Merano, Tyrol

72

Head of a Man

VERSO: Indeterminate sketch in opposite direction, possibly of a draped torso

Pencil, some stumping, on wove paper; pentimento in chin.

5 7/8 x 4 1/2 in. (144 x 113 mm).

Numbered on verso, *IV,15*.

PROVENANCE: Fragmentary collector's mark in purple ink at lower left; sale, Hamburg, E. Hauswedell, 23–25 April 1953, no. 1929; Sven A. Bruntjen, San Francisco; Galerie Arnoldi-Livie, Munich.

LITERATURE: Grönvold 1915, II, repr. p. 44; Nathan 1954, no. 458.

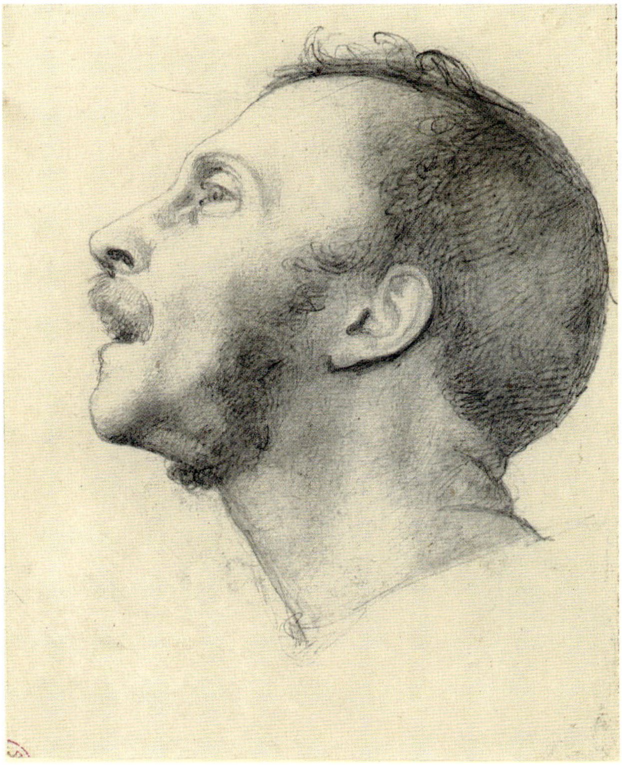

72

After completing his studies in Hamburg and Dresden, Wasmann went to Munich for two years, 1830–31, then the Tyrol, 1832–35, before making a journey to Rome in 1832, where he became involved with the Nazarenes. Under the influence of Johann Friedrich Overbeck, he converted to Catholicism. He remained in Italy for three years, sketching in the Campagna, in the mountains around Subiaco, and in the Alban Hills.

In this very typical pencil drawing, Wasmann posed a studio model—most probably as a shepherd—gazing upward. Stylistically the work must date to around 1835, when he was still in Italy. Like many German artists of this period, Wasmann specialized in rustic landscapes, often populated with shepherds and farm animals. A fine draftsman, the artist executed a number of other works that are closely comparable to the present drawing, such as a child's portrait in the Wallraf-Richartz Museum, Cologne (see Rennes 1994, no. 59, repr.). Here, too, he rubbed the surface of the drawing, softening the pencil contours to suggest atmosphere.

Much celebrated in Germany, the artist has been the subject of a number of monographs and exhibitions. His drawings were included in the great exhibition of German painting in Paris in 1976–77 (see, for example, Paris 1976–77, no. 252, repr.) as well as a recent exhibition devoted to open air painting (Washington and elsewhere 1996–97, no. 123, repr.). CDD

FRIEDRICH GAUERMANN

Austrian, Miesenbach 1807–1862 Vienna

73

Plant Study

VERSO: Unfinished mountain landscape with a church

Oil over black chalk on wove paper.

5⅛ x 6⅝ in. (132 x 169 mm).

PROVENANCE: Thomas le Claire, Hamburg.

EXHIBITION: Hamburg 1989, no. 51, repr.

The third son of the landscape painter Jacob Gauermann (1773–1843), Friedrich was greatly influenced in his stud-

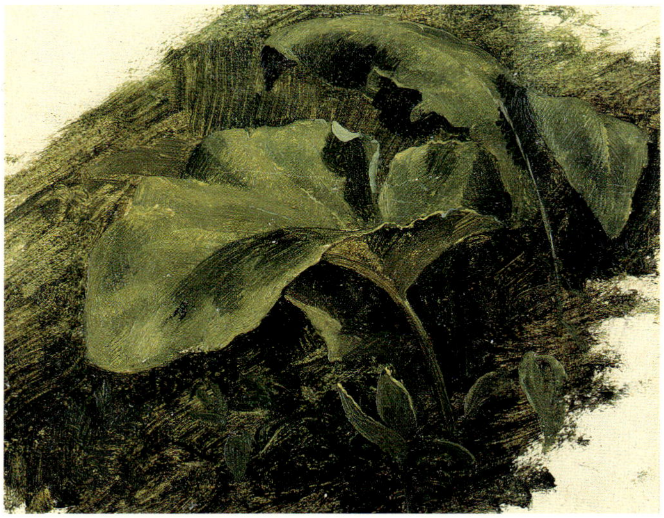

73

ies at the Vienna academy by Netherlandish animal and landscape painting. This study of dock leaves may well have been preparatory for one of his many landscape paintings, since these coarse and weedy plants often appear in the foreground of such works. It is not unlike the plant in the foreground of the artist's 1828 painting *Weideiidyll am Traunsee,* a pastoral with cows, goats, and shepherds in a mountainous setting, which sold at the Dorotheum, Vienna, on 18–29 September 1979. He painted a view from the church in his native town of Scheuchenstein, *Two Goats Near the Church of Scheuchenstein* (Feuchtmüller 1987, p. 269, no. 3), a study for which is on the verso of this sheet. A preparatory drawing for *View of Scheuchenstein* is preserved in the Vienna academy (Nr. 7008; brush and wash, inscribed, *ausgefuhrt 1828 in Leipzig fur Herr Hillig*) and another is in the Historical Museum of the City of Vienna (Nr. 10.039; wash and pen, inscribed *Hillig*).

CDD

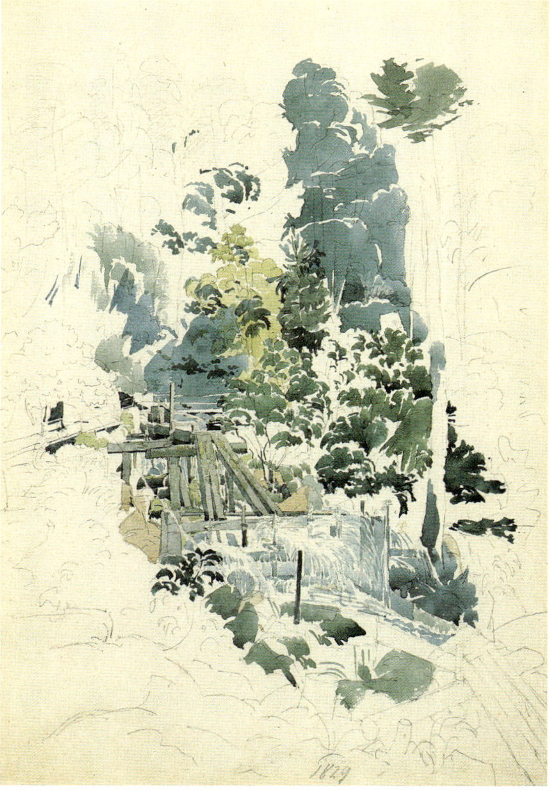

74

RUDOLF VON ALT

Austrian, Vienna 1812–1905 Vienna

74
A Forest Stream

Watercolor and pencil.
9½ x 6⅝ in. (240 x 168 mm).
Dated at lower right, in pencil, *1829*.
PROVENANCE: Galerie Arnoldi-Livie, Munich.

The Viennese painter, draftsman, and printmaker Rudolf von Alt was perhaps the most accomplished watercolorist in the nineteenth-century German-speaking world. He would have learned the art of watercolor painting from his father, Jacob von Alt (1789–1872), a landscape and watercolor painter. Rudolf accompanied his father on his travels and, along with his brothers and sisters, colored his father's drawings. In 1833 he and his father traveled to Italy; Venice made a particularly lasting impression on him. Two years later he visited Rome and Naples and, under the influence of the strong southern light, developed a much wider range of color. Eventually he changed his subject matter from topographical views to scenes of rural or urban life. The artist was only seventeen years old when he worked in the sketchbook from which this sheet was removed. The page is blank except for the detailed watercolor of a stream, evidently an early study for a larger rural landscape. CDD

CHRISTOFFER WILHELM ECKERSBERG

Danish, Blåkrog, southern Jutland, 1783–1853 Copenhagen

75

View of Furesø from Rudersdal

Pencil; framing lines in pencil.

7⅛ x 11⅜ in. (180 x 290 mm).

Dated at lower right, in pencil, *3.Juli 1833*.

PROVENANCE: Sale, Copenhagen, Kunst Hallen, *Aeldre Kunst Antikviteter,* 9 September 1998, no. 45, repr.; Thomas le Claire, Hamburg.

Eckersberg occupies a uniquely important place in the history of Danish painting. Not only was he one of the two or three most talented artists of Denmark's golden age, but through his many students he exercised tremendous influence upon subsequent generations of Danish painters. A pupil in Copenhagen of Nicolai Abildgaard (1743–1809), Eckersberg later studied in Paris under Jacques-Louis David (1748–1825) and spent the years 1813 to 1816 in Rome, where he shared a house with the Danish sculptor Bertel Thorvaldsen

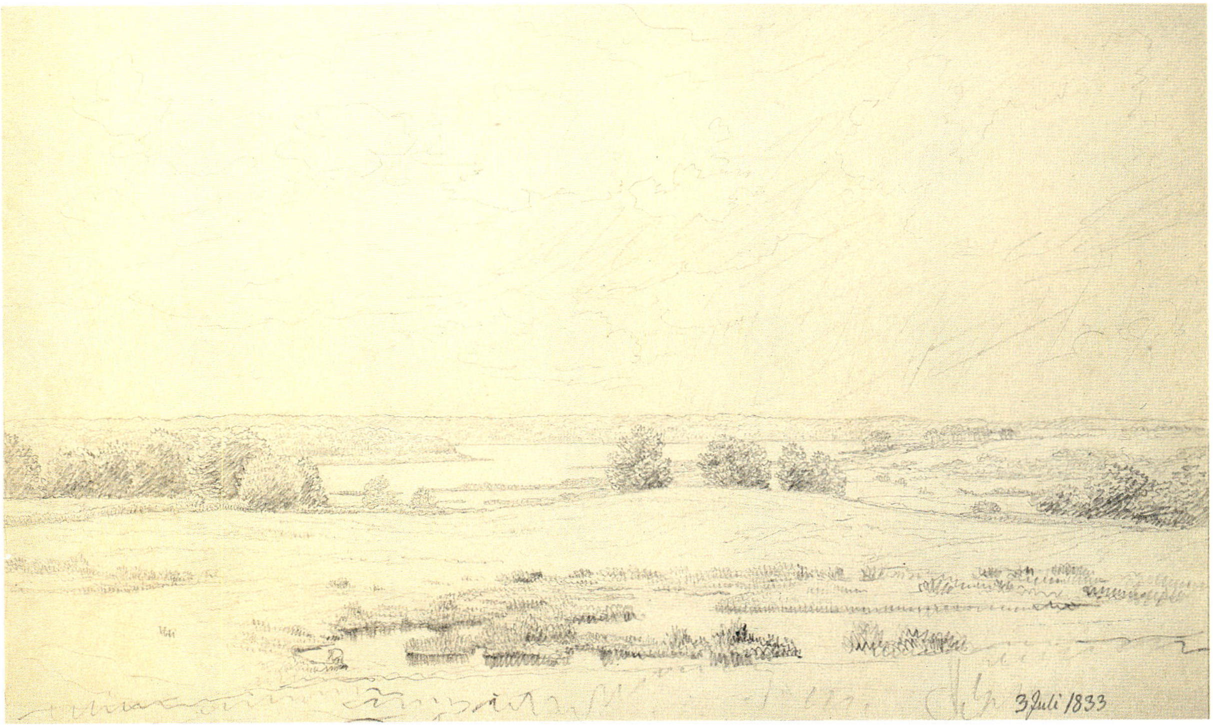

75

(1768/70–1844) and produced a number of carefully composed paintings of Roman monuments. After his return to Copenhagen, he became a member of the Akademi for de Skønne Kunster (Kunstakademi), where he was appointed professor in 1818 and served as director from 1827 to 1829.

This drawing is related to one of the artist's most important small paintings, *View of Furesø from Rudersdal,* now in the Statens Museum for Kunst, Copenhagen (Hannover 1898, no. 481, fig. 138). Furesø, the deepest lake in Denmark, is located about ten miles northwest of Copenhagen and is bordered on its south shore by a forest. The view in the painting is from the Kongevejen, the principal road from Copenhagen to Frederiksborg.

According to the artist's diary, he painted a similar view of Furesø from the Kongevejen, *en plein air,* on 27 May 1831 (Hannover 1898, p. 386, under no. 481). Two years later, on Wednesday, 3 July 1833, Eckersberg, his son Erling (1808–1889), and his students Constantin Hansen (1804–1880), Christen Købke (see Nos. 79–81), and Wilhelm Marstrand (see No. 86) made another excursion to the lake, where they were joined by another of Eckersberg's pupils, Adam Müller (1811–1844; photocopy of Eckersberg's diary, 1 January 1832–end September 1834, Statens Museum for Kunst). There, Eckersberg made the present drawing, in which the approaching rainstorm he describes in his diary is clearly visible in the middle distance. In the finished work, which Eckersberg completed in his studio on 3 September 1833 (Hannover 1898, p. 386, under no. 481), the landscape is similar to that in the drawing, although a seated woman has been added in the foreground. WMG

76

View over the Holmenskanal to the Stock Exchange, Christiansborg, and the Slotskirken, Copenhagen

Pen and gray and some brown ink, gray wash, over pencil, on buff paper; lightly squared in pencil.

8¾ x 12½ in. (223 x 311 mm).

Monogrammed and dated in pen and ink, *E / 1846*.

PROVENANCE: Baron Otto Ditlev Rosenørn-Lehn, Schloss Oreby, Denmark; Galerie Arnoldi-Livie, Munich.

EXHIBITION: New York 1995b.

As Poul Grinder-Hansen has pointed out (correspondence, 13 October 1999), this characteristically detailed drawing represents some of the principal buildings of Copenhagen as they appear from Asiatisk Plads in Christianshavn, on the other side of the harbor. On the left is the early-seventeenth-century Stock Exchange (Børsen), readily identifiable from its bizarre spire composed of the entwined tails of three dragons. The classical building in the center of the composition is Christiansborg Palace, erected in 1820 by Frederik VI on the site of a structure that had burned to the ground in 1794. The building in the drawing also burned down, in 1884, and in 1907 it was replaced with the neobaroque edifice that now houses Denmark's parliament. To the right of Christiansborg Palace is Holmens Kirke, a late-sixteenth-century structure that was converted into a church under Christian IV (r. 1588–1648) in 1619.

The drawing is a study for a painting of 1846 that is now in the Bymuseet, Copenhagen (Hannover 1891, no. 593). In the painting the view is exactly the same, but several additional figures appear in the foreground and the prow of a boat is visible at the far right.

A drawing of a similar view, signed and dated 27 July 1832, was on the art market in Denmark during the early 1930s (sale, Copenhagen, Winkel and Magnussen, 19 October 1933, no. 180, repr.). WMG

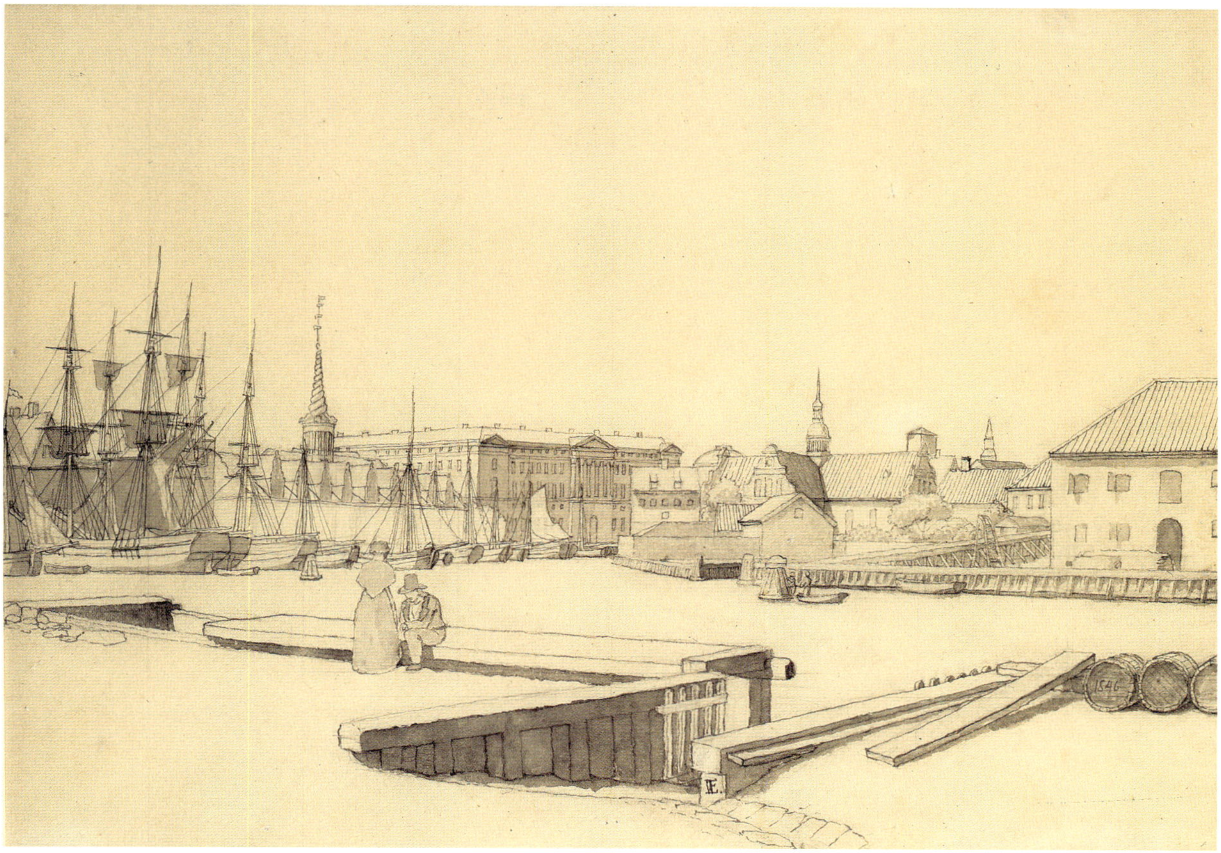

76

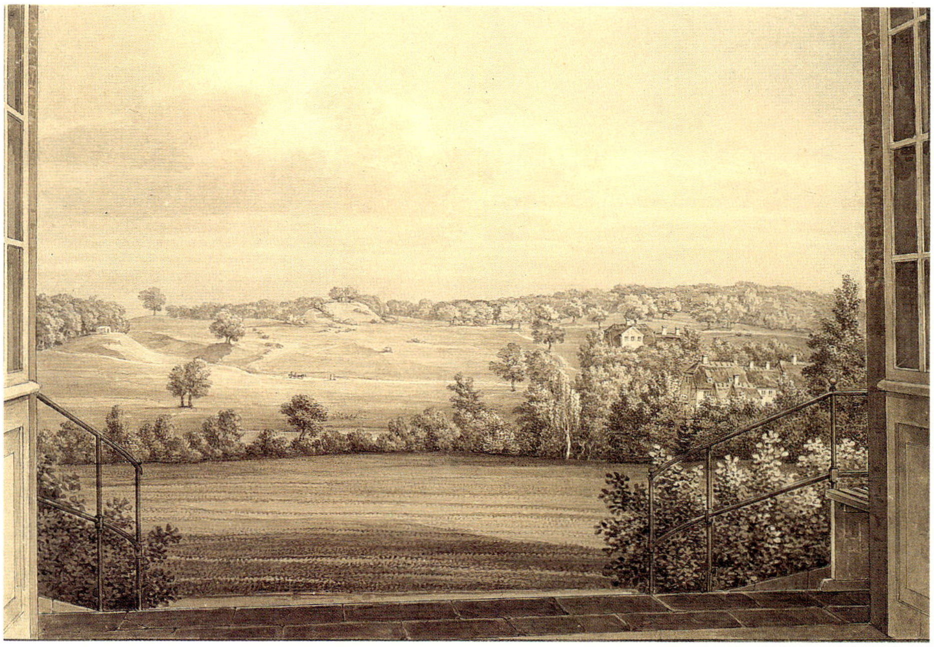

77

HEINRICH GUSTAV FERDINAND HOLM

Danish, Berlin 1803–1861 Copenhagen

77

View from a Door at Frederiksdal

Pencil, brown and gray wash; framing lines in gray wash; laid down on old mount.

6 11/16 x 9 9/16 in. (170 x 248 mm).

Inscribed on verso, *View from the Window at / Frederik'sdal / July 1827.*

PROVENANCE: William Drummond, London.

EXHIBITION: New York 1995b.

One of a family of artists, Holm specialized in precisely rendered topographical prints of Copenhagen and the Danish countryside. This drawing represents the garden at Frederiksdal, an elegant, small house near Furesø that was designed for Denmark's foreign minister in 1744 by the court architect Niels Eigtved (1701–1754). As Poul Grinder-Hansen has observed (correspondence, 13 October 1999), the view in the present drawing is from the central doorway facing the garden. On the right is the Hjortholm mill, and behind the trees and bushes that separate the garden from the open fields and woods is the river Mølleå. Frederiksdal was a popular subject, and Holm executed more than a dozen views of the property (see Housted 1994, pp. 399–400, nos. 6.047–6.064).

WMG

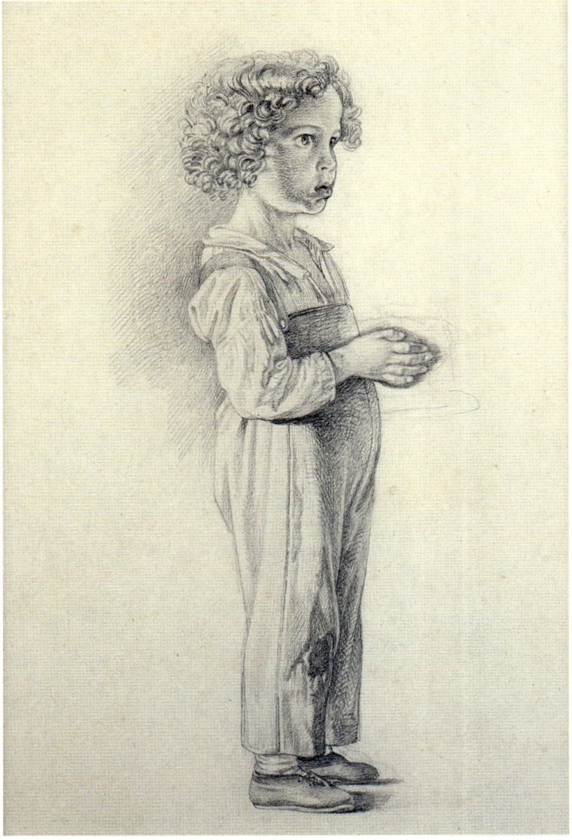

78

ERNST MEYER

Danish, Altona 1797–1861 Rome

78

A Boy, Standing, with Hands Clasped

Pencil.

11 1/4 x 7 9/16 in. (287 x 191 mm).

PROVENANCE: Galerie Fischer-Kiener, Paris; W. M. Brady and Co., New York.

A pupil in Copenhagen of Christian August Lorentzen (1749–1828) and C. W. Eckersberg (see Nos. 75–76), Meyer settled in Rome in 1824, remaining there until 1841. For the next decade he traveled throughout Europe, but in 1852 he returned to Italy, where he continued to work until his death nine years later. The majority of his paintings are of Italian subjects. Although later criticized for being excessively sentimental, Meyer's images of everyday Roman life were extremely popular in Denmark and were avidly collected even by his great contemporary, the neoclassical sculptor Bertel Thorvaldsen (1768/70–1844).

Meyer appears to have been an indefatigable draftsman, and an enormous number of his drawings are preserved in Den Kongelige Kobberstiksamling, Copenhagen. The present work comes from a group of some thirty sheets that appeared on the art market in Paris in 1996. Most of these depicted individual figures in Italian costume, although the group also included compositional drawings and a few landscapes.

The child in this drawing is typical of those in Meyer's works on canvas, and a similarly posed little girl, facing left instead of right, appears in his painting *A Bearded Religious Distributing Pictures of Saints* (sale, Copenhagen, Arne Bruun Rasmussen, 31 May 1967, no. 192, repr. p. 33). WMG

CHRISTEN KØBKE

Danish, Copenhagen 1810–1848 Copenhagen

79

Portrait of Peter Petersen

Pencil.

6¼ x 5⅜ in. (160 x 136 mm).

PROVENANCE: David K. R. Thompson, Toronto; John and Paul Herring, New York.

LITERATURE: Kent 1993, p. 177, fig. 7; Nørregård-Nielsen 1996, II, pp. 57–58, fig. 53, III, p. 209.

EXHIBITION: New York 1995b.

With Eckersberg (see Nos. 75–76), Købke was the leading painter of Denmark's golden age, during which there emerged in Copenhagen a vital, distinct, and stylistically cohesive national school. Talented as both landscape painter and portraitist, Købke approached both genres with the same forthright naturalism and keen attention to detail.

At the Kunstakademi Købke studied first under the landscape and portrait painter Christian August Lorentzen (1746–1828) and then with Eckersberg, whose work was to have a profound impact upon the younger artist's style. Købke received few commissions, and in the absence of more lucrative work, he often portrayed members of his family. This drawing represents his mother's brother, Peter Petersen, a poor merchant who enjoyed none of the success of his more prosperous brother Nicolai Wilhelm, a merchant and politician also portrayed by Købke.

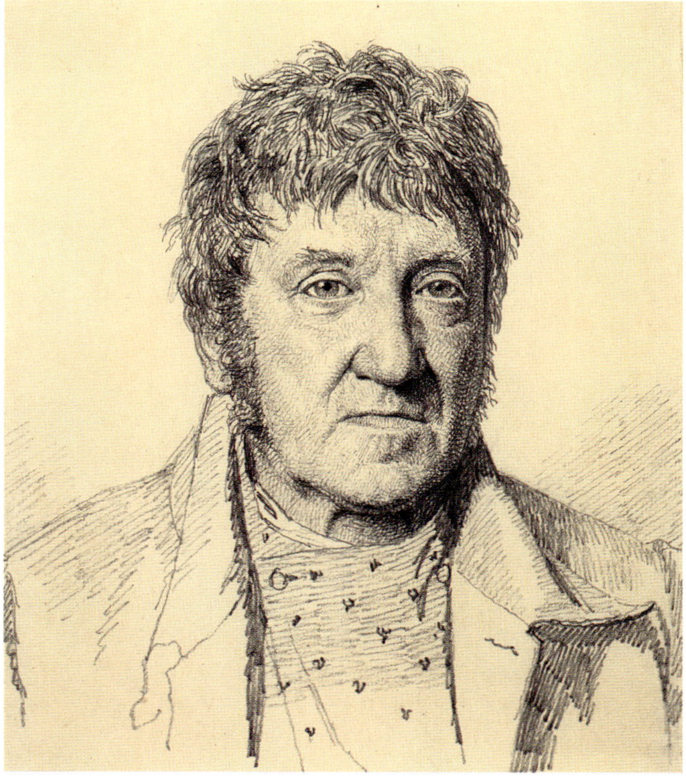

79

Hans Edvard Nørregård-Nielsen has proposed that the present work may have been executed in Odense during the mid-1830s. Another, painted portrait of the same sitter, datable about 1845, is in a private collection (Nørregård-Nielsen 1996, III, fig. 162, p. 269, no. 188). WMG

80

Portrait of Sophie Frimodt at the Age of Four

Pencil.

5⅜ x 4⅜ in. (137 x 112 mm).

PROVENANCE: Hazlitt, Gooden and Fox, London.

LITERATURE: Nørregård-Nielsen 1996, II, pp. 109–11, fig. 106.

EXHIBITION: New York 1995b.

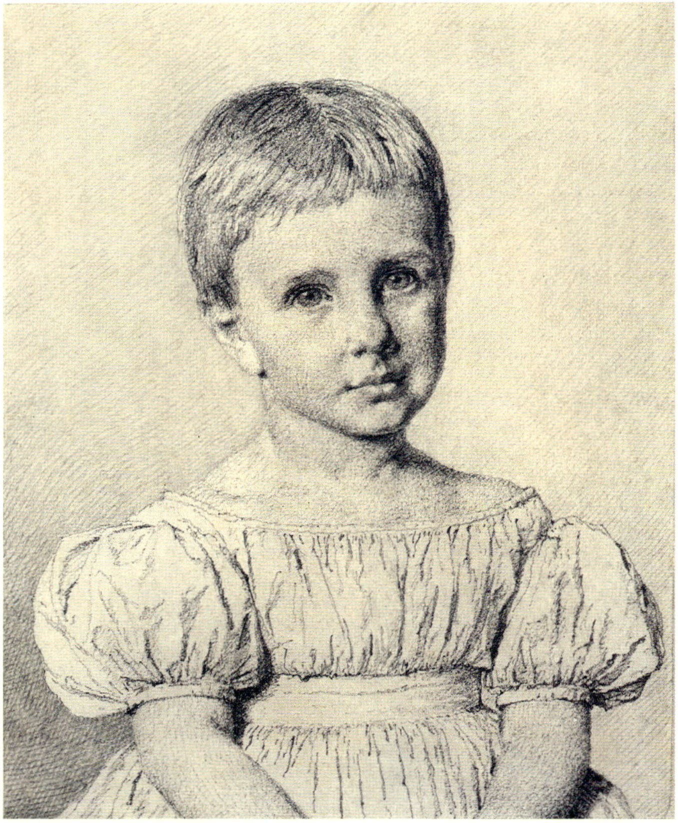

80

In 1836 Henrik Nicolai Clausen (1793–1877), a professor of theology and later a politician, commissioned Købke to draw portraits of his two sons and daughter. This sensitive drawing is Købke's portrait of the four-year-old Sophie (1832–1908), who in 1857 would marry a priest, Jens Christian Rudolph Fridmodt (1828–1879), with whom she would have six children. Købke's drawing of the eldest of Henrik Clausen's children, also called Henrik (b. 1825), is in Den Kongelige Kobberstiksamling, Copenhagen (Nørregård-Nielsen 1996, II, fig. 104); his portrait of Johannes (1830–1905) is in the Kunstmuseum, Århus (Nørregård-Nielsen 1996, II, fig. 105). All three drawings are of the same size and are comparable in style, their painstaking execution belying the subtlety of Købke's characterization of his young sitters.

Købke's aptitude for portraying children is similarly apparent in another drawing in the collection of Charles Ryskamp, a pencil study of *Julius and Betzy Eckersberg* (Nørregård-Nielsen 1996, I, fig. 126A), which is signed and dated February 1831 and which the artist may have utilized in connection with his *Portrait of Julius Eckersberg* in the Statens Museum for Kunst, Copenhagen. Julius wears the same costume in both works. WMG

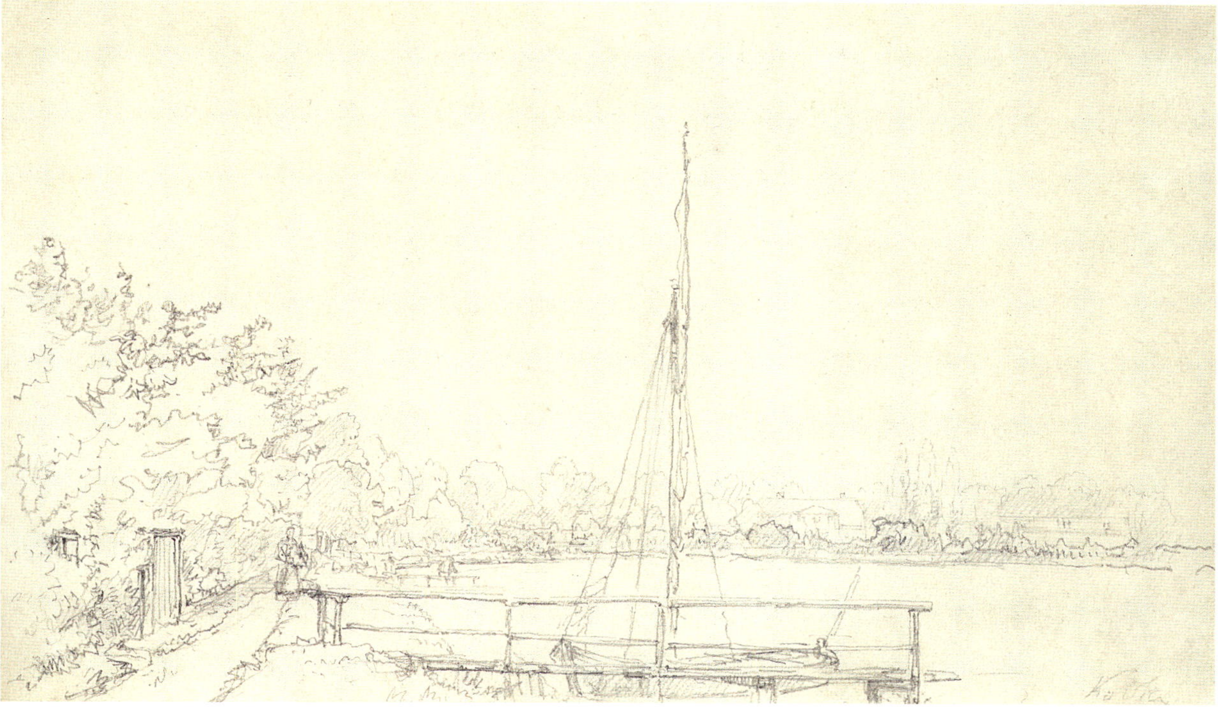

81

81

View of Dosseringen at Sortedamssøen

Pencil.

4⅞ x 8½ in. (125 x 217 mm).

PROVENANCE: David K. R. Thompson, Toronto; John and Paul Herring, New York.

LITERATURE: Copenhagen 1996, pp. 270–71 (the "compositional drawing" described as being in a private collection?).

EXHIBITION: New York 1995b.

About 1834 Købke's family moved to a house on the northwestern shore of Lake Sortedam (Sortedamssøen), and during the next several years he executed a number of views of the area. This sketch depicts a view from the pathway along the shore of the lake toward the town of Østerbro, which was then on the suburban fringes of Copenhagen.

The drawing is preparatory for Købke's 1838 painting *View from Dosseringen Near Lake Sortedam Toward Østerbro,* now in the Museum Oskar Reinhart am Stadtgarten, Winterthur (Nørregård-Nielsen 1996, II, fig. 179, III, p. 260, no. 125). There are important differences between the sketch and the finished work, in which the dock in the foreground is enlivened with figures. Other preparatory drawings include a sheet of studies for the sailboat and drawings of the boy and three women who appear on the dock (all Den Kongelige Kobberstiksamling, Copenhagen; Nørregård-Nielsen 1996, II, figs. 180–83). An oil sketch of the dock and embankment, similar in composition to the present sheet, and in which the dock is similarly devoid of figures, is in the Kunstmuseum, Århus (Nørregård-Nielsen 1996, II, fig. 184, III, p. 260, no. 124). WMG

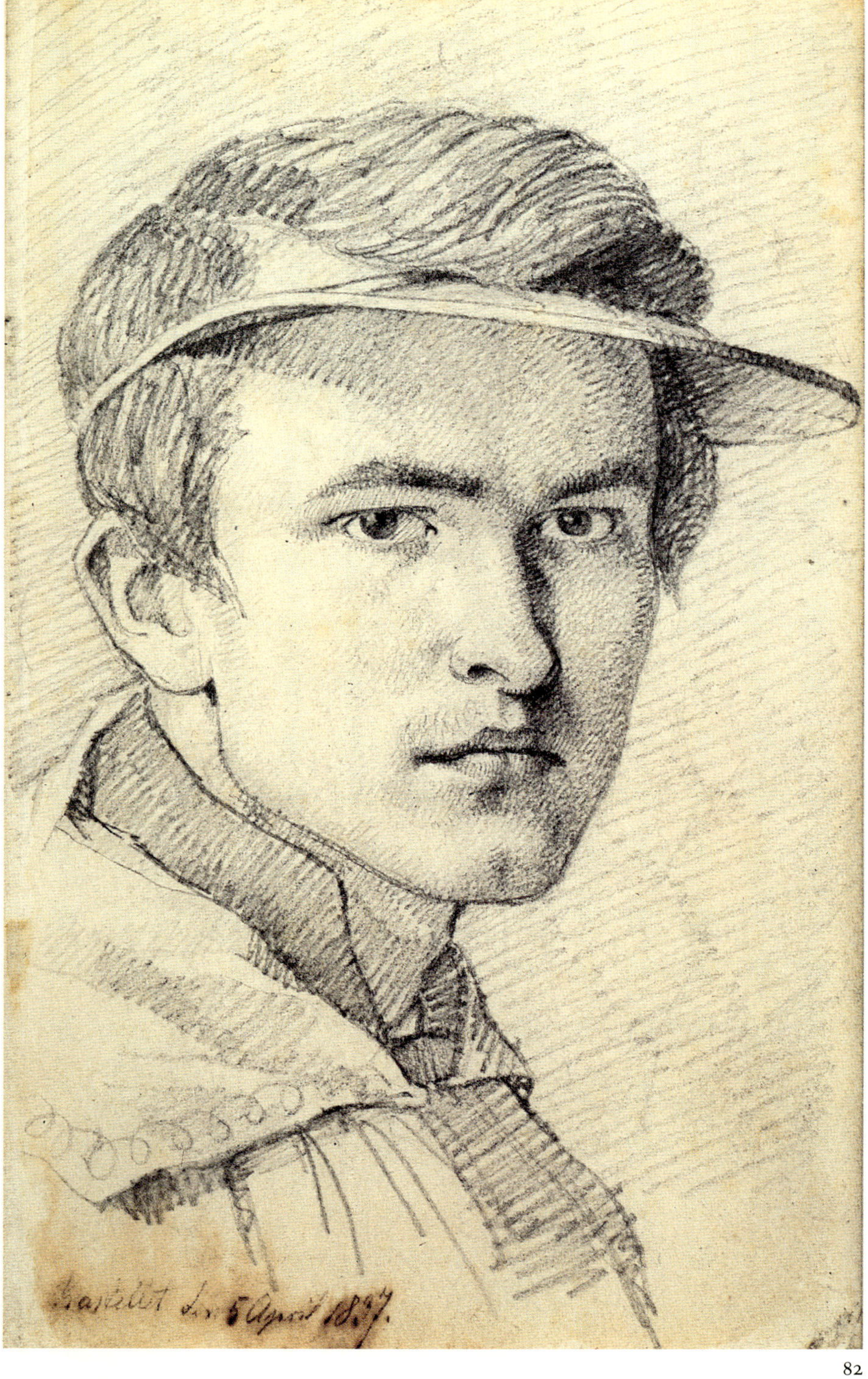

82

JOHAN THOMAS LUNDBYE

Danish, Kalundborg 1818–1848 Bedsted

82

Self-Portrait

VERSO: *Sketches of Male Heads*

Pencil.

6¾ x 4⅜ in. (172 x 111 mm).

Inscribed in pencil, *Kastellet den 5 April 1837*; on verso, in pencil, *Alf. Jacobsen* [?].

PROVENANCE: Lorenz Frölich; Thomas le Claire, Hamburg.

LITERATURE: Madsen 1895, repr. p. 23; Brünniche 1953, repr. frontispiece; Copenhagen 1989, repr. p. 52.

EXHIBITIONS: New York 1994b, no. 35, repr.; Copenhagen 1994, p. 221, no. 74, repr. p. 99; New York 1995b.

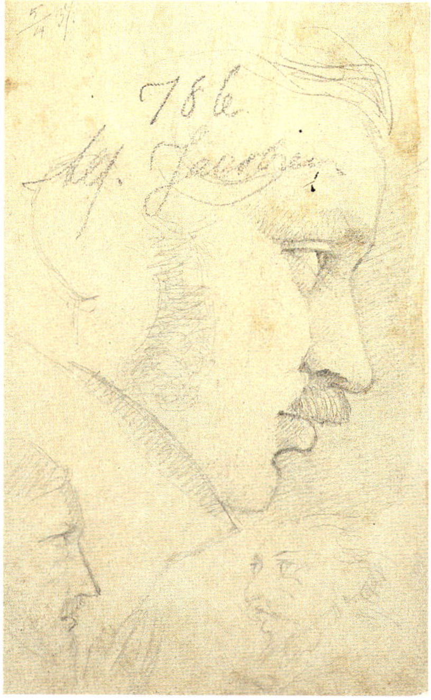

82V

Lundbye is best known for his romantic depictions of the Danish landscape, but he also painted animals and people, making numerous self-portraits, of which this drawing is among the earliest and most powerful (for other self-portraits by Lundbye, see Copenhagen 1998–99, pp. 124–27, nos. 1–6, repr.). In Lundbye's painted *Self-Portrait,* dated 1841 and now in the Ny Carlsberg Glyptotek, Copenhagen, the artist's pose and intense expression are the same as in this work, although he wears a beard and moustache and is recognizably older.

Marianne Saabye has suggested that the head in profile on the verso may represent the artist's brother Carl (verbal communication, 30 November 1999). Lundbye frequently drew members of his family, and although it can be difficult to distinguish among his various brothers, the head on the present sheet may be compared to a drawn portrait of Carl, also dated 1837, in Den Kongelige Kobberstiksamling, Copenhagen (Copenhagen 1998–99a, no. 17, repr.).

WMG

83

Portrait of P. C. Skovgaard

Pen and black ink.

8½ x 6⅝ in. (215 x 167 mm).

WATERMARK: A beehive.

Inscribed by the artist at lower left, in pen and black ink, *5 Martz 40;* by another hand (?), at lower right, in pencil, *J. Th. Lundbye;* by another hand, at lower left, in pencil, *Portrait of Skovgaard.*

PROVENANCE: Sale, Copenhagen, Arne Bruun Rasmussen, 21 January 1987, no. 502; Galerie Arnoldi-Livie, Munich.

EXHIBITION: New York 1995b.

Lundbye evidently enjoyed making portraits of his fellow artists, and his frequent companion, the landscape painter P. C. Skovgaard (see No. 84), is the subject of a number of such works. In addition to the present sheet,

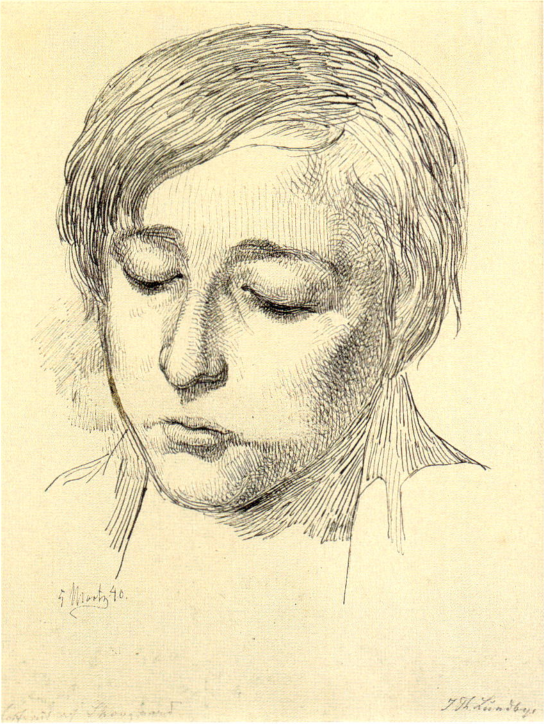

83

there are, among others, an early drawing of Skovgaard in Den Kongelige Kobberstiksamling, Copenhagen; two pen sketches, dated 20 June 1840 and 10 April 1845, in Den Hirschsprungske Samling, Copenhagen (Copenhagen 1998–99, nos. 47, 50, repr.); a watercolor representing the artist in fancy dress, dated 26 February 1844 (Den Hirschsprungske Samling; Copenhagen 1998–99, no. 48, repr.); and another watercolor, dated 22 March 1845 (Den Hirschsprungske Samling; Copenhagen 1998–99, no. 49, repr.). In the earliest of these drawings the artist is clean-shaven; in the rest he sports muttonchops.

Other, stylistically similar studies of Lundbye's artist friends include a portrait of Lorenz Frølich (1820–1908), dated 12 March [1840] (Den Kongelige Kobberstiksamling, Copenhagen; Copenhagen 1998–99, no. 41, repr.), and a drawing of Thorald Læssøe (1816–78), in pen and wash and dated 6 December 1839, that was on the art market in Germany in spring 1993. WMG

PETER CHRISTIAN SKOVGAARD

Danish, Ringsted 1817–1875 Copenhagen

84

Landscape

Watercolor, pen and brown ink.

3⅜ x 11½ in. (85 x 292 mm).

Dated at lower right, in pen and brown ink, *29 Sept: 1851.*

PROVENANCE: Thomas le Claire, Hamburg.

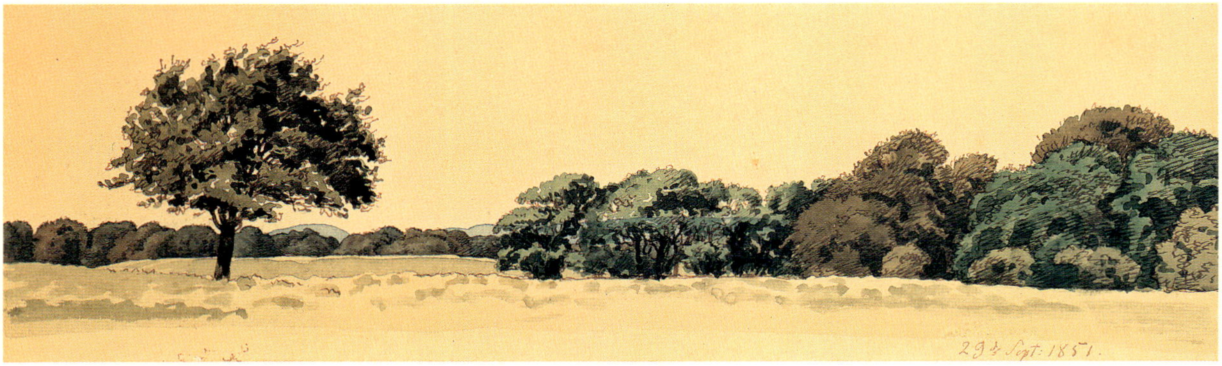

84

A pupil of Johan Ludwig Lund (1777–1867), Skovgaard is celebrated for his monumental depictions of the Danish countryside. His best-known works are large-scale paintings of Denmark's great beech forests. Although carefully composed and highly idealized, these reflect the artist's intense study of nature, often conducted in the company of his friend Johan Thomas Lundbye (see Nos. 82–83), with whom he made frequent sketching trips throughout Zealand.

The motif in this study of a sun-drenched field on the edge of a wood is typical of Skovgaard's paintings and sketches, while its elongated horizontal format recurs in other works by the artist. WMG

C. F. EMANUEL LARSEN

Danish, Copenhagen 1823–1859 Copenhagen

85

Harbor Scene with Soldiers Bathing

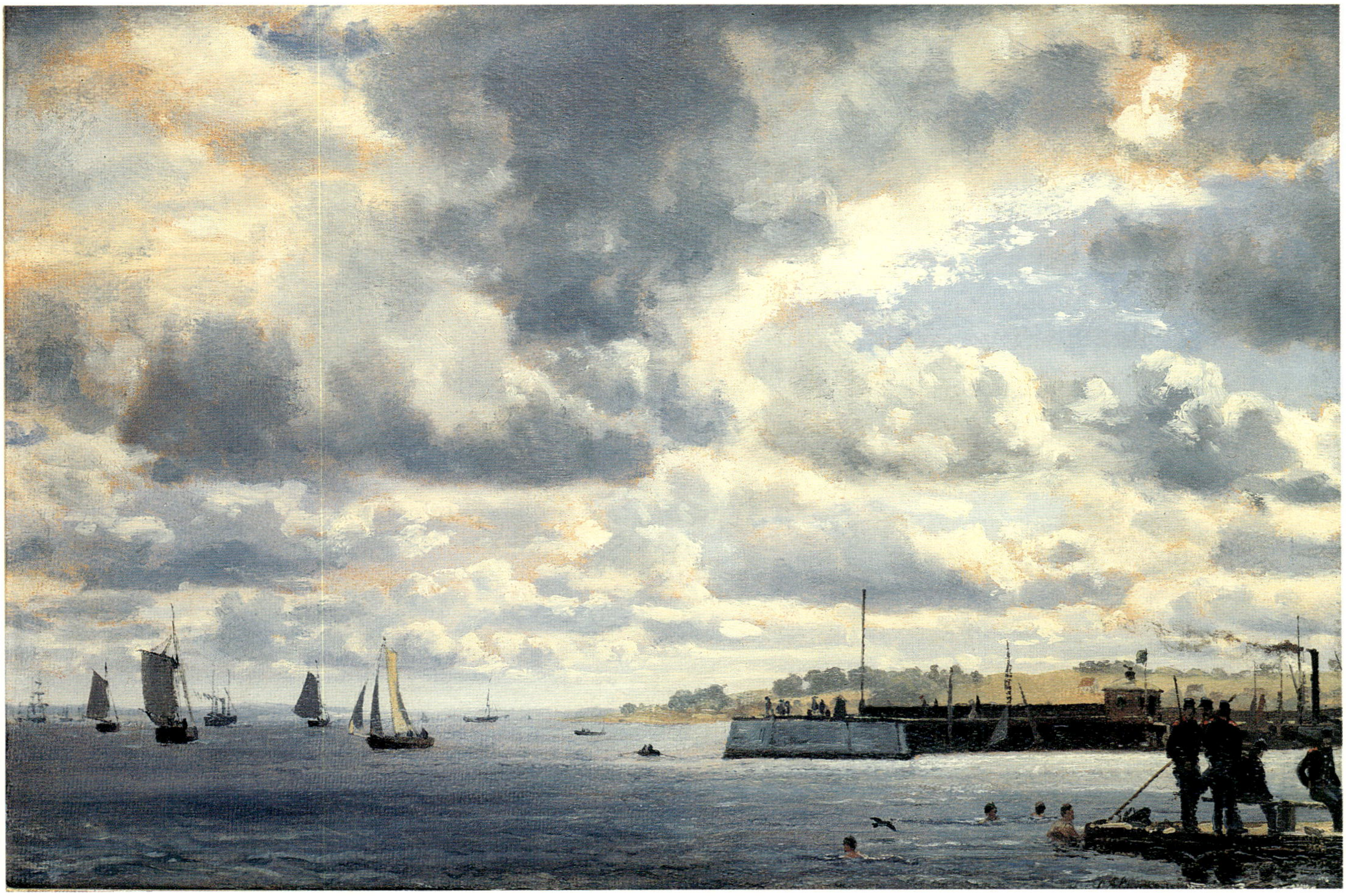

85

Oil on paper, mounted on canvas.

$12^{1/4}$ x $18^{1/4}$ in. (310 x 465 mm).

Signed at lower right, *Emanuel Larsen.*

PROVENANCE: Private collection, England; Per Kolind, Copenhagen; Artemis Fine Arts, Inc., London.

EXHIBITION: New York 1999a, no. 13, repr.

A pupil of C. W. Eckersberg (see Nos. 75–76) and the German-born marine painter Friedrich Theodor Kloss (1802–1876), Larsen devoted himself exclusively to marine subjects. These naturally reflect the influence of Eckersberg, but works by Larsen are much more freely painted than those of his older contemporary and sometimes display an interest in meteorological phenomena that is more closely related to the comparatively romantic work of Kloss as well as that of the Norwegian artist Johan Christian Dahl (1788–1857).

The present sketch appears to have been made not in the course of the artist's extensive travels but in his native Denmark. In this respect it is typical of Larsen's work. Moreover, both that it is on paper and its pictorial handling suggest it may have been executed outdoors rather than in the artist's studio, as were the majority of his larger and more finished paintings of comparable subjects. WMG

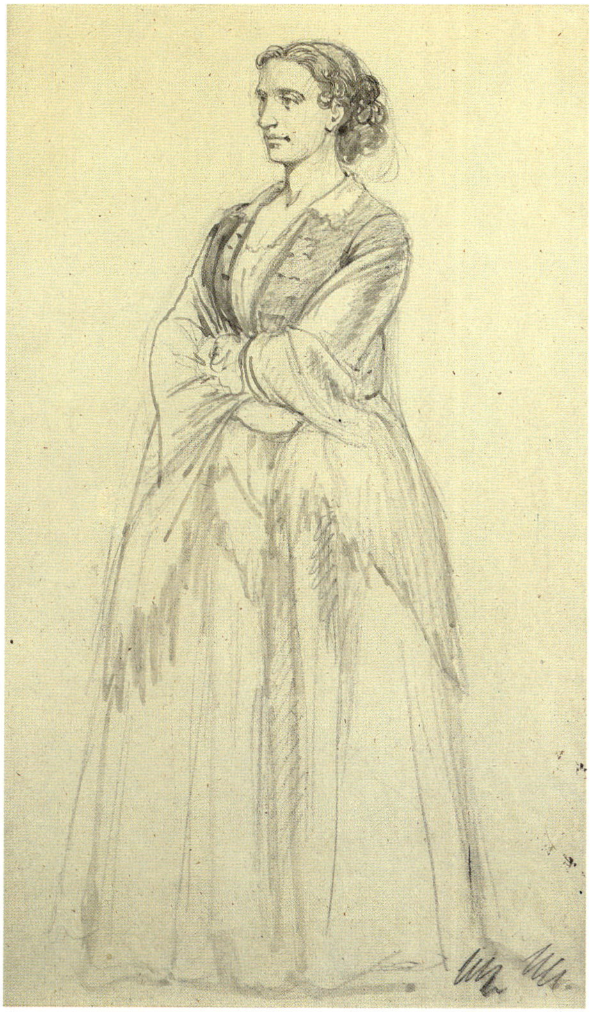

86

WILHELM N. MARSTRAND

Danish, Copenhagen 1810–1873 Copenhagen

86

Portrait of Johanne Luise Heiberg

Pencil, gray wash, on light green paper.

$13^{3/4}$ x $8^{1/4}$ in. (350 x 210 mm).

PROVENANCE: J. Rump (?); Galerie Bork, Copenhagen.

EXHIBITION: New York 1995b.

A painter as well as an illustrator, Marstrand was a pupil of C. W. Eckersberg (see Nos. 75–76) and eventually became a professor at the Kunstakademi, Copenhagen, where he was director from 1853 to 1857 and again from 1863 until his death ten years later. Throughout his life he was attracted to the theater, and many of his works reflect his fascination with the stage.

This drawing is a study for a major painting, Marstrand's full-length *Portrait of Johanne Luise Heiberg,* signed and dated 1859 and now in the museum at Frederiksborg Castle (Madsen 1905, repr. p. 333; other studies for the painting repr. pp. 331–32). Johanne Luise Heiberg (1812–1890) was the most famous actress of the Danish golden age. She was the inspiration for Søren Kierkegaard's 1847 essay "Crisis and a Crisis in the Life of an Actress," and many of the plays written by her husband, Johan Ludvig Heiberg, included roles he had designed for her. Marstrand's portrait was executed about the time the actress resumed her career after having temporarily retired from the stage in response to the 1858 dismissal of her husband as director of the Royal Theater.

WMG

DAVID COX

British, Deritend, near Birmingham, 1783–1859 Harborne

87

Thames Estuary with Fishermen in Small Boats

Watercolor over black chalk.

6¼ x 9¼ in. (162 x 254 mm).

Signed on verso, in pencil, *D. Cox* (according to London and New York 1976; not visible through lining).

PROVENANCE: Colnaghi, New York and London; Davis and Langdale, New York, 1976.

EXHIBITIONS: London and New York 1976, no. 9; New York 1985, no. 33, repr.

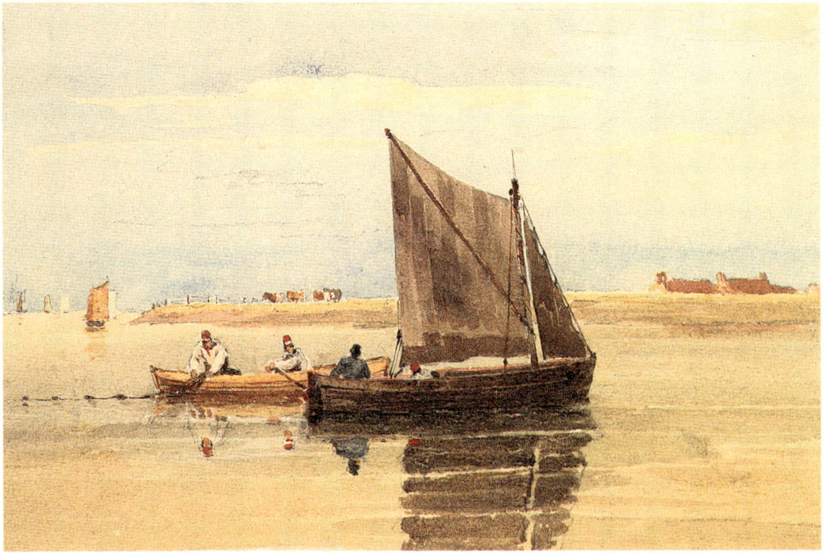

87

Although the Thames figured prominently in Cox's oeuvre throughout his long and highly successful career, this view of the river may be dated about 1812 and exemplifies his great skill in the handling of watercolor. Here, with deceptive simplicity, he brushed a few subtly nuanced strokes of color to indicate the pale water and shore as well as the shadow of the sail cast on the low waves, leaving sliverlike reserves of the white paper to indicate clouds in the sky and the play of light on the water. The low rooflines of cottages along with cows and more boats define the distant horizon.

Taught by several masters, most notably Cornelius Varley (see No. 63), Cox, a member of the Old Water-Colour Society and a constant exhibitor until 1859, taught drawing for many years. Benefiting from long school holidays, he painted landscapes of river scenery and toured Wales and other parts of the country. He also prepared a practical book, *A Treatise on Landscape Painting and Effect in Water-Colours,* 1814, which appeared in several editions. One that was published as late as 1841 is illustrated with soft-ground etchings and fifteen colored aquatints. Cox states in his text that close touch with nature was the primary inspiration for his watercolors. The book was followed in 1816 by another, *A Series of Progressive Lessons in Water-Colours,* which also was published in multiple editions.

CDD

EDWARD LEAR

British, London 1812–1888 San Remo, Italy

88

Trees Near Sorrento

Black chalk on light green paper.

13½ x 9¾ in. (343 x 248 mm).

Inscribed at right, in black chalk, *Sorrento;* dated in graphite, *Augt 20 1838.*; inscribed at lower right, *Trunk [dove] colors— / 1. B Sienna. 2. [cream] white. / Upper foliage dark—lower light green. / branches brown gray.*

PROVENANCE: Sale, London, Christie's, 17 June 1969, no. 159.

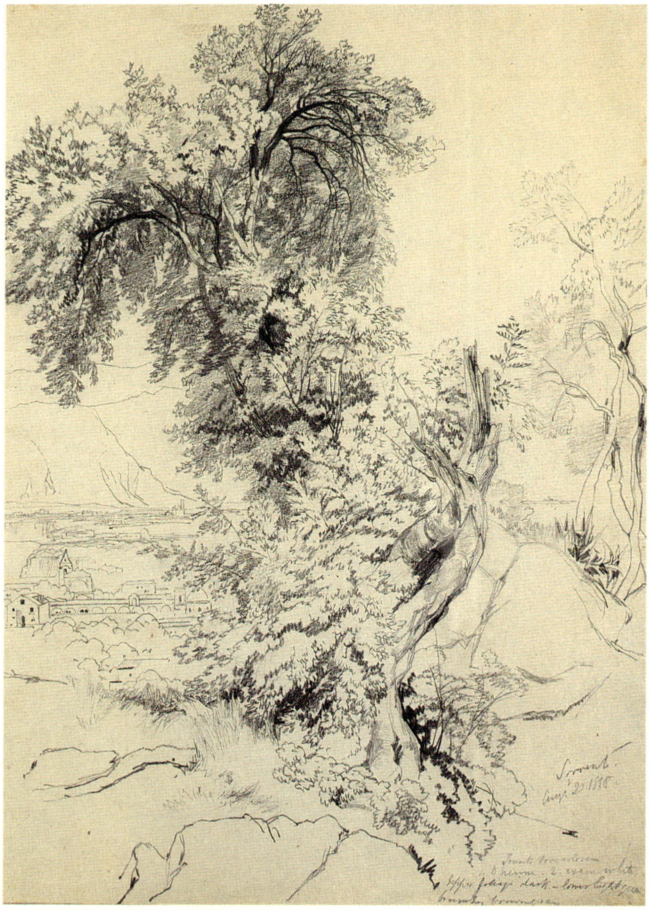

88

This sheet is similar in technique to the drawings made by Lear during his first Italian journey. The artist worked basically in line, and in this example his use of soft black chalk on pale green paper is characteristic of his manner of drawing at the time. Perhaps best known for the nonsense rhymes that he wrote and illustrated, Lear made his living for some years as a topographical draftsman; the present work, made in 1838, a year after his arrival in Rome, may or may not have been executed in connection with the first of his seven travel books, *Views in Rome and Its Environs*, London, 1841. Lear was only twenty-six when he made this rather lyrical drawing of some trees in southern Italy near Sorrento. *A Panoramic View of Tivoli* (acc. no. 1972.12, Thaw Collection, The Pierpont Morgan Library; New York and elsewhere 1975–76, no. 113, repr.), drawn in much the same technique, was not used in the lithographs for this volume, either. CDD

JOHN LINNELL

British, London 1792–1882 Redhill, Surrey

89

Portrait of the Reverend F. Thomas

Point of brush and brown wash, over black chalk.

7⅛ x 5 5/16 in. (181 x 133 mm).

Signed at lower right, in black chalk, *J Linnell.*

PROVENANCE: The artist; his son James Thomas Linnell; by descent to his granddaughter Mrs. G. C. Bollard; sale, London, Sotheby's, 13 November 1980, part of no. 2; William Drummond, London.

EXHIBITION: London 1981a.

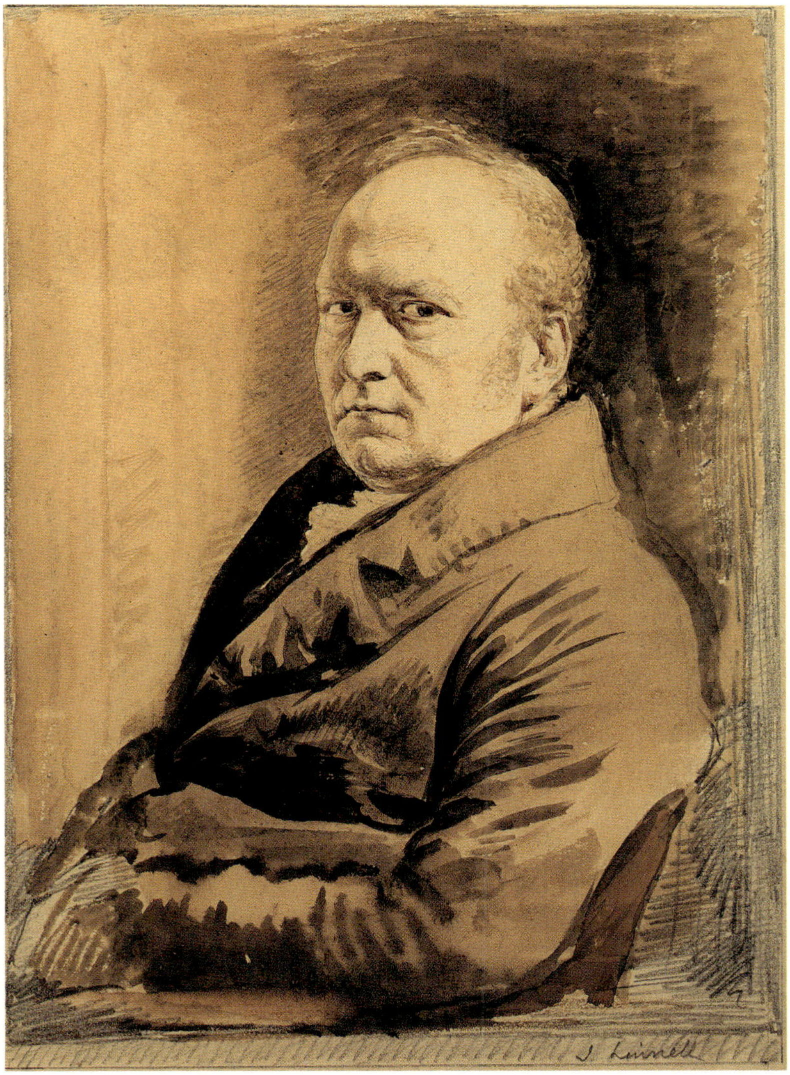

89

In 1812, under the influence of Cornelius Varley (see No. 63), Linnell became a Baptist. The Reverend F. Thomas, portrayed here so forthrightly, was a minister of the church, one of many subjects Linnell drew for engravings that appeared in *The Baptist Magazine,* a monthly published in London from 1809 to 1904. The artist included the drawing on a list of works given to his son in 1879, noting that it was executed in 1817, for the cost of one pound, one guinea (Linnell 1994, no. 19, p. 386). It was one of at least four portraits of ministers done by Linnell that year. Nothing much is known about the sitter; he may have been one of the eleven members of the family of the Reverend Joshua Thomas (1719–1797) to have entered the Baptist ministry. Joshua Thomas was the author of, among other works, a history of the Baptists in Wales. As pastor of the Baptist church in Leominster, he also ran a day school.

This drawing was eventually sold at auction in London in 1980 as part of a folio of portraits and figure studies by the artist. Among the others portrayed are Lady Belgrave, Mrs. Farrant, Mrs. Johnstone, Col. Moore, Priscilla Ravenscroft, Mr. Selby Lowndes, Mrs. Edward Sheppard, and Sibella Stephen. The folio also included a portrait of Linnell's wife that Charles Ryskamp gave to the Morgan Library (acc. no. 1993.12). It was after Linnell's marriage in 1817 that the artist took up portraiture with a good deal of success, acquiring royal and aristocratic patronage as well as Baptist commissions. CDD

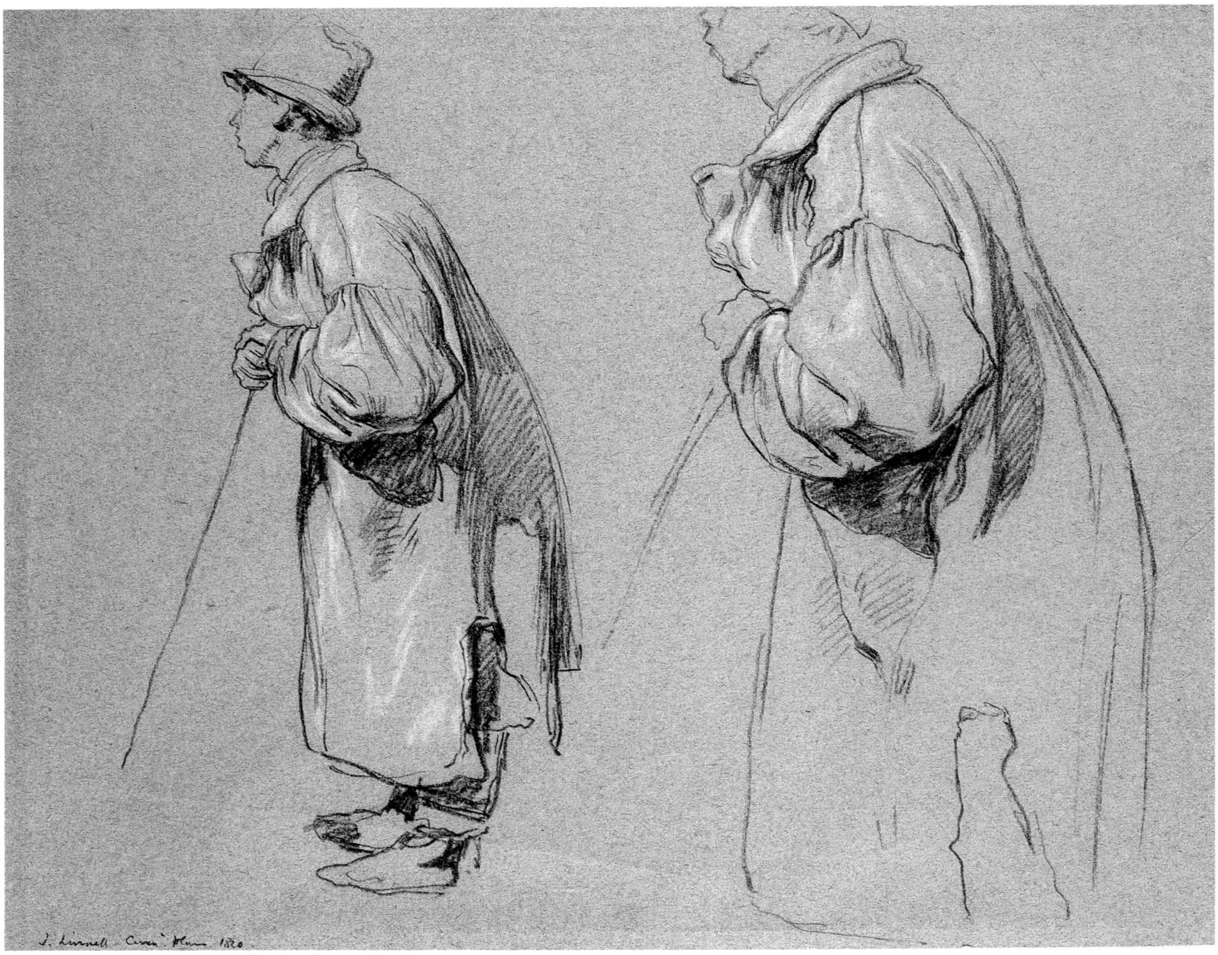

90

90
Two Studies of a Shepherd

Black chalk, heightened with white, on gray paper.

10⅝ x 13¾ in. (270 x 349 mm).

Signed, inscribed, and dated at lower left, in pen and brown ink, *J. Linnell Ciren! place 1820.*

PROVENANCE: Stephen Somerville Ltd., London.

Linnell made this study in connection with *The Dairy–Welsh Farmyard*, a good-sized oil on panel (20 x 30 inches) exhibited at the British Gallery, 1830. A smaller sketch of this painting, dating to 1847, also exists. Although the artist loved watercolor, he made a better living from his oil paintings. He studied the effect of light on the shepherd's smock twice, beginning at the top of the page with an outline of the entire figure leaning forward slightly on a thin stick or crook. He wears a smock and a high crowned hat. In the second study, which takes up the full length of the sheet, the artist made a separate, more intensive study of the smock alone. Similar if not exact figures appear in such works as *The Last Glean Before the Storm* (1848) and *A Hillside Farm* (1816 and 1847). This kind of careful preparation recalls Linnell's acute interest in and admiration of Renaissance art and even suggests the kind of detailed preparations routinely undertaken by Italian artists. CDD

91
Corn Stooks

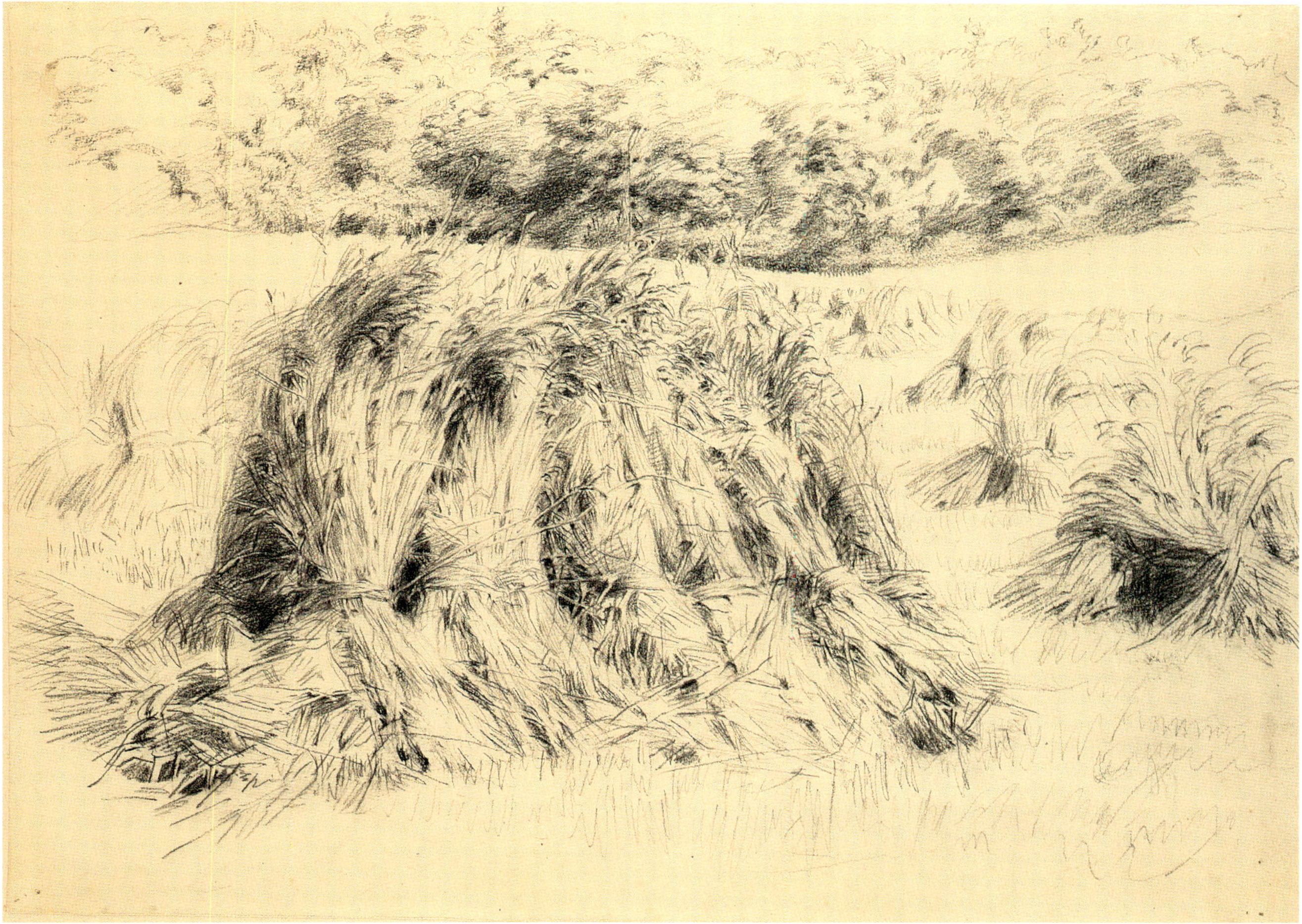

91

Black chalk.

12¾ x 18$\frac{9}{16}$ in. (324 x 470 mm).

PROVENANCE: O. Coleman Dunn, Salt Lake City; Colnaghi, London.

EXHIBITIONS: Salt Lake City 1964, no. 18; London 1970a, no. 122; New York 1992b, no. 59, fig. 18; Brussels 1994–95, no. 61, repr.; New York 1998, no. 96, repr.

After entering the Royal Academy School, Linnell became the student of John Varley (1778–1842), who encouraged his students to draw directly from nature. Through Varley he met Cornelius, the artist's brother, who introduced him to the naturalist movement of the early nineteenth century. A successful artist, Linnell was able to give William Blake (see Nos. 48–49) a regular income at the end of Blake's life. He commissioned the engravings for the *Book of Job* in 1823 and the watercolors for Dante's *Divine Comedy* in 1824. He also introduced Samuel Palmer (1805–1881) to Blake in 1824, having already encouraged Palmer to make studies from nature.

The simplicity and directness of his observations are evident in this black chalk drawing of corn stooks. This kind of study was merely a preparation for Linnell's more finished paintings and was never exhibited by the artist. In 1849 he bought Redstone Wood in Redhill, Surrey, where he and his family moved into a new home in 1851. This move to the country had a great impact on the artist's work from this time, and cornfields became prominent in his paintings. As Stephanie Wiles suggested (New York 1998, no. 96), this fine drawing may have been a study for a work such as *Reapers at Noon*, a replica of which was made the following year (Tate Gallery, London). Another, similar study of *Corn Stooks* was sold at auction in 1998 (sale, London, Sotheby's, 8 April 1998, no. 139, repr.) CDD

JAMES THOMAS LINNELL

British, 1826–1905

92

Landscape in Surrey

Watercolor and bodycolor, especially in wheat field, over black chalk, on blue paper.

14½ x 20$\frac{15}{16}$ in. (368 x 535 mm).

PROVENANCE: Somerville and Simpson Ltd., London.

Although this very fresh sheet closely resembles the work of John Linnell (Nos. 89–91), it is more in character with that of James Linnell, his second son. It has been identified as a landscape in Surrey, probably near Redhill, the house in which John Linnell and his family lived. In this sweeping landscape, James varied the concentration of brilliant colors to suggest a beautiful late summer day in the country. The densest application is reserved for the wheat in the foreground, which he stroked on in a pale but brilliant yellow, using lighter washes of dark green for the foliage and deep blue for the background of farms and receding hills.

Like his three brothers, James exhibited at the Royal Academy between 1850 and 1888. According to the list in Algernon Graves, *The Royal Academy of Arts, A Complete Dictionary of Contributors and their work . . .*, 1905, James seems to have been the most prolific of Linnell's four sons, exhibiting almost every year. It is apparent from the list that he began exhibiting biblical subjects at the Royal Academy in the 1850s, but landscape painting would become his principal interest by the 1860s. CDD

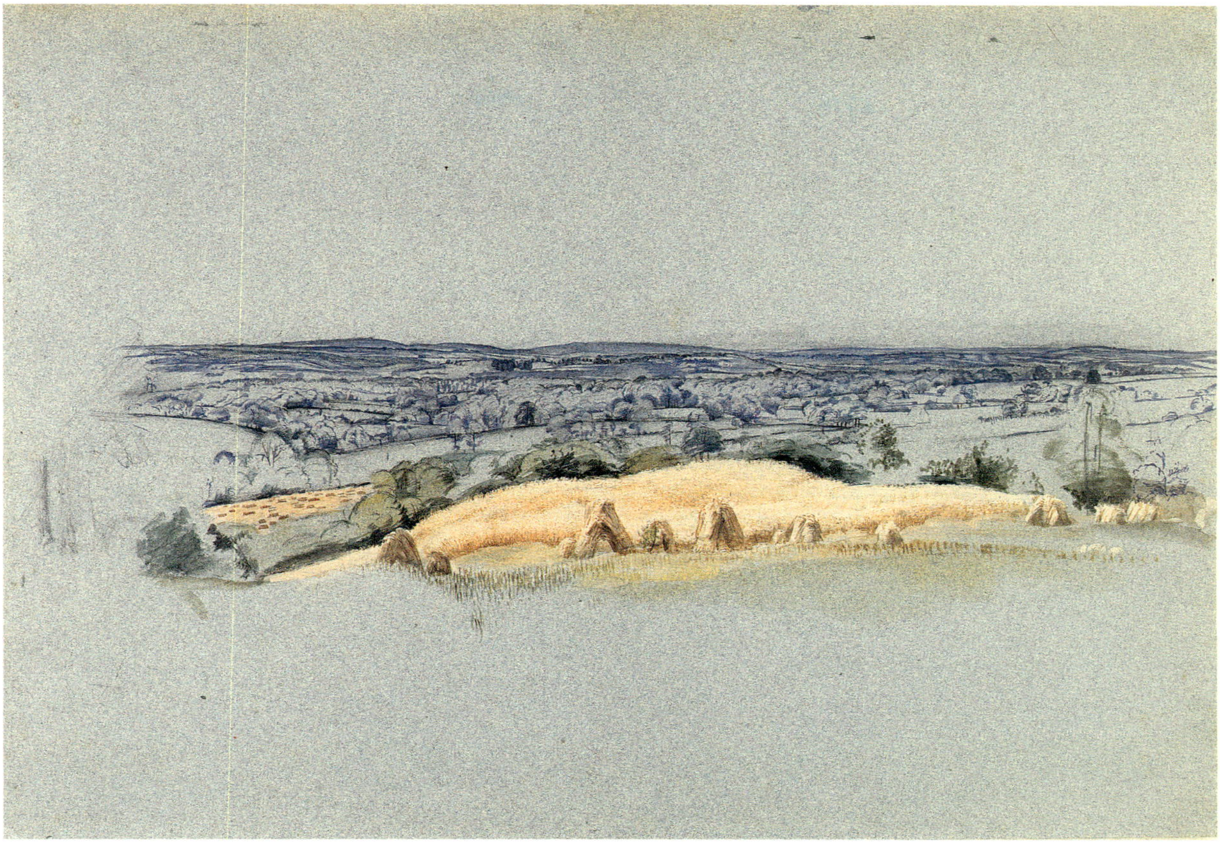

92

WILLIAM HENRY HUNT

British, London 1790–1864 London

93

A Doorway in Bushey Church

Watercolor, reed pen and brown ink.

12⅞ x 8½ in. (328 x 217 mm).

WATERMARK: J. Whatman, Turkey Mill, 1820 (cropped along bottom).

PROVENANCE: John Baskett Ltd., London.

LITERATURE: Witt 1982, no. 154 (as *Doorway on the North Side of Aldenham Church*).

Hunt began his artistic career as a watercolorist apprenticed to the landscape painter John Varley (1778–1842) from 1804 until 1811, often embarking on sketching excursions along the Thames with his friend and fellow student John Linnell (Nos. 89–91). He and Linnell also attended Dr. Thomas Monro's informal drawing academy in Bushey, Hertfordshire. Following his student days, Hunt often visited Monro at his home near Bushey and drew subjects from the surrounding town and countryside.

In a 1980 letter to Charles Ryskamp, Sir John Witt identified the subject of the present drawing as Bushey

Church. In his 1982 catalogue of Hunt's oeuvre, however, Witt listed the subject as the nearby Aldenham Church. Although the two churches are difficult to distinguish in Hunt's drawings, the present sheet probably depicts Bushey Church. Monro often commissioned Hunt to draw sites around Bushey, such as this interior of the parish church, one of several the artist executed in the 1820s (see Witt 1982, nos. 17–18, 104, 108, 172, 197, 251, and sale, London, Sotheby's, 27 November 1975, no. 145; sale, London, Sotheby's, 14 July 1988, no. 30). Hunt's early style is distinguished by the use of a reed pen and brown ink with heavy outlines over watercolor, a technique that can be attributed to the influence of copying the Canaletto drawings in Monro's collection. JT

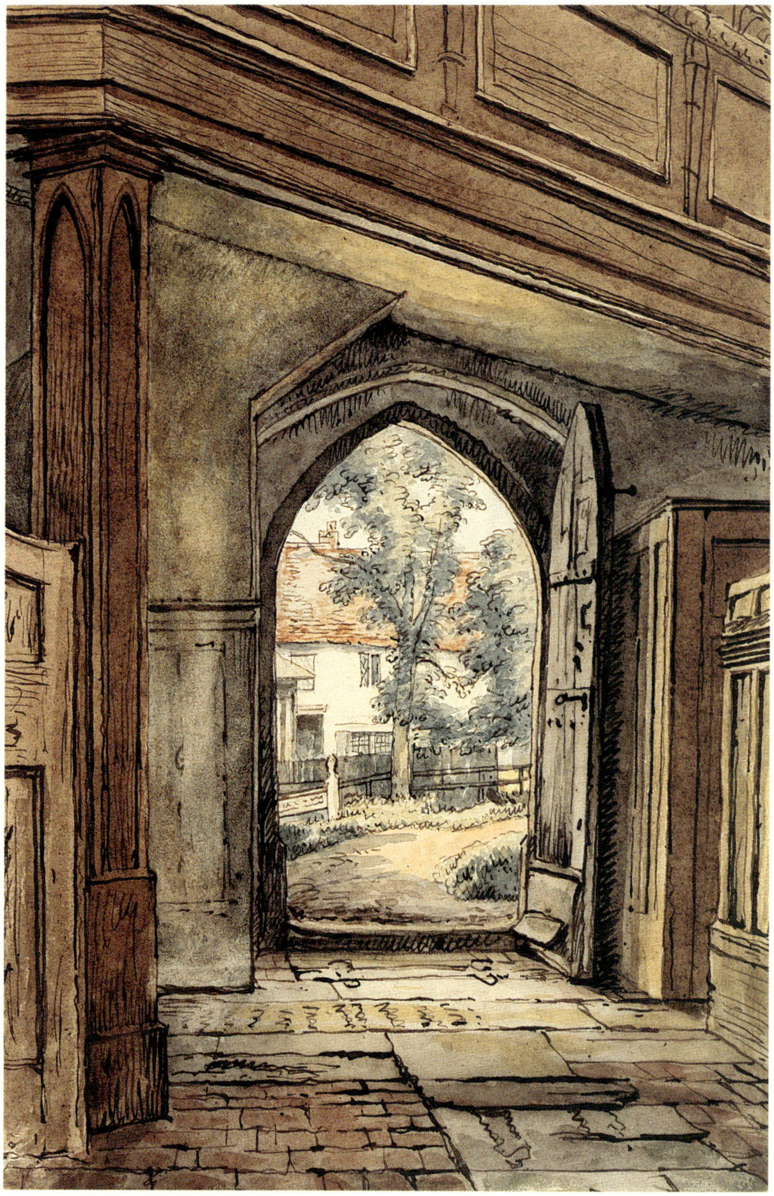

93

94

Boy in a Pantry

Watercolor and pencil, with gouache, on cream card.
11 1/16 x 7 1/2 in. (281 x 190 mm).
PROVENANCE: Cyril Fry, London.
LITERATURE: Witt 1982, no. 498.

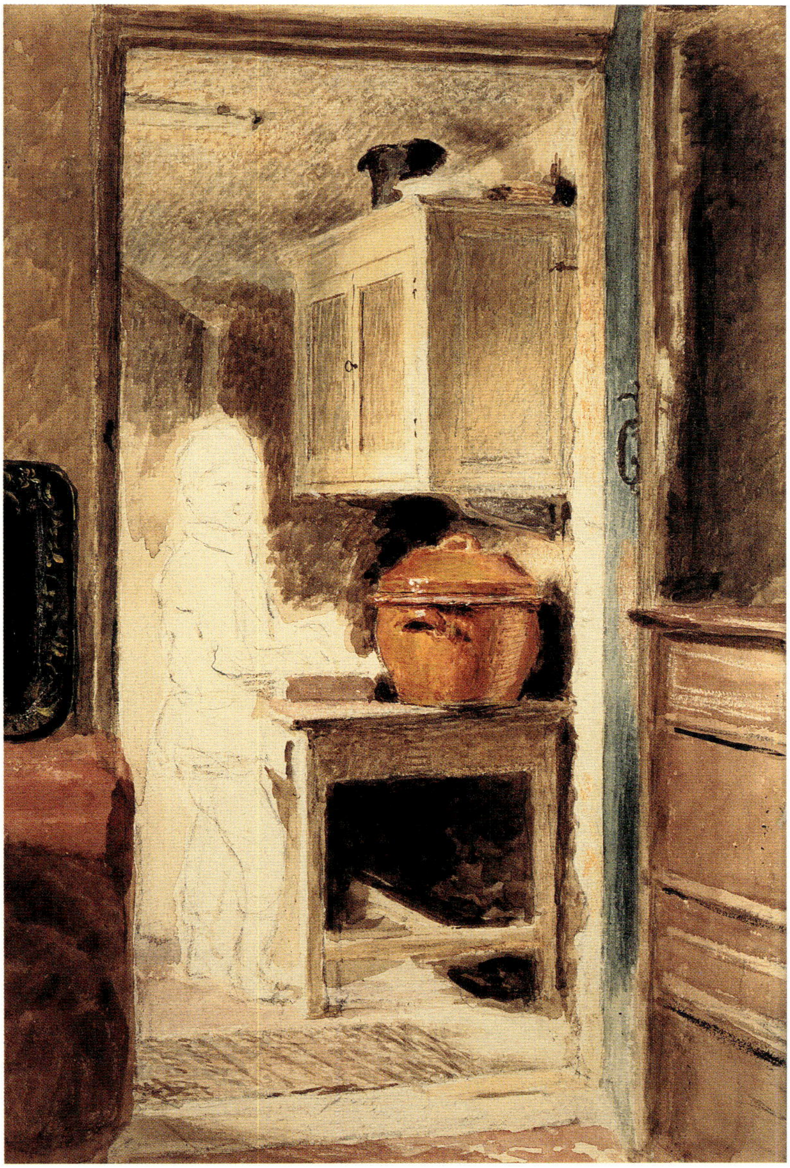

94

After becoming a member of the Society of Painters in Water-Colours in 1826, Hunt increasingly drew genre scenes and exquisitely executed still lifes that inspired the nickname "Bird's Nest Hunt." He also turned away from using heavy reed pen outlines to work in pure watercolor.

This drawing is typical of Hunt's rustic genre scenes, which often depict a single figure in an interior. In 1831 the artist met the Swain family at Hastings, where he wintered. The three young Swain brothers served as models for the artist's anecdotal scenes, assuming different costumes and attitudes suggested by Hunt. Sir John Witt has identified the model in the present drawing as one of the Swain boys and dates the drawing to the early 1830s, Hunt's "second period," during which his drawing technique is characterized by small, separate strokes of wash, creating a flickering, stippled surface. Hunt's interest in the subject as a still life rather than as a figure study is revealed through the contrast of the finished setting, especially the pot and platter, with the unfinished figure of the boy. JT

JOHN FREDERICK LEWIS

British, London 1805–1876 Walton-on-Thames

95

An Interior with Armor and Weaponry

Watercolor.

7¾ x 11¹⁵⁄16 in. (196 x 287 mm).

PROVENANCE: W. M. Brady and Co., New York.

Lewis came from a family of painters and printmakers, and his talents developed naturally within the family circle. By 1827, however, he had turned to watercolor, developing an accomplished technique that owes something to David Wilkie (see Nos. 66–67), who specialized in large, historical paintings and whose style he especially admired. Lewis decided to concentrate on topographical views and picturesque genre subjects. He began to travel widely in search of motifs, first in Scotland and then to Spain and Morocco, producing a series of flamboyant watercolors that brought him a great deal of attention. His future course was decided in 1837, however, when he left England for an extended tour of Europe and the Near East, not returning to London until 1851, by which time he had received wide critical acclaim for his views of markets, bazaars, and, above all, harem subjects.

It is very possible that the drawing represents the artist's studio, which might have contained such paraphernalia as the suits of armor, sword, crossbow, rich draperies, frames, and large Oriental vase depicted in this work. To judge from the style, it may well have been executed around 1835. CDD

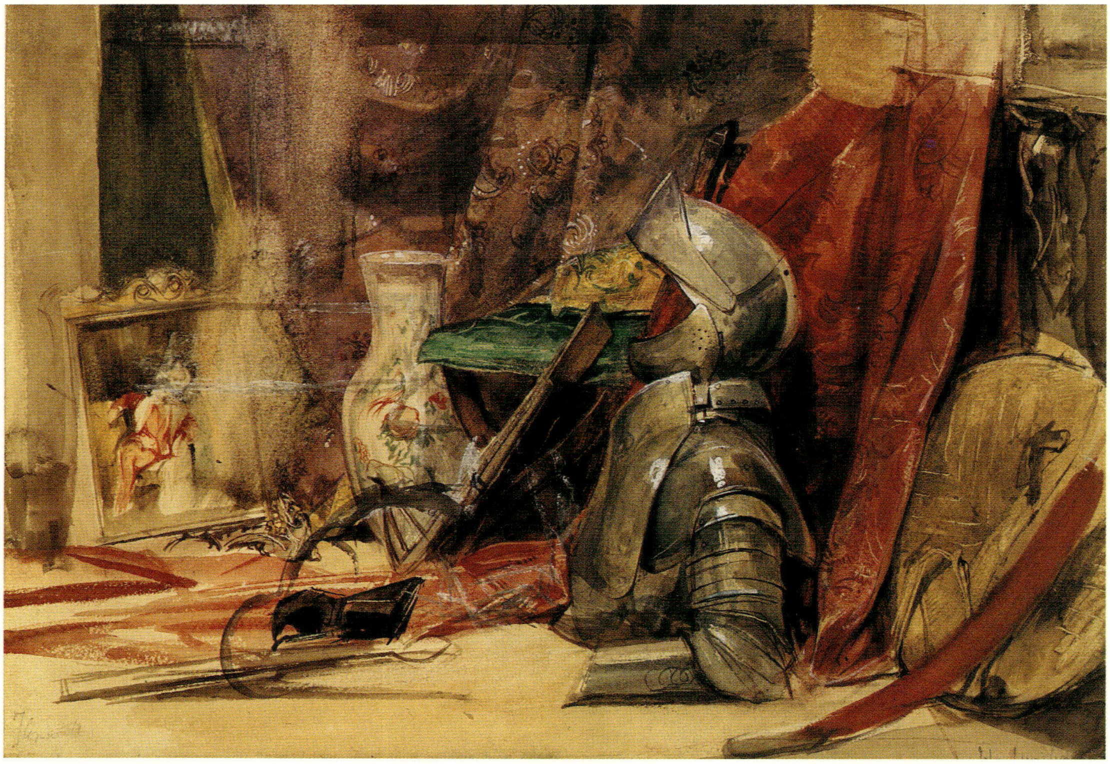

95

ALEXANDRE-MARIE COLIN

French, Paris 1798–1875 Paris

96

Interior of the Artist's Studio

Watercolor on cream paper.

9⅞ x 7⅛ in. (251 x 200 mm).

WATERMARK: J. Whatman, Turkey Mill, 1857.

Signed at lower left, in black ink, *A. Colin;* inscribed at lower right, in black ink, *HG* or *46*.

PROVENANCE: W. M. Brady and Co., New York.

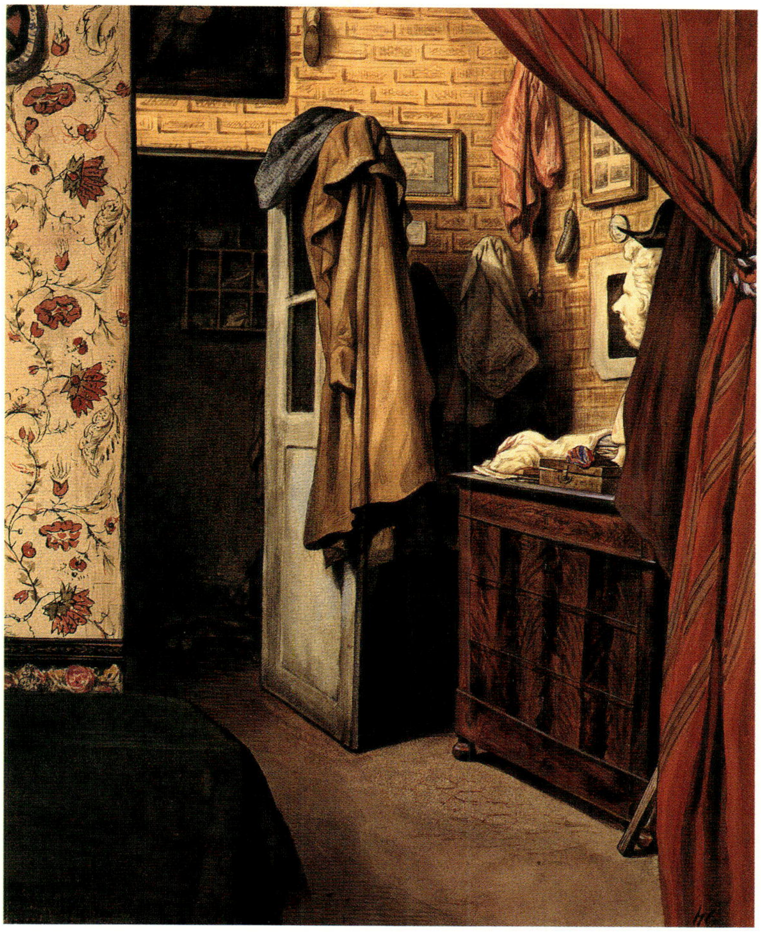

96

Described by Paul Joannides as "one of the forgotten figures of French Romanticism" (Joannides 1983, p. 496), Colin was an intimate friend of Eugène Delacroix (No. 97) and Richard Parkes Bonington (1802–1828). A student of Anne-Louis Girodet (1767–1824) at the Ecole des Beaux Arts (ca. 1814), Colin first exhibited at the Salon of 1819 and continued to do so regularly for the rest of his life. In 1824 he traveled with Théodore Géricault (1719–1824) to England. The same year Colin accompanied Bonington to Dunkirk on a sketching expedition, drawing several portraits of his friend. In 1831 he became a professor of drawing at the Ecole des Beaux-Arts at Nîmes, although he returned to Paris after the death of his first wife seven years later. Having reestablished himself in Paris with a second wife and family, Colin began traveling. On trips to Italy, Spain, and the Netherlands, the artist made copies after the old masters with the hope of founding a museum of copies in France.

Although primarily a painter and draftsman, Colin also was active as a lithographer. At the height of Colin's career, Géricault commissioned him to execute a lithograph of the *Raft of the Medusa* to be distributed at the Salon (see preface to Colin sale, Paris, Hôtel Drouot, 2 February 1876). Colin also made a series of lithographs after Géricault's drawings, some of which were in his personal collection. As a painter, his style was close to that of Delacroix, and his subjects were frequently literary and historical, but he also painted genre scenes and portraits.

In this intimate view of his studio, the artist reveals evidence of his activity as a collector, including a marble bust, a painting above the doorway, and several drawings on the brick walls. The watermark indicates that the sheet must have been executed in 1857 or later, during Colin's maturity. JT

EUGÈNE DELACROIX

French, Charenton-Saint-Maurice 1798–1863 Paris

97

Moroccan House

Watercolor and pencil.

4 x 6 in. (102 x 152 mm).

Inscribed variously, in pencil, *daurer; drap; au avant / bords ou / al frauger / vert loin; oisax; rouge / bo / bleu / r/ b.*

Estate stamp at lower left.

PROVENANCE: Edgar Degas; his sale, Paris, Hôtel Drouot, 15–16 November 1918, no. 93.1; Jean Guiffrey; Eugene V. and Clare E. Thaw, New York.

LITERATURE: Ives et al. 1997, no. 273, repr.

EXHIBITIONS: New York 1986, no. 63; New York 1997–98a, fig. 413; Frankfurt 1998–99, one of nos. 49–52.

Delacroix's fascination with Oriental subjects, a characteristic theme of the romantic movement, is manifest in his early paintings, such as *The Death of Sardanapalus* of 1827. Five years later, at the age of thirty-four, Delacroix embarked on his first journey to North Africa. Upon his arrival in Morocco, the artist wrote, "I am like a man in a dream, seeing things he's afraid will vanish from him." The artist's excitement at seeing first-hand the exotic world he had previously experienced only through literature inspired him to draw incessantly. This would be one of the few periods during which he worked directly from life.

The purpose of Delacroix's visit was to accompany a diplomatic mission to Moulay Abd al-Rahman, sultan

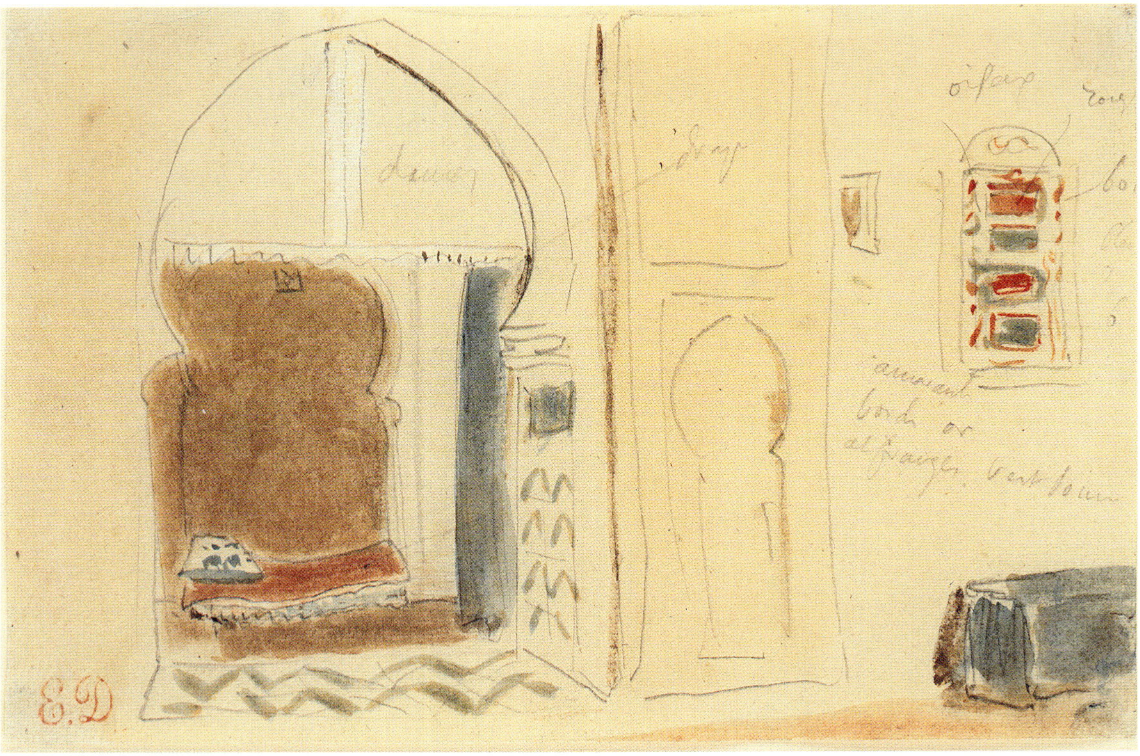

97

of Morocco, led by Comte Charles de Mornay at the behest of Louis-Philippe (1773–1850; r. 1830–48). The artist arrived in Morocco on 25 January 1832 and stayed through 10 June before traveling to Oran and Algiers. When he returned to France in July, Delacroix brought with him seven sketchbooks containing drawings in pencil and watercolor of the people, costumes, and architecture he observed on his trip. These would serve as aide-mémoire in his later depictions of Oriental themes and furnished material for such subjects throughout his career.

Only four of Delacroix's sketchbooks have survived intact: two are in the Louvre, one is in the Musée Condé, Chantilly, and one was sold at Sotheby's, Monaco, on 26 June 1983. The other three have been dispersed or lost, but individual sheets occasionally surface.

Once in the collection of Edgar Degas, the present sheet is typical of the studies found in Delacroix's Moroccan sketchbooks and must have come from one of the dispersed albums. The loose, free execution suggests that the drawing was made on site, an observation supported by the descriptive phrases and color notations on the sheet.

JT

ACHILLE-JACQUES-JEAN-MARIE DEVÉRIA

French, Paris 1800–1857 Paris

98

Three Studies of the Children of Alexandre-Marie Colin

Pencil.

4⅛ x 3⅛ in. (150 x 80 mm), inscribed on verso, in pencil, *Paul Colin / par Achille Devéria*; 3⅞ x 5⅛ in. (98 x 130 mm), initialed, at lower left, *AD*, inscribed on verso, in pencil, *Paul Colin / par Achille Devéria*; 3¹⁵⁄₁₆ x 3¹⁄₁₆ in. (100 x 78 mm), inscribed on verso, in pencil, *Isabelle Colin / par Achille Devéria*.

PROVENANCE: W. M. Brady and Co., New York.

Achille Devéria was a pupil of Anne-Louis Girodet (1767–1824) and a lifelong friend of Delacroix (No. 97). After leaving Girodet's studio, Devéria became a prolific illustrator and popular printmaker. His talent as a portraitist is evident in his numerous depictions of famous romantic artists, writers, and musicians, such as Victor Hugo, Alexandre Dumas père, Franz Liszt, and Camille Roqueplan. Devéria also used his friends as models for plates in his series of lithographs *The Times of the Day* and *Historical Costumes*. As a result of his expertise as a printmaker, Devéria was appointed to the Cabinet d'Estampes at the Bibliothèque Nationale in 1849 and became its curator in 1857.

In this group of three small studies, Devéria portrayed the children of the artist Alexandre-Marie Colin (No. 96), who also was a colleague of Delacroix and an intimate friend of Devéria; the two had met while they were students in Girodet's atelier. According to the artist's inscription, the two studies of a boy depict Paul Alfred Colin (1838–1916), Colin's only child from his second marriage. The difference in the sitter's age between the two portraits suggests that they were done some years apart. Paul Colin became a painter of landscapes and marine subjects and eventually married Devéria's daughter Sarah. The third portrait is inscribed Isabelle Colin. None of Colin's four daughters was named Isabelle. It is possible that she was one of his grandchildren—all his daughters are believed to have been married before 1850—although this cannot be confirmed.

JT

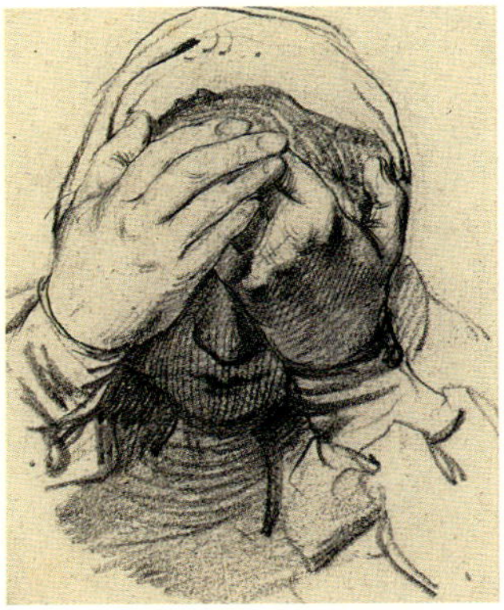

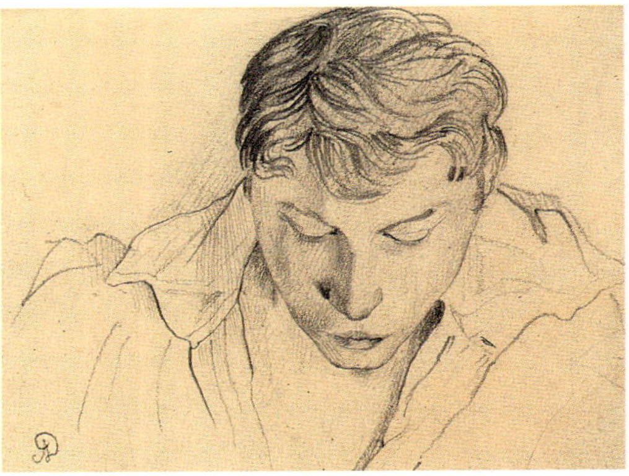

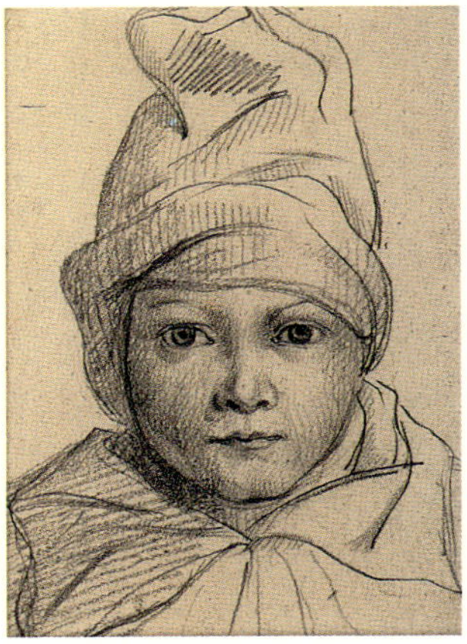

98

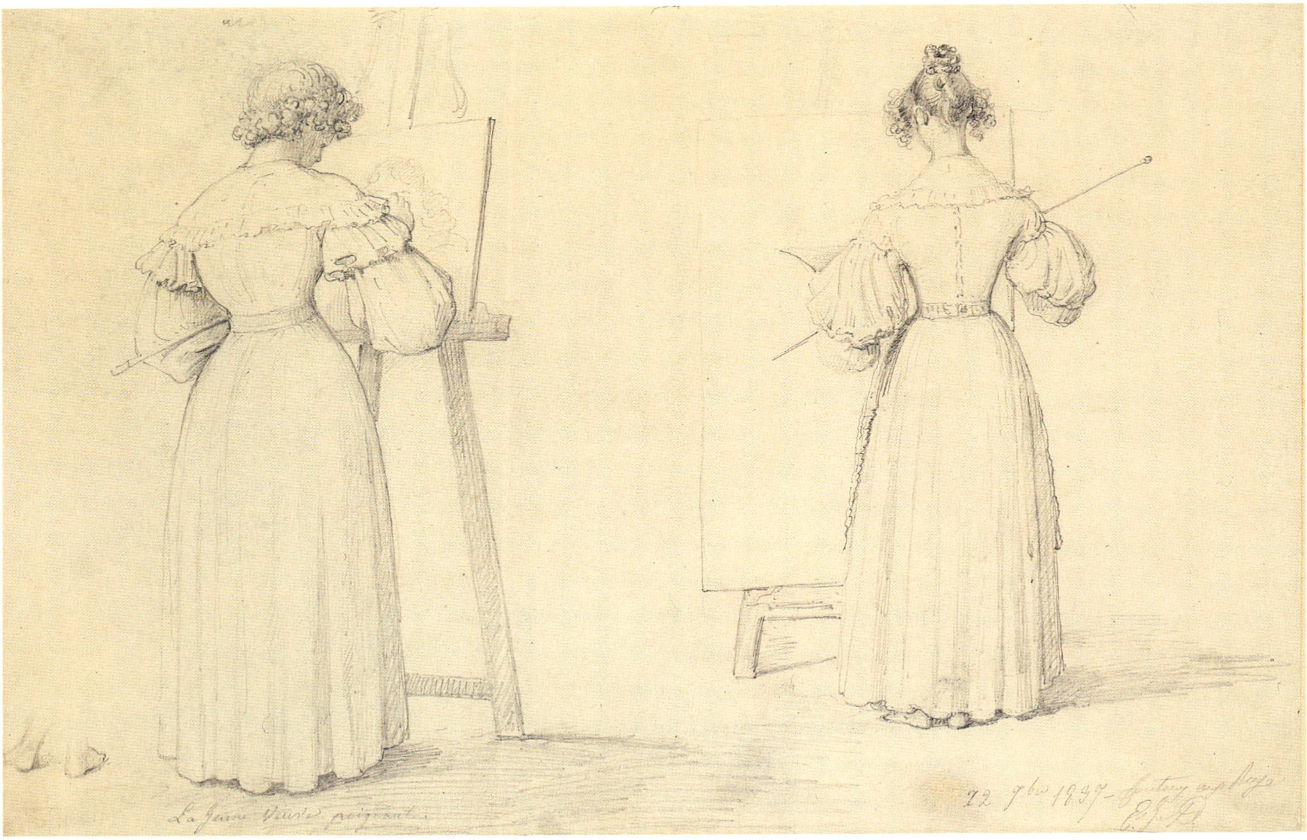

99

EUGÈNE-FRANÇOIS-MARIE-JOSEPH DEVÉRIA

French, Paris 1805–1865 Pau

99

Two Studies of Women Painting

Pencil.

8⅞ x 13⅞ in. (224 x 352 mm).

Inscribed by the artist at lower left, in pencil, *La Jeune Veuve peignant.*; dated, inscribed, and initialed at lower right, in pencil, *22 9bre 1837—fontenay aux Roses / EFD.*

PROVENANCE: Hazlitt, Gooden and Fox, London.

EXHIBITION: London 1977, no. 23, pl. 23.

Like his older brother, Achille (No. 98), Eugène Devéria was a student of Anne-Louis Girodet (1767–1824). Whereas Achille gained fame as a printmaker of fashionable subjects, Eugène built his reputation on large-scale history paintings in the romantic style. Along with Delacroix, Devéria was a leader of the romantic movement and was honored with numerous official and religious commissions. He first exhibited at the Salon in 1824 and continued to send paintings to Paris until the last few years of his life.

A talented portraitist, Devéria often depicted his family and friends in drawings and paintings. This sheet contains two studies of women painting, both seen from behind. The study at left depicts a woman painting a portrait on a high easel; beneath her image the artist wrote *La Jeune Veuve peignant*. At right another young woman stands before a large, blank canvas, holding a maulstick and palette. According to Devéria's inscription at the lower right, the drawing was executed in 1837 at Fontenay-aux-Roses, a town just outside Paris. A year later Devéria left Paris to stay in Avignon, before settling permanently in Pau, a village in the Pyrenees, in 1841.

The intimate perspective suggests that the women depicted were members of Devéria's family or close friends. One of the figures may tentatively be identified as the artist's sister Laure (1813–1838), a flower painter who debuted at the Salon in 1836 and would have been twenty-four years old at the time, although it is not known whether she was a widow in 1837. JT

BENOIT BLANC

French, Gémenos, near Marseille, 1812–1862 Paris

100

Portrait of Mme. Léonie Bouchage

Conté crayon, some stumping, on cream wove paper.

12¾ x 10¼ in. (325 x 260 mm).

Inscribed, dated, and signed, at right center, in black chalk, *Sergines, Juin 1858 / Benoni Blanc;* inscribed and signed on verso, in black chalk, *Mme Léonie Bouchage, / épouse de Mr Arthur Bouchage, / receveur de l'Enregistrement et des domaines, / à Sergines, (Youne) / Portrait fait à Sergines, en Juin 1858, / par B. Blanc de Gémenos, près Marseille, (Provence).*

PROVENANCE: Richard Day Ltd., London.

EXHIBITION: New York and London 1988, no. 47, repr.

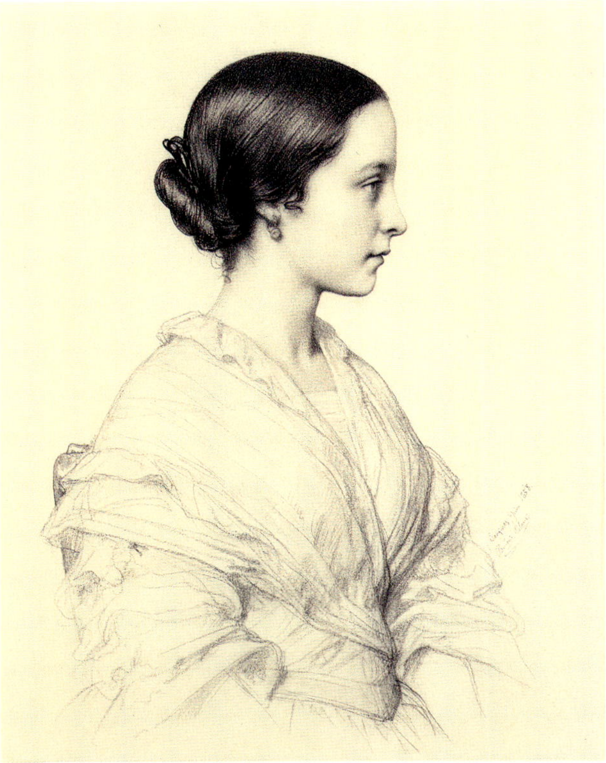

100

A talented youth, Blanc entered the Ecole Publique et Gratuite de Dessin in Marseille at the age of eight. At sixteen he left Marseille for Paris, where he entered the atelier of Horace Vernet (1789–1863), a history painter noted for the naturalism of his figures. When Vernet was appointed director of the Villa Medici in 1829, Blanc traveled with him to Rome. Upon returning to Paris three years later, he entered the atelier of the history painter Paul Hippolyte Delaroche (1797–1856), whom he may have met while in Italy, and began to sign his works Benoni. In order to earn a living, Blanc cultivated his talent as a portraitist, producing works distinguished by their fine, detailed execution and fidelity to the sitter.

In 1858 Blanc ventured outside Paris to the forest of Fontainebleau, where he drew *en plein air,* maintaining the same precision and loyalty to his subject as in his portraits. It was during his stay at Sergines, a town near Fountainebleau, that Blanc executed the present portrait. According to the artist's inscription on the verso of the drawing, the sitter was the wife of Arthur Bouchage, the property tax collector at Sergines. This sheet is a rare example of Blanc's work as a portraitist; the whereabouts of his portrait drawings and paintings are, for the most part, unknown. A significant number of his landscape drawings are to be found in Aix-en-Provence: over fifty are in the Bibliothèque Méjane, and two others are in the Musée d'Arbaud.

JT

FRANÇOIS BONVIN

French, Vaugirard 1817–1887 Saint-Germain-en-Laye

101

A Kitchen Maid

Watercolor, heightened with gouache, over charcoal, on blue paper prepared with brown wash.

11½ x 6½ in. (292 x 165 mm).

Signed and dated, at lower left, in black ink, *F. Bonvin 48.*

PROVENANCE: M. Pasteur, Paris; Galerie Fischer-Kiener, Paris; private collection, New York; W. M. Brady and Co., New York; private collection, New York.

EXHIBITIONS: New York 1989b, no. 32, repr. (as private collection, New York City).

The realist painter Bonvin showed an early predilection for still lifes and scenes of everyday life. To a great extent he was self-taught, but he was encouraged by both François Granet (1775–1849), who was director of the

Louvre in the 1840s, and the great realist painter Gustave Courbet (1819–1877). The present work was executed in 1848, when the artist would have been about thirty years old. In 1849 the art critic Champfleury compared Bonvin's work to that of Jean-Siméon Chardin (1699–1799), the artist whose work Bonvin most admired. Bonvin became well known for his small still lifes and intimate genre scenes, which he continued to paint and draw throughout his life. Here, he uses a somewhat somber palette lightened by bright passages of white gouache to suggest the effect of sunlight in an otherwise dark room. Bonvin is equally well-known for his depictions of simple, everyday objects, such as pots and pans, fully worked in charcoal or black and red chalk to suggest the play of light and shadow he found so interesting. CDD

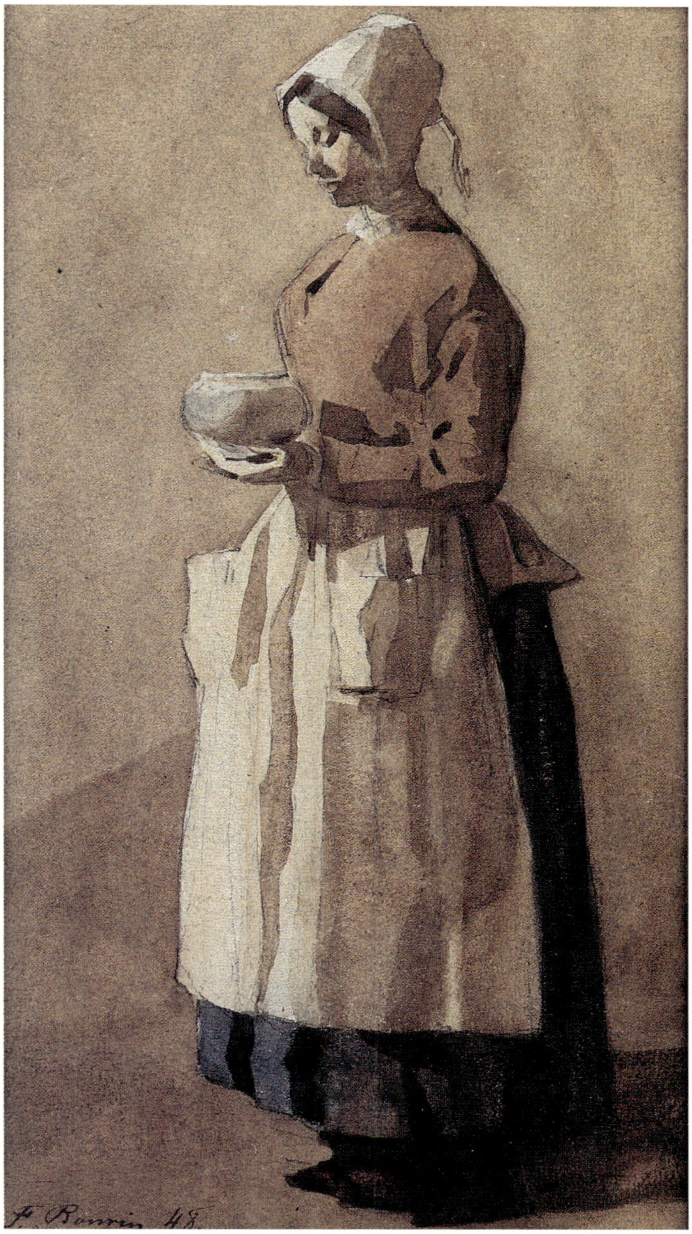

101

ADOLPH MENZEL

German, Breslau 1815–1905 Berlin

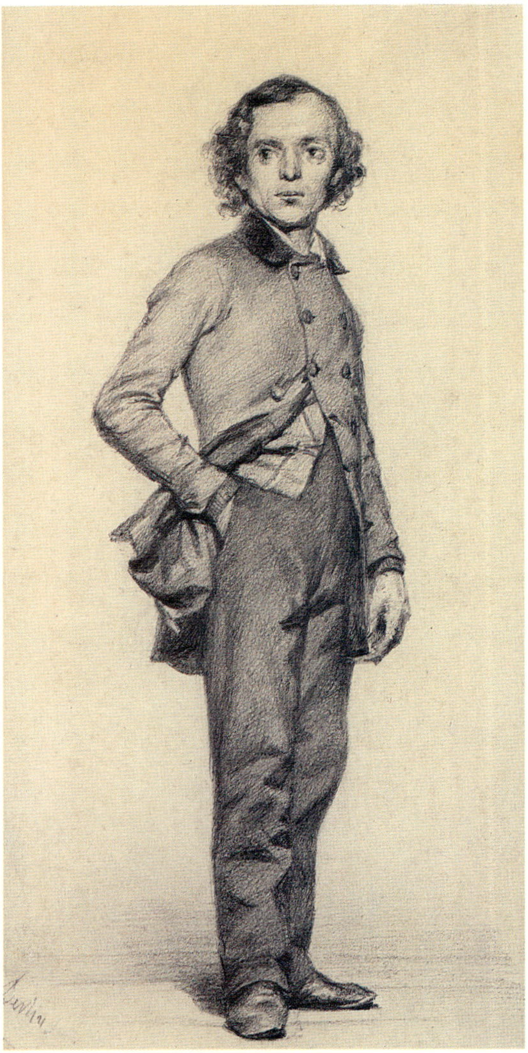

102

102

Standing Youth

Pencil.

9¼ x 4¾ in. (235 x 120 mm).

Inscribed by the artist at lower left, in pencil, *Berlin*.

PROVENANCE: C. H. Arnold, by descent; Thomas le Claire, Hamburg.

This young man has been identified as Carl Johan Arnold (1829–1916), Menzel's pupil and a son of friends, whom the artist praised in a letter to the boy's father: "He keeps painting and drawing from morning until night." The young man stayed with Menzel, who treated him like a nephew, for a two-year period and was frequently the subject of drawings and paintings. In a study that must date to around 1846–47, now in the Thaw Collection, The Pierpont Morgan Library, Menzel depicted a somewhat younger Arnold, asleep on a sofa. Another sketch, which must date to the same moment, depicts him still on the sofa, but awake (Wirth 1965, p. 64, repr.). To judge from the boy's appearance in the present work, Menzel must have made this study at a later date, since he looks somewhat older and thinner. Menzel signed and dated 1847 a pensive portrait of the youth, turned to the left in three-quarter profile and executed in pastel (Berlin 1955, no. 161, repr.).

Arnold subsequently would gain a reputation as a genre and animal painter, eventually becoming court painter at Weimar. CDD

103

Two Studies of a Hand Holding a Glass

Pencil, stumped.

5 x 8⅛ in. (127 x 206 mm).

Initialed and dated at lower right, in pencil, *AM 90*.

PROVENANCE: Dr. Wolfgang Ratjen, Munich; David Lachenmann, Munich; Katrin Bellinger, Munich; Flavia Ormond Fine Arts Ltd., London.

EXHIBITION: New York 1999b, no. 22, repr.

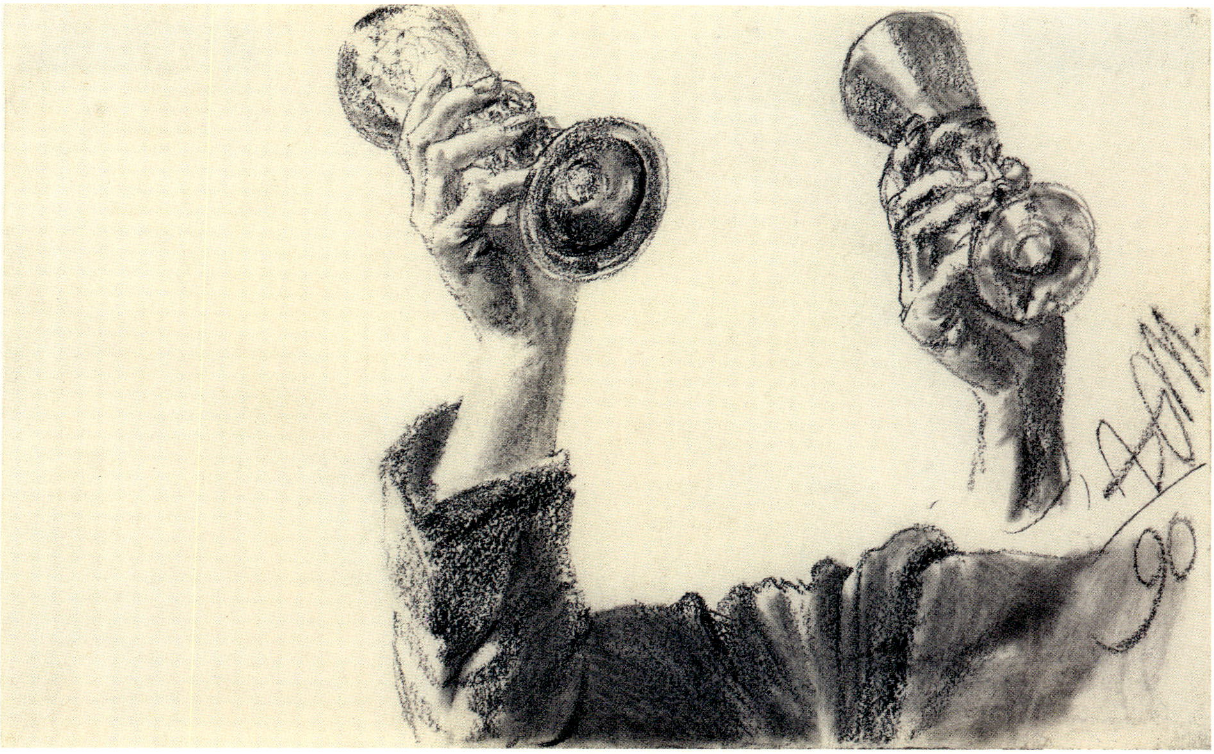

103

In this brilliant, nearly photographic work, Menzel twice drew the upraised arm of a woman holding a goblet: once in a full study of her arm and shoulder and once simply from the wrist to the hand holding the goblet. A similar work depicting a bearded man who holds a wineglass in his upraised right hand was formerly with Sabrina Förster (Düsseldorf 1987, no. 22, repr.). Arguably the greatest German draftsman of the century, Menzel may be characterized as a realist because of the everyday character of his subjects. Beginning with his career as an illustrator, he developed a distinctive manner of drawing in pencil, alternating fine strokes with dramatic accents laid on in a heavier pencil, suggestive of the effects he achieved as an illustrator in lithography. CDD

104

Three Studies of Elderly Women

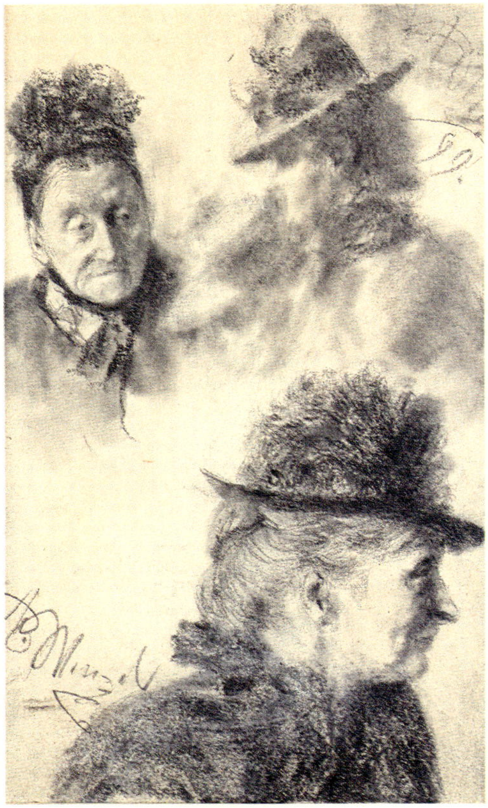

104

Pencil, stumped, with some white chalk, on paper, laid down on board.

8¼ x 5³⁄₁₆ in. (210 x 132 mm).

Initialed and dated at upper right, in pencil, *AM / 99;* signed at lower left, in pencil, *A. Menzel.*

PROVENANCE: Dr. Richard Doetsch-Benziger, Basel; sale, Kunstkabinett Stuttgart, 20–21 May 1960, no. 389, repr.; Benjamin Sonnenberg, New York; Mrs. Benjamin Sonnenberg; her estate sale, New York, Sotheby Parke Bernet, Inc., 21 November 1980, no. 133, repr. (withdrawn from sale; purchased privately from estate).

EXHIBITIONS: Basel 1943, no. 189; Basel 1956, no. 85, repr.; Newark 1961, no. 30; Princeton 1997, no. 193.

Menzel filled this sheet almost completely with studies of the heads of two elderly women, one wearing a short-brimmed hat trimmed with feathers and the other, a little round hat tied under her chin with ribbons. At the upper right a smaller study of the woman wearing the brimmed hat is broadly drawn in pencil. This one lacks the clarity of detail of the principal studies because Menzel went over all the lines with a stump, almost as if to erase it. A late work, this drawing was executed in 1899, when the artist would have been in his eighty-fifth year. The expressions of the women, who seem lost in their thoughts, appear to be candid, as though the artist drew them without their knowledge. CDD

WILHELM GENTZ

German, Neuruppin 1822–1890 Berlin

105

Arabs Approaching the Sea

Graphite.

6⅝ x 12⅜ in. (167 x 315 mm).

Signed at lower center, in pencil, *W. Gentz;* inscribed on verso, in pencil, *Wilhelm Karl Gentz 1822 Neuruppin / † 1890 Berlin.*

PROVENANCE: Dr. Matthias Konrad Hubrecht Rech, Bonn (Lugt S. 2745a; on associated fragment of old mat); David Lachenmann, Munich.

A pupil in Berlin of the history and portrait painter August Karl Friedrich von Kloeber (1793–1864), Gentz continued his studies in Antwerp and then, from 1846 to 1852, in Paris, first with Charles Gleyre (1808–1874)

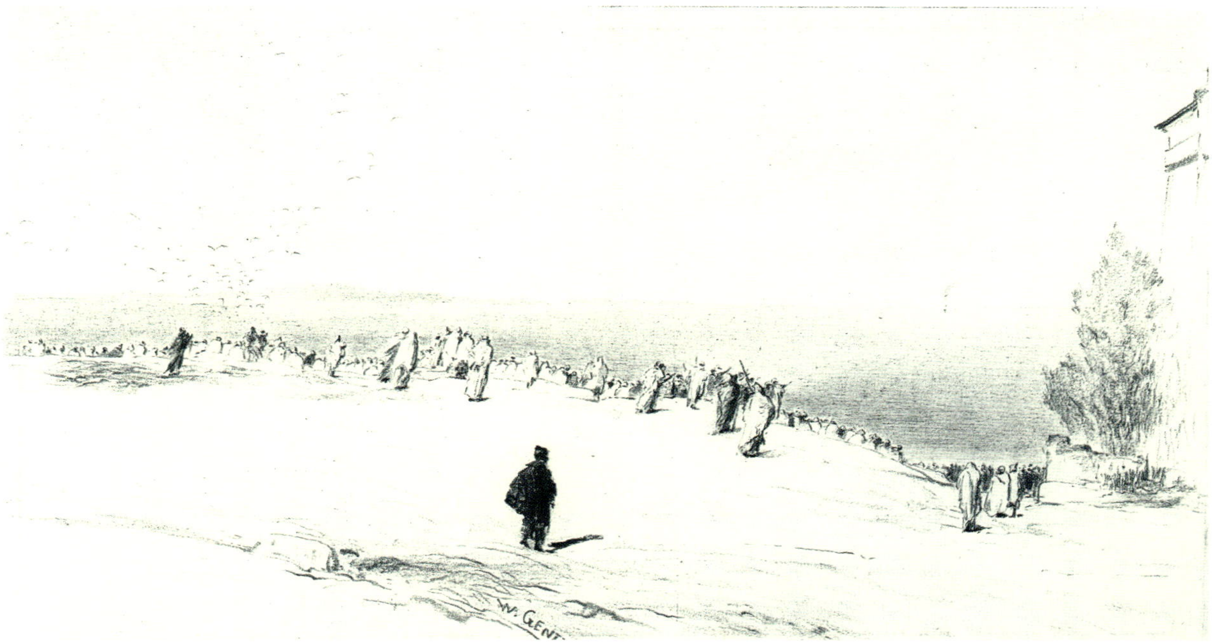

105

and subsequently with Thomas Couture (1815–1879). He thereafter traveled extensively in North Africa and enjoyed considerable success as a painter of subjects inspired by his experiences in Egypt and the Arab world. The catalogue of an exhibition of works by Gentz that was held in Berlin in 1890 lists no fewer than 232 drawings (Berlin 1890, nos. 340–571).

While the precise subject of this enigmatic depiction of Arabs descending a slope toward the sea remains unidentified, the theme is typical of works executed after Gentz's return from North Africa. WMG

HILAIRE GERMAIN EDGAR DEGAS

French, Paris 1834–1917 Paris

106

Study for a Male Nude with a Sword; Study for the Musculature of the Figure's Right Thigh

Pencil on dyed rose-colored paper.

11 x 8$\frac{1}{16}$ in. (280 x 205 mm).

Inscribed variously by the artist in pencil identifying the muscles of the thigh, *d'orb anterieur; l'adducteur; d'orb interne; triceps; couturier; l'adducteur.*

PROVENANCE: Degas atelier stamp (Lugt 657); Christian Humann, Paris; Galerie Arnoldi-Livie, Munich.

EXHIBITION: New York and London 1982, no. 60, repr.

It has been suggested that this study of movement and musculature may be connected to *The Young Spartans Exercising*, a painting by Degas now in the National Gallery, London. A working drawing that includes a pentimento sketch for the left leg, it is plausibly part of the artist's preparations for this rather early painting (1860–62). However, none of the youthful male figures in the painting is posed quite in this manner. The drawing, nevertheless, must date to the same period, when Degas had just returned from a long sojourn in Italy, where he studied from the middle to late 1850s. The Italian paper also supports this date for the work. The artist's inscriptions on the écorché at the upper left of the sheet are anatomical notes of the musculature of the thigh, indicating his careful, if not studious, approach to figure drawing.

Neoclassical in both subject and treatment, this drawing is reminiscent of the work of Jean Auguste Dominique Ingres (1780–1867), whom Degas greatly admired. CDD

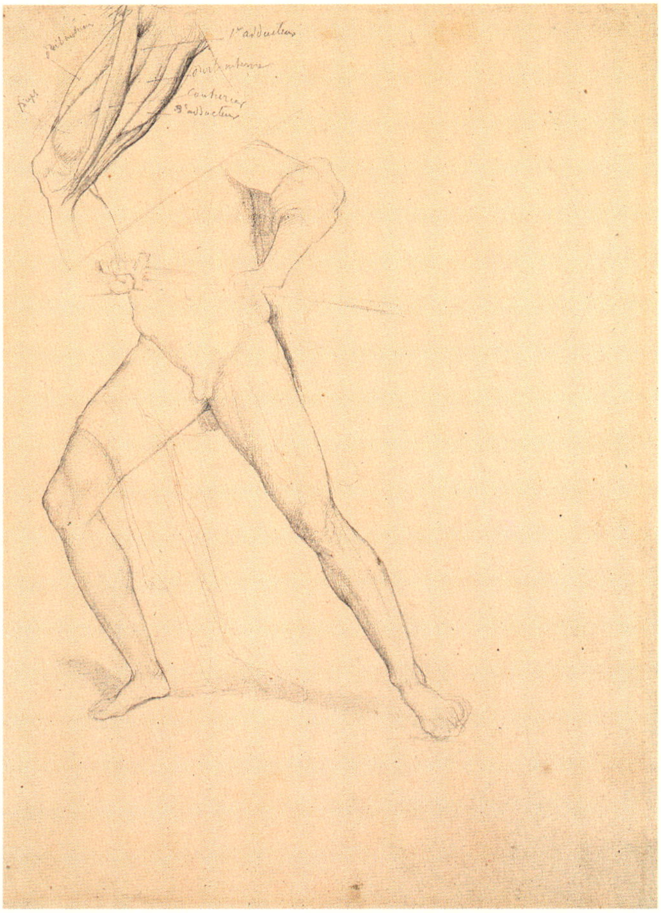

106

107
Flowerpots

Oil on paper, laid down on canvas.

5⅞ x 5⅛ in. (150 x 130 mm).

PROVENANCE: Henri Fèvre, the artist's nephew (according to inscription on stretcher); Marcel Guerin (according to Neal Fiertag); Eric G. Carlson, New York.

This work belongs to a very small group of still lifes executed by Degas when he was in Italy in 1856 and 1857. Executed in oil on paper, these little paintings all have a curiously modern air about them, owing in large measure to the artist's reduction of the subjects to simple, almost abstract, forms. Two of these still lifes are in the Louvre (Brame and Reff 1984, nos. 13–14, repr.), while yet another was on the New York art market in 1995. In these works, Degas was interested in the rendering of volume in the simplest terms. Studied at very close range, the objects depicted might have been selected precisely because of their lack of detail. The terra-cotta flowerpots in the present work, for example, have completely smooth surfaces. Similarly, one of the still lifes in the Louvre comprises two studies: above, some simple carpenter's tools are piled on a plain wooden block, and below, a spherical form lies on a table. The most recent such work to appear on the New York art market depicts an apple, turned upside down, the reflection of which can be seen in the small rectangular mirror upon which it sits. It is lit by a small windowlike opening at left. CDD

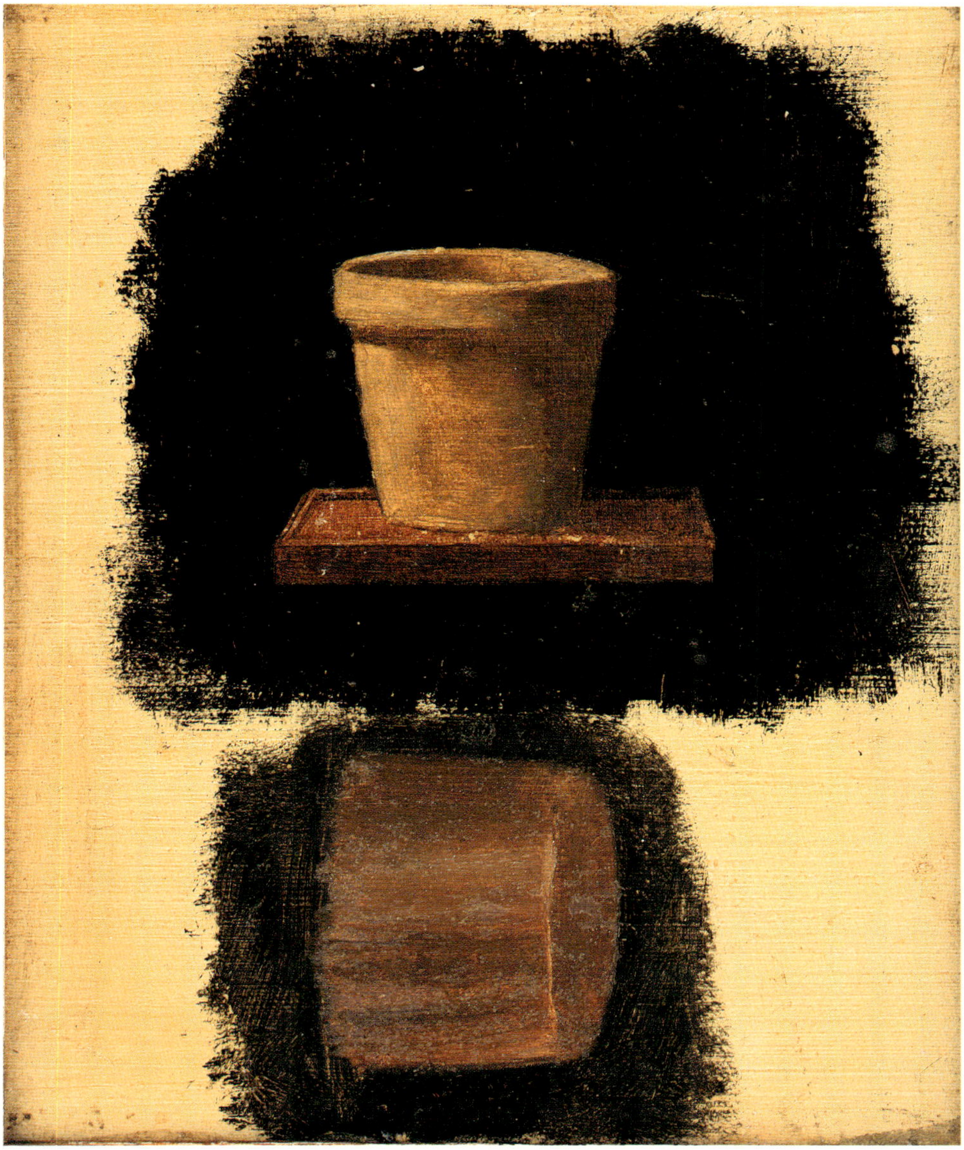

107

AUGUSTE-HILAIRE LÉVEILLÉ

French, Joué-du-Bois, Orne, 1840–1900 Paris

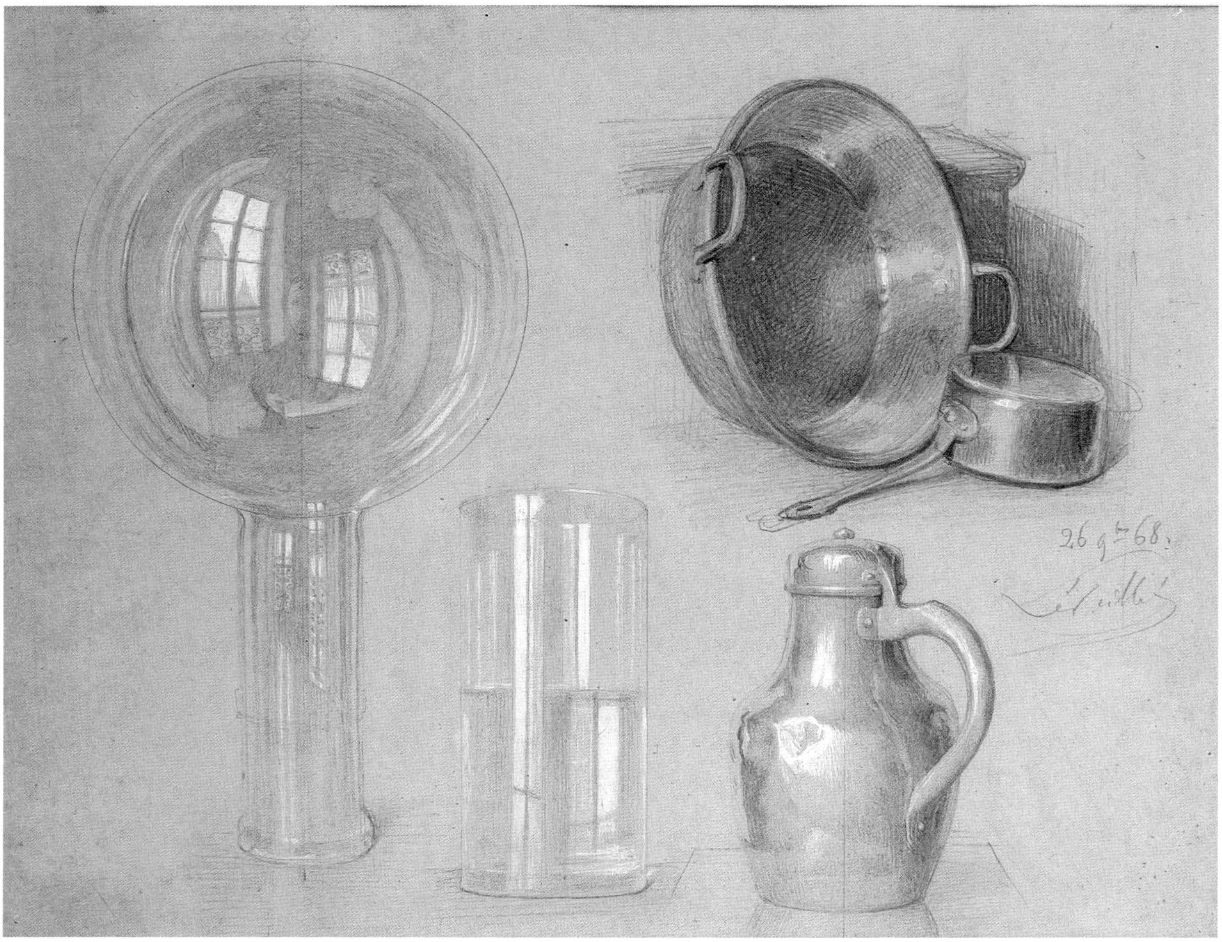

108

108

Studies of Surface Reflections

Graphite, heightened with white gouache, on gray card.

9½ x 12⅜ in. (242 x 315 mm).

Dated and signed at right center, in graphite, *26 9 bis 68 / Léveillé.*

PROVENANCE: Eric G. Carlson, New York; W. M. Brady and Co., New York.

Primarily a wood engraver, Léveillé produced illustrations for such journals as *L'Art* and *Le Monde illustré* as well as for *Le Magasin pittoresque*, *La Revue illustrée*, and *La Gazette des Beaux-Arts*. He began his career as a student of the wood engravers Adolphe-Jean Best (1808–1879), head of the atelier of engravers at *Le Magasin pittoresque*, and Laurent Hotelin and exhibited at the 1889 Exposition Universelle along with fellow wood engravers

Charles Baude (1853–1935) and Auguste Lepère (1849–1918). As a reproductive engraver, he made engravings after contemporary paintings and sculpture and was the primary engraver of Rodin's work.

The present sheet contains studies of surface reflections on an upturned glass beaker, a jar, a metal jug, and some pots and pans. Dated 1868, the sheet was executed when the artist was twenty-eight years old and reveals the skill at close observation that would later make Léveillé such a talented reproductive engraver. With great technical precision, he used a compass to draw the round beaker, large pot, and cylinder before shading the objects and highlighting the surface to capture the reflections. Léveillé depicted his own reflection in the beaker at the upper left of the sheet. JT

ALBERT-CHARLES LEBOURG

French, Montfort-sur-Risle, Eure, 1849–1928 Rouen

109

Still Life with Washtub, Barrel, Candlestick, and Skillet

Conté crayon, heightened with white, on blue-gray paper.

12½ x 9⅝ in. (318 x 244 mm).

Signed and dated, at lower left, in black conté crayon, *A. Lebourg 68;* inscribed on verso, in black conté crayon, *Monfort, Avril 68;* stamped at upper right, *A. Lebourg, Paris, 60 Rue de Clichy.*

PROVENANCE: By descent through the family of the artist; W. M. Brady and Co., New York.

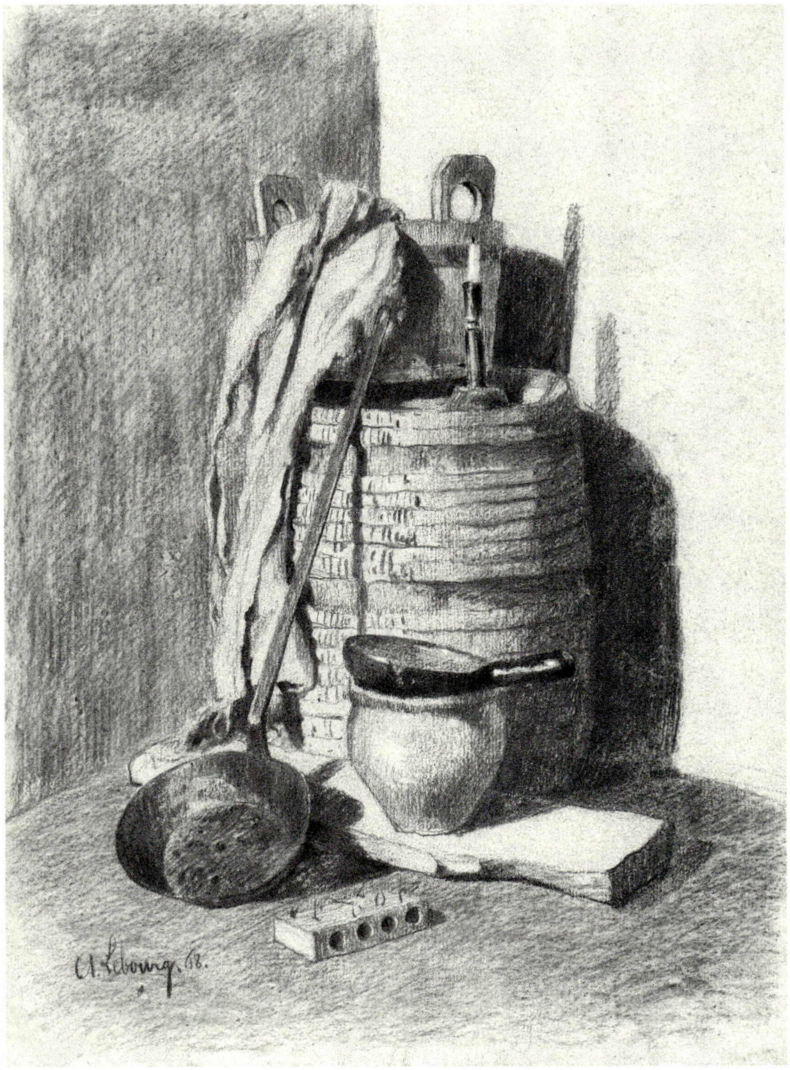

109

After entertaining an early interest in architecture, Lebourg entered the Ecole Municipale de Peinture et Dessin in Rouen and studied with the history painter and curator of the Musée des Beaux-Arts, Rouen, Gustave Morin (1809–1886). In 1872 Lebourg accepted the post of professor of drawing at the Société des Beaux-Arts, Algiers, where he remained for five years before returning to France. During his time in Algiers, he developed his talent as a landscape painter. Shortly after his return to Paris, he discovered Impressionism and exhibited with the Impressionists in 1879 and 1880.

This drawing belongs to a group of realist depictions of still-life subjects dating from the late 1860s and early 1870s, many of which were executed while Lebourg was studying in Rouen. It was done when the artist was only nineteen years old, and, according to the inscription, it was executed in his hometown of Monfort-sur-Risle. Gabriel Weisberg compares Lebourg's early still lifes to works by Léon Bonvin from the 1850s, which reveal "a young artist perfecting his ability to observe by studying simple forms from his environment" (Cleveland 1980, p. 156). As reflected here, the realist tradition of still-life subjects revived earlier prototypes by such masters as Jean-Siméon Chardin (1699–1779), who popularized the depiction of familiar objects. Indeed, Lebourg lends monumentality and beauty to such common objects as a washtub and barrel through his masterful execution and arrangement of forms. A comparable sheet was formerly in the collection of Frederick J. Cummings, Detroit (see Cleveland 1980, no. 126, repr.). Charles Ryskamp's collection also includes another sheet of still-life studies from Lebourg's student years in Rouen. JT

JEAN-MICHEL CELS

Belgian, The Hague 1819–1894 Brussels

110

Cloud Study in the Late Afternoon

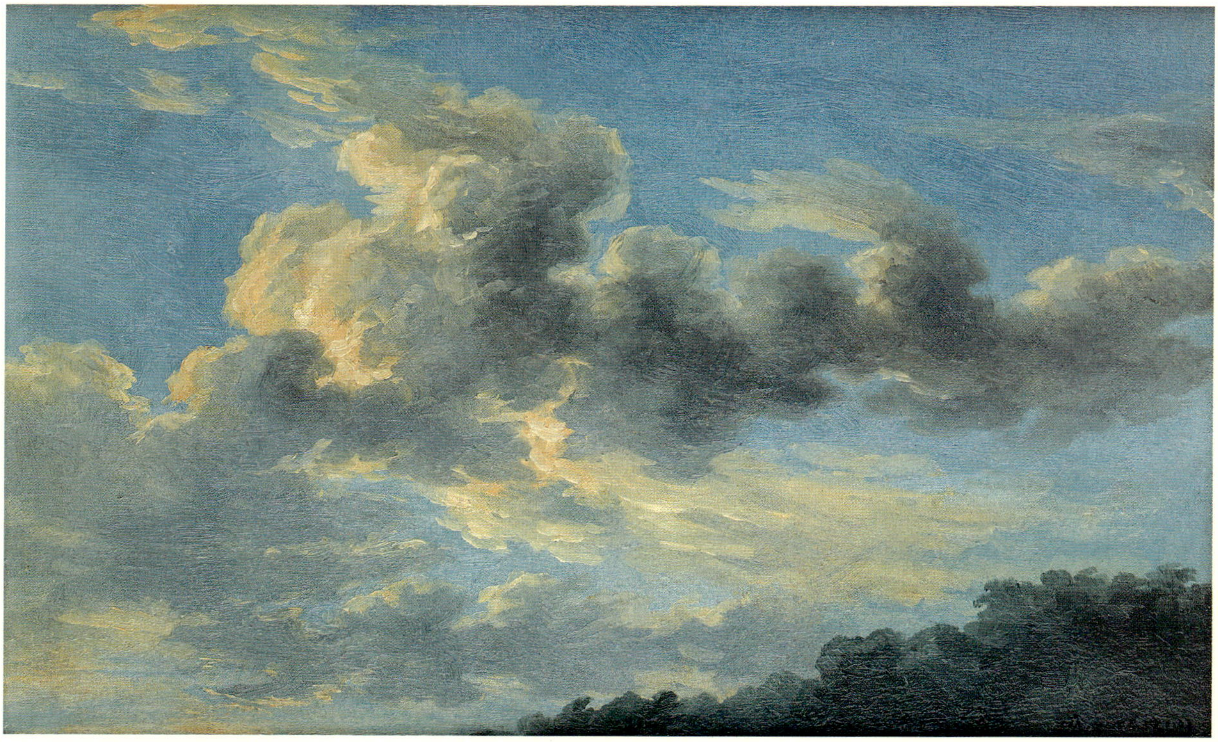

110

Oil on paper.

Sight measurements: 8⅛ x 13³⁄₁₆ in. (206 x 335 mm).

Signed with the artist's monogram and dated, at lower right, *JMC 8 OCT 1840*.

PROVENANCE: Sale, South Kensington, London, Christie's, 16 April 1997, part of no. 310; W. M. Brady and Co., New York.

Cels learned the art of the oil sketch from his father, Cornelis Cels (1778–1859), a Belgian neoclassical painter who studied in Italy for seven years. Artists there had begun sketching landscapes in oil *en plein air* as early as the seventeenth century, but it was not until the late eighteenth century, particularly through the efforts of Pierre-Henri de Valenciennes (1750–1819), that it became established practice.

Cloud studies in oil were among the exercises Valenciennes recommended in his influential treatise of 1800, *Elémens de perspective pratique*. One of the early practitioners was Simon Denis (1755–1812), a Belgian artist whose delicately painted cloud studies with their narrow strip of earth anchoring the bottom of the composition follow the formula advocated by Valenciennes (Washington and elsewhere 1996–97, no. 37, repr.). Closer to Cels's generation was John Constable (see No. 64), who assiduously painted heavily brushed, atmospheric sky studies during the period 1821–22, many of them from a viewpoint within the clouds (Reynolds 1984, no. 22.21, pl. 350).

Compared with these earlier examples, Cels's cloud studies are often more abstract in form and nonnaturalistic in color, with thickly impastoed surfaces; see, for example, *Sky Study with Birds* of 1842 in the Gere collection (London 1999, no. 12, repr.). In the present work, forms are built up in a series of layered dabs of paint, the closely modulated tones resembling the texture of a mosaic. Like tesserae, the dabs of paint are distinct, each stroke in a color slightly different from the one next to it. At the left different shades of ocher are dabbed onto gray, blending in the eye of the viewer to become the greenish gray of storm clouds. To the right of center, where the paint is thinly applied, an almost dry brush of ocher is dragged over cerulean to produce the effect of wisps of cloud shot through with streaks of light. Following Valenciennes, Cels has left a suggestion of the tops of trees along the lower edge of the sheet. KS

ANTON MAUVE

Dutch, Zaandam 1838–1888 Arnhem

111

A Stable with Carts by the Ruins of Castle Brederode

Watercolor over black chalk.

10⅝ x 15⁹⁄₁₆ in. (269 x 395 mm).

WATERMARK: Fragment.

Initialed in watercolor, at lower right, *AM;* inscribed on verso, at left center, in pen and black ink, *939*.

PROVENANCE: The artist's studio (Lugt 143); sale, The Hague, Kleykamp, 22–23 May 1917; art market, Amsterdam, 1958; Hans van Leeuwen (b. 1911), Amsterdam (Lugt S. 2799a); sale, Amsterdam, Christie's, 10 November 1999, no. 168, repr.

LITERATURE: Engel 1967, no. 27(c).

EXHIBITIONS: Utrecht 1959–60, no. 15; Laren 1963, no. 81; Bonn and elsewhere 1968, no. 96; Amsterdam 1988, no. 4.

One of the finest artists of the Hague school, an internationally acclaimed movement active from around 1870 until 1900, Mauve apprenticed from age sixteen with the Haarlem animal painter Pieter Frederik van Os

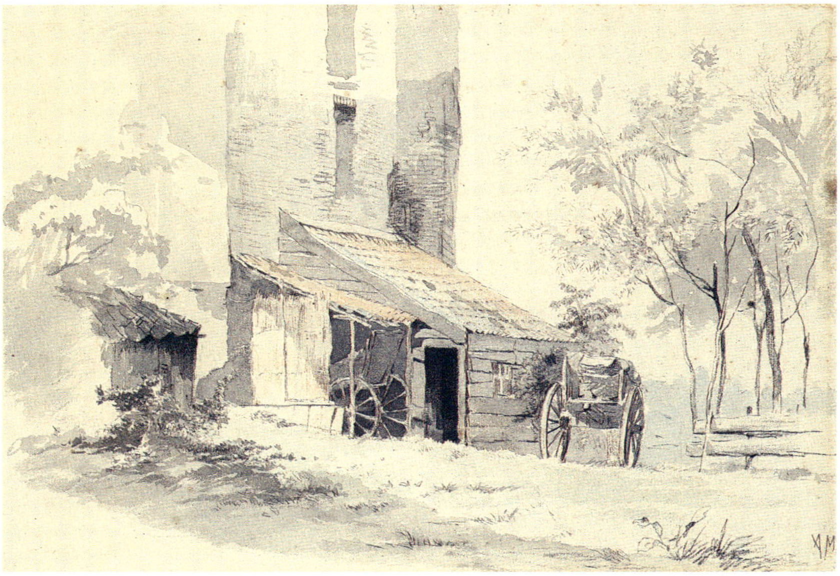

111

(1808–1892). In 1858 Mauve settled in Oosterbeek, a kind of Dutch Barbizon on the Rhine, where he began to draw in the often moody, highly atmospheric style that would characterize his mature work. That same year he made the present drawing (Engel 1967, no. 27[c]), which depicts the ruins of Castle Brederode in Santpoort, near Haarlem. Founded in the thirteenth century and named for a noble family whose line began in 1244 and died out in 1679, Brederode was destroyed and rebuilt numerous times over the centuries. When Mauve depicted the castle, which he made the subject of one other drawing and two paintings, all executed in 1857–58 (Engel 1967, nos. 17, 27[a,b]), it had lain in ruins since the siege of Haarlem by the Spanish in 1573.

KS

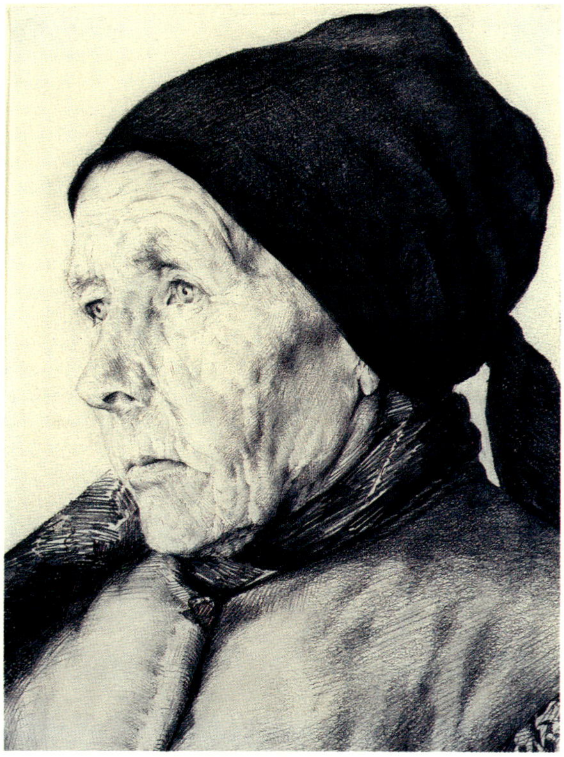

112

ATTRIBUTED TO WILHELM LEIBL

German, Cologne 1844–1900 Würzburg

112

Portrait of an Old Woman

Pencil.

8¾ x 7 in. (220 x 180 mm).

PROVENANCE: Eduard Selzam; from whom purchased by Kunsthandel Bauer, 1906/7; sale, London, Christie's, 19 June 1992, no. 22, repr.; Peter Nahum, London.

LITERATURE: Waldmann 1919, p. 164, fig. 22.

EXHIBITION: London 1995, no. 86, repr.

Leibl trained to be a locksmith and then hoped to become a precision instrument maker. His interest turned to art after a month of study. Following five years of training in Munich, he found himself most interested in postromantic realist art and spent the year 1869 in Paris. He was particularly impressed by the art of Edouard Manet (1832–1883) and Gustave Courbet (1819–1877).

While both Courbet and Leibl may be characterized as realists, Courbet was more interested in atmospheric effects in his landscapes than was Leibl, who was primarily concerned with detail. The outbreak of the Franco-Prussian War forced him to return to Germany, where he settled first in Munich before finding his subject matter in the peasants and landscape of the surrounding countryside.

The old woman in this drawing appears to be the eldest of the three peasant women in Leibl's most famous work, *Three Women in Church*, a painting of 1878–82, now in the Kunsthalle, Hamburg. If anything, she appears to be older in the present work, and she may even be Leibl's ideal model, a fine-featured, sharp-eyed peasant woman, whose worn face and black kerchief appear throughout his mature work. Known as Die Tumin, she appears in many works of the early 1890s, notably *Die Spinnerin*, the 1892 painting now in the Museum der bildenden Kunst in Leipzig and in *Bauernjägers Einkehr*, 1893, now in the Wallraf-Richartz Museum, Cologne (Munich and Cologne 1994, nos. 128, 131, repr.). There are a number of loose chalk and pen studies of the same model (Munich and Cologne 1994, nos. 129–30, 132–33, repr.), which demonstrate Leibl's interest in depicting the elderly, whose faces reveal their life experience. The painstaking technique of this sensitive portrait is quite different from Leibl's customary graphic manner, however, and it has even been suggested that the work may instead be by the painter and printmaker Eduard Selzam, who once owned the drawing. CDD

JEAN-BAPTISTE-EDOUARD DETAILLE

French, Paris 1848–1912 Paris

113

Le Spahi

Watercolor on cream card.

11 3/16 x 6 7/8 in. (283 x 174 mm).

Signed and dated at lower left, in pencil, *Ed. Detaille/1901*.

PROVENANCE: Robert Noortman Gallery, London; sale, London, Sotheby's, 22–23 June 1988, no. 706, repr.; W. M. Brady and Co., New York.

The star pupil of Ernest Meissonier (1815–1891), Detaille is known as a painter of military life. He began specializing in military subjects early in his career and always studied his models from life. In 1870 he traveled to Algeria to sketch and obtained a staff position. When the Franco-Prussian War broke out, he enlisted in the Eighth Mobile Battalion, Fourth Company. He served as secretary first to General Pajol and later to General Appert, which enabled him to observe military life firsthand and afforded him time to sketch. Detaille's work focused on his interest in the uniforms, customs, and activities of soldiers, especially the

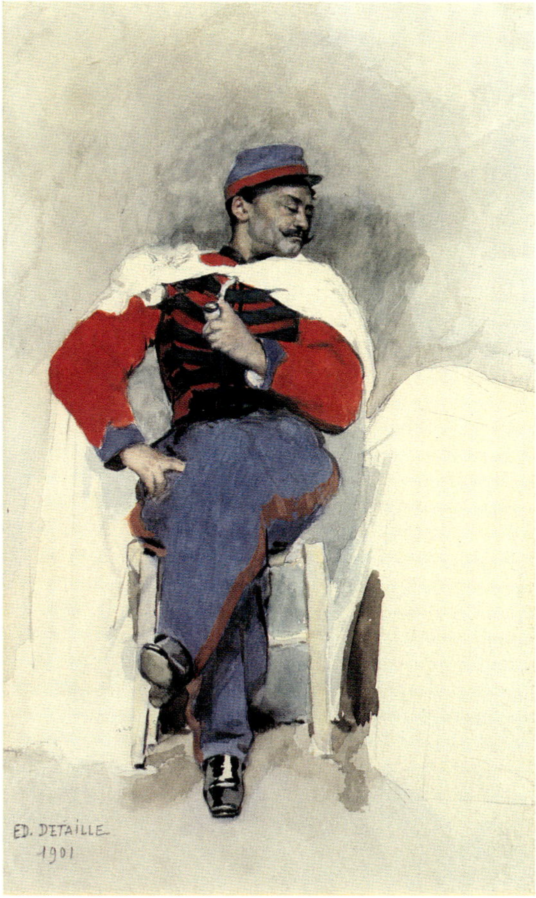

113

French, and in 1883 he published *Types et Uniformes*, an illustrated two-volume set describing the dress and classifications of the French army from the Revolution through the 1870s. From 1879 until 1890 Detaille regularly exhibited his watercolors at the Salon des Aquarellistes.

This drawing is characteristic of the artist's costume studies, which are typically executed in gouache and depict a single figure in full uniform. These studies, done from life, were occasionally used by Detaille as source material for paintings but just as often were done for their own sake. Although the present drawing is dated 1901, the sitter appears in a costume worn by officers of indigenous Algerian troops of the French army from about 1840 until 1870. The uniform may have belonged to Detaille's vast collection (now in the Musée de l'Armée, Paris). JT

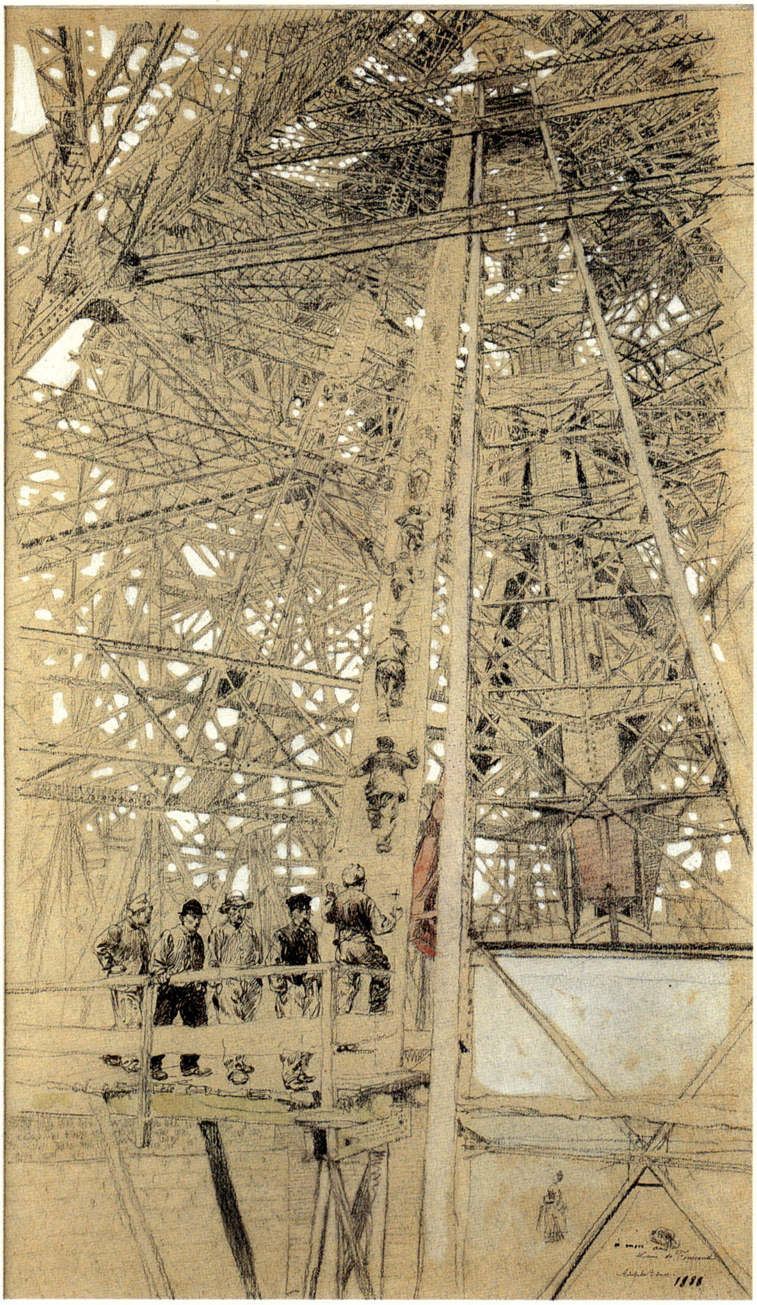

114

ADOLPHE-GUSTAVE BINET

French, La Rivière Saint-Sauveur, Calvados, 1854–1897 Saint-Aubin-sur-Quilleboler

114

Construction of the Eiffel Tower

Conté crayon, pen and brown ink, pink and green watercolor, and white gouache, on blue paper faded to light brown.

17 15/16 x 12 9/16 in. (456 x 319 mm).

Inscribed, signed and dated at lower right, in pen and brown ink, *à mon ami / Louis de Fourcaud / Adolphe Binet / 1888.*

PROVENANCE: W. M. Brady and Co., New York.

A student of Jean-Léon Gérôme (1824–1904) at the Ecole des Beaux-Arts, Binet specialized in portraiture and scenes of Parisian life. Binet absorbed Gérôme's realism and effectively applied it to the contemporary street scenes that he exhibited at the Salon in the 1880s.

This sheet depicts workers scaling a stairway to the unfinished upper section of the Eiffel Tower, which served as a gateway to the 1889 Exposition Universelle, when it was visited by nearly two million people. Construction of the tower was begun in January 1887 and completed on 31 March 1889. Judging from photographs documenting the construction of the tower, this drawing was probably executed between June and August 1888. The tower's immense scale is sensitively revealed through the relative proportions of the workers as well as the presence of a woman on the ground at lower right. The steep interior view of the tower further dramatizes the scene, as the workers climb a perilously vertical ladder from one level to the next. Binet must have begun this sheet on site, mapping the complex, weblike network of beams, later highlighting the fragments of dazzling sunlight piercing the tower's open structure.

Binet dedicated this drawing to his friend Louis de Fourcaud (1851–1914), an art historian and professor at the Ecole des Beaux-Arts, who wrote about such contemporary artists as François Rude (1784–1855) and Théodule Ribot (1823–1891). Fourcaud collected drawings and paintings, including works by Ribot, Auguste Rodin (1840–1917), Léon Lhermitte (1844–1925), and Jules Bastien-Lepage (1848–1884), and he befriended many artists.

JT

PEDER SEVERIN KRØYER

Danish, Stavanger 1851–1909 Skagen

115

The Prow of a Boat

Black chalk.

10 3/16 x 13 3/8 in. (259 x 340 mm).

WATERMARK: J. Whatman, 187 [cut off].

PROVENANCE: Estate of the artist (stamp on verso, P. Kroyer 1910, encircled), Niall Hobhouse Ltd., London; W. M. Brady and Co., New York.

A pupil in Copenhagen of Frederik Vermehren (1823–1910) and Wilhelm Marstrand (see No. 86), Krøyer joined the artists' colony at the fishing village of Hornbæk during the mid-1870s. He subsequently studied in Paris, under Léon Bonnat (1833–1922), and traveled to Spain and Italy before returning to Denmark in 1881. Krøyer spent most of the rest of his life in Copenhagen and at another artists' colony, Skagen, where he painted impressionistic scenes of the everyday life of his artist friends and the local fishermen.

As Marianne Saabye has pointed out

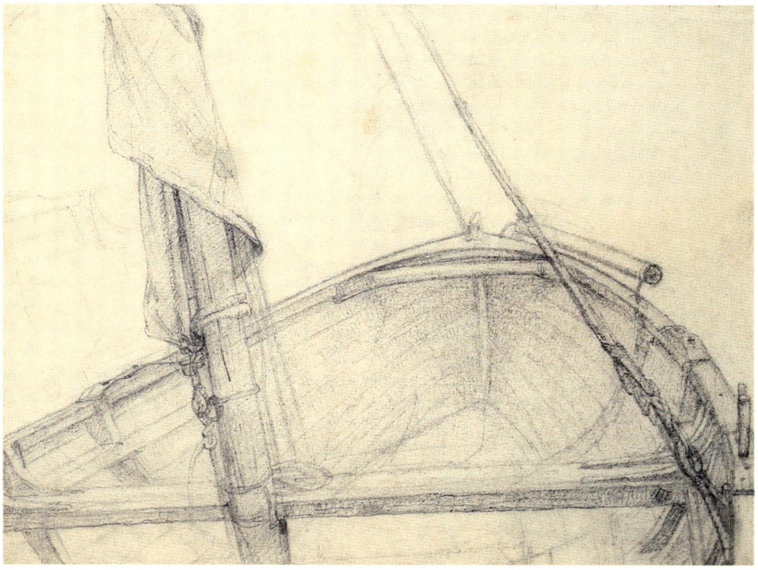

115

(verbal communication, 30 November 1999), this drawing is a study with minor differences for the prow of the boat in Krøyer's major early painting *Hornbæk Fishermen: Early Morning*, signed and dated 1877 and today in a private collection (Århus 1992, repr. p. 163, incorrectly dated to 1876). In the finished work the boat is on the open sea, three fishermen struggle to raise a net, and the stern of the vessel is filled with herring.

Krøyer's painstaking preparation for the painting is reflected in a series of studies on paper and in oil on canvas. In addition to the present work, H. Chr. Christensen cites a charcoal drawing in the Skagens Museum and a watercolor formerly in the collection of J. P. Lund (Christensen 1923, p. 27, under no. 157). The author also describes no fewer than seven painted studies for the picture, including an oil sketch for the entire composition, now in Den Hirschsprungske Samling, Copenhagen, as well as individual studies in oil on canvas for each of the three fishermen (Christensen 1923, pp. 26–27, nos. 149–56). WMG

VINCENZO GEMITO

Italian, Naples 1852–1929 Naples

116

Two Studies of a Skeleton

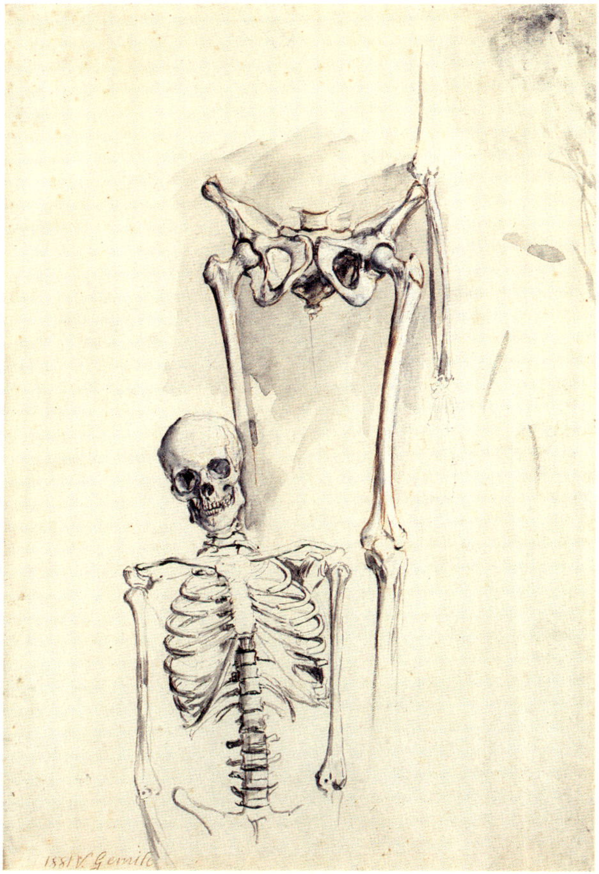

116

Pen and brown and gray ink, gray wash.

12 x 8⅝ in. (304 x 219 mm).

WATERMARK: Anchor in a double circle.

Signed and dated at lower left, in pen and brown ink, *1881 V. Gemito.*

PROVENANCE: Colnaghi, New York and London.

LITERATURE: Di Giacomo 1988, repr. p. XVIII.

EXHIBITION: New York and London 1992, no. 52, repr.

Perhaps the most gifted Italian sculptor of the second half of the nineteenth century, Gemito also was a talented draftsman, and many of his figure studies and portrait drawings are preserved in public and private collections in Europe and the United States. In 1877, having already enjoyed a degree of success in Naples, he traveled to Paris, where he was to remain until 1880. This drawing, the macabre subject of which appears to be unparalleled in Gemito's oeuvre, must have been executed shortly after his return to Italy.

It almost certainly was made in front of an actual skeleton, rather than having been copied from a print. The intended function of the drawing is unknown, but the way in which the forms overlap and the rather perfunctory treatment of the spine and rib cage suggest that Gemito's interest in the subject was more likely personal and artistic than straightforwardly scientific.

WMG

Pencil
5 13/16 x 4 1/8 in. (148 x 105 mm)

Adolph Siebert (German, Halberstadt 1806–1832 Rome)
Portrait of the Painters Alhborn and Hopfgarten
Pencil
5 x 7 3/4 in. (127 x 195 mm)

Denis Stuart (Dutch, Bussum, b. 1961)
Englischer Garten, Munich, by Night, 1997
Oil on paper
7 7/8 x 11 3/8 in. (200 x 288 mm)

Giovanni Battista Tiepolo (Italian, Venice 1696–1770 Madrid)
Young Man Holding a Book
Pen and brown ink, brown wash
8 5/8 x 5 7/16 in. (211 x 138 mm)

Cornelius Varley (British, London 1781–1873 London)
Joshua Cristall Sketching on the River Wye
Pencil
9 x 14 1/4 in. (124 x 366 mm)

3 3/16 x 5 3/4 in. (77 x 146 mm)

Charles François Eustache (French, Paris 1820–1870 Cherbourg)
A View of the Harbor at Cherbourg
Black chalk heightened with white chalk on blue paper
8 x 23 1/8 in. (208 x 585 mm)

Paul Huet (French, Paris 1803–1869 Paris)
Sunset
Watercolor
4 5/8 x 6 7/8 in. (117 x 175 mm)

Moïse Jacobber (German, Rhénanie 1786–1863 Paris)
Study of Pears
Oil on paper
4 1/4 x 5 1/2 in. (108 x 140 mm)

Adolph Kaiser (German, Geisa 1804–1861 Weimar)
Study of a Cypress at Tivoli
Pen and black ink over preliminary indications in graphite
14 3/4 x 10 1/2 in. (375 x 270 mm)

The World Observed
Five Centuries of Drawings from the Collection of Charles Ryskamp
Drawings Exhibited Ex-Catalogue

Carl Vilhelm Balsgaard (Danish, Copenhagen 1812–1893 Copenhagen)
Portrait of the Painter Emanuel Larsen
Oil on board
6 x 4 7/8 in. (152 x 125 mm)

Jean-Victor Bertin (French, Paris 1797–1871 Paris)
Landscape at Fontainebleau
Black chalk and pencil
13 1/4 x 17 1/2 in. (330 x 440 mm)

Paul Hippolyte Delaroche (French, Paris 1797–1856 Paris)
Man Seated on a Bench
Black chalk, stumped, heightened with white gouache
9 x 6 in. (229 x 152 mm)

An Unmade Bed
Watercolor over faint traces of pencil

Louis Lafitte (French, Paris 1770–1828 Paris)
A Man Sketching a Ruined Tower
Pencil
7 x 9 1/2 in. (179 x 240 mm)

Attributed to Guillaume de Marcillat (French, active in Italy, La Châtre, near Bourges, 1467/70–1529 Arezzo)
Landscape with a Fortified Village by a River; verso: *Half-Length Portrait of a Woman*
Pen and brown ink on tan paper
3 7/8 x 2 3/8 in. (98 x 60 mm)

Adolf Menzel (German, Breslau, 1815–1905 Berlin)
Man with a Toothache
Pencil
3 7/16 x 3 1/2 in. (88 x 90 mm)

Ernst Ferdinand Oehme (German, Dresden 1797–1855 Dresden)
Landscape with Ruins
Watercolor
3 7/16 x 3 13/16 in. (88 x 98 mm)

Jørgen Roed (Danish, Ringsted 1808–1888 Copenhagen)

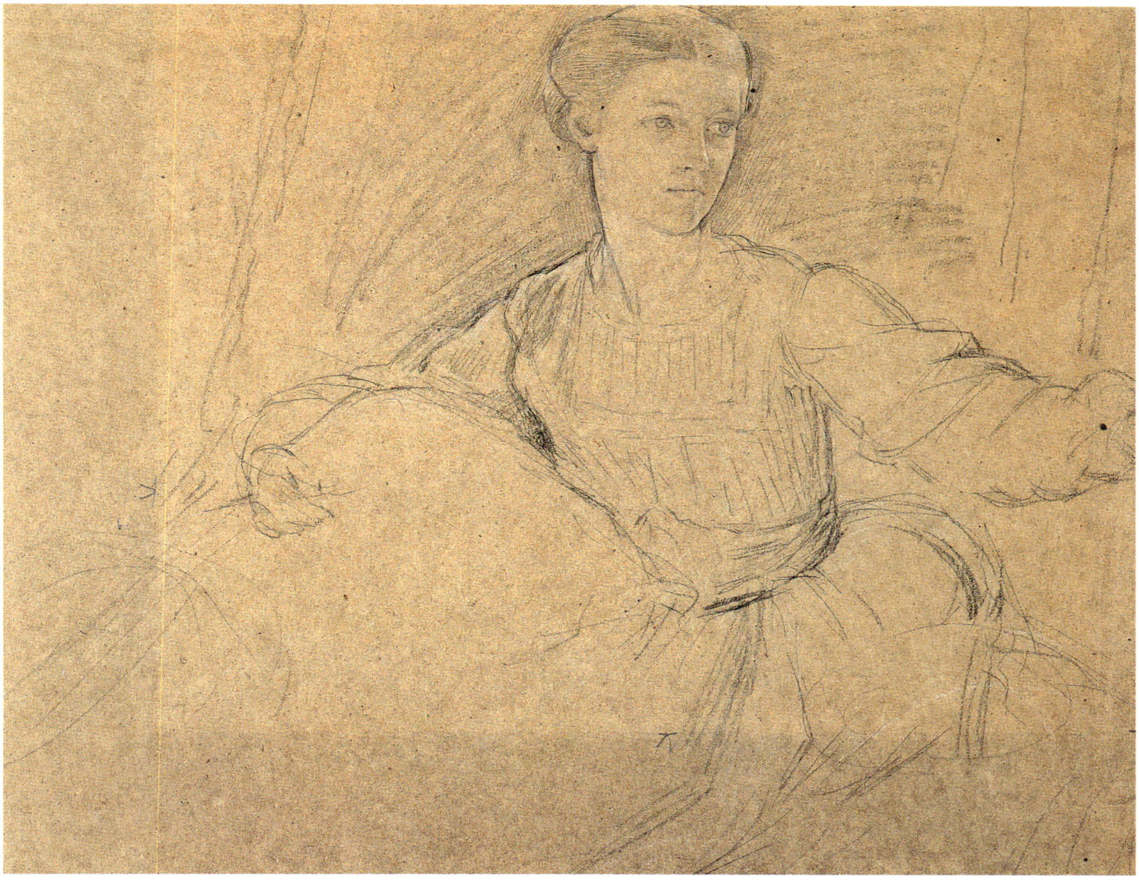

117

WILLIAM BLAKE RICHMOND

British, London 1842–1921 London

117

Portrait of a Young Lady

VERSO: Partial study for a composition

Black chalk, heightened with white chalk, on brown wove paper.
Irregular, 12⅞ x 16⅜ in. (327 x 416 mm).
PROVENANCE: Anthony d'Offay Fine Art, London.

William Blake Richmond was the son of artist George Richmond (1809–1896), who was an intimate of William Blake. As a young man, Richmond was a protégé of another of his father's friends, John Ruskin (1819–1900), but he later rejected Ruskin's strict teaching in favor of history painting and portraiture. At the age of seventeen, he began his formal training at the Royal Academy, exhibiting there as early as 1861. Today he is best remembered for his mosaic decoration of the choir, sanctuary, and ambulatory of St. Paul's Cathedral, carried out between 1891 and 1907.

Richmond, however, was one of London's leading portrait painters, albeit out of financial necessity; his career as a portraitist peaked in the 1880s. He particularly excelled at portraits of children and society ladies and was remarkably adept at capturing female beauty. His painted and drawn portraits are invariably elegant and often tinged with a Pre-Raphaelite melancholy. Richmond is frequently associated with other Victorian neoclassical artists, such as Frederic Leighton (1830–1896) and Lawrence Alma-Tadema (1836–1912).

The subject of this portrait has not been identified, and the drawing cannot be connected to any known painting by the artist. According to Simon Reynolds, this attractive sheet dates to the late 1870s or 1880s. JT

(HELEN) BEATRIX POTTER

British, London 1866–1943 Near Sawrey, Cumbria

118

Leaves and Flowers of the Orchid Cactus

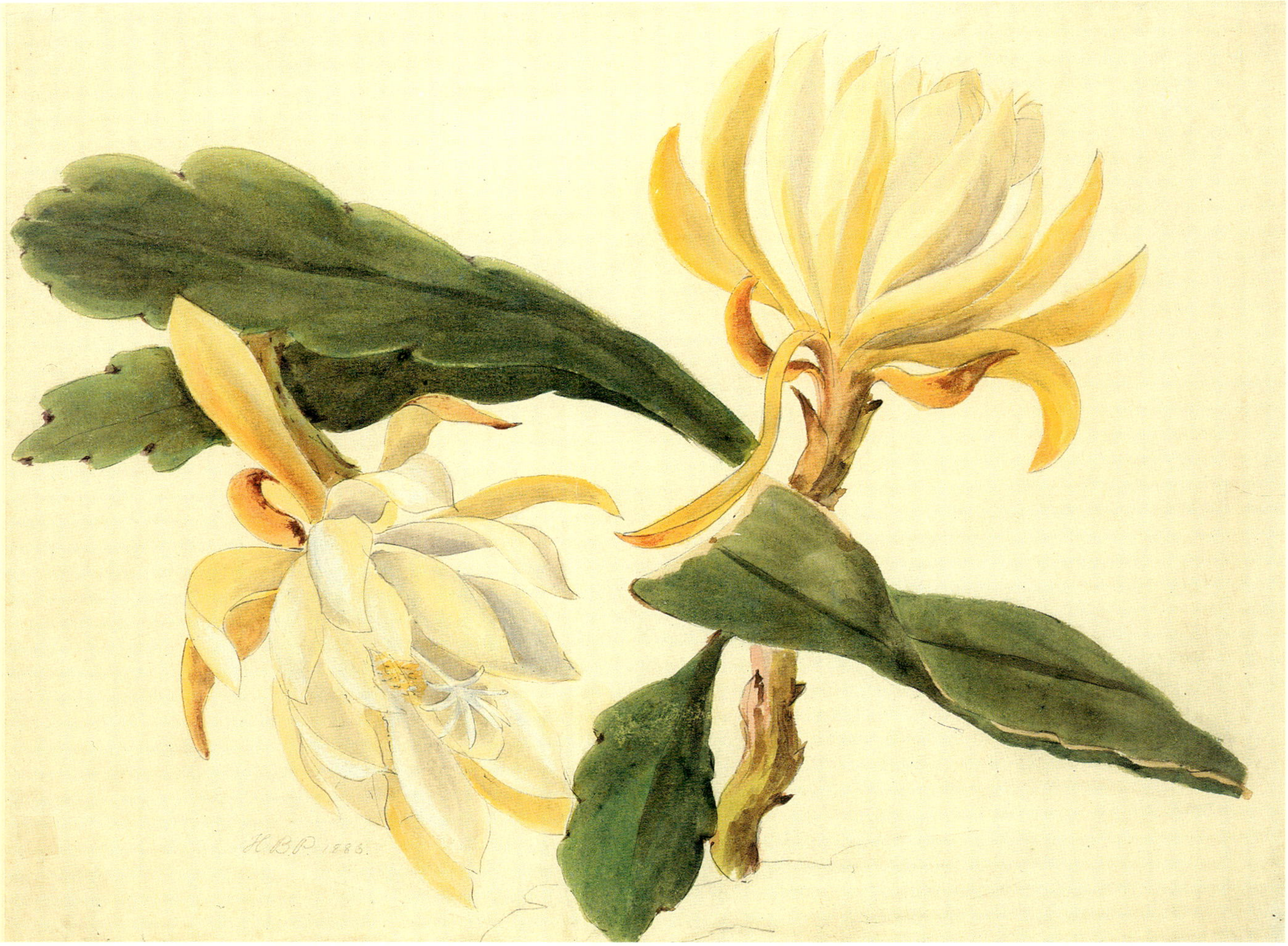

118

Watercolor and pencil.

11⅛ x 14⅞ in. (283 x 377 mm).

Signed at lower left, in pencil, *H.B.P. 1886*; inscribed on verso, at lower left, in pencil, *At Camfield / Given to Miss Hammond. '87 / Helen Beatrix Potter.*

PROVENANCE: Sale, London, Sotheby's, 6 April 1979, no. 633.

From early childhood the study of nature held a powerful fascination for Beatrix Potter. Beginning about age seven she copied from her father's illustrated books on natural history and from the same age she kept notebooks in which she made precise drawings in pencil and watercolor of the flora and fauna in her family's and friends' gardens. A precocious and largely self-taught young artist, by the age of ten she was capable of producing a credible likeness of a narcissus (Victoria and Albert Museum, BP. 273; *Potter* 1985, no. 44, repr.).

The range of Potter's drawings of flowers and plants—from freely drawn sketches with color applied in broad strokes of the brush, to closely observed studies in watercolor and pen and ink or pencil, in the tradition of botanical illustration—suggests something of her working methods in preparing drawings for her illustrated children's books. For example, a watercolor sketch of onions in a vegetable patch that served as a background study for an illustration in *The Tale of Benjamin Bunny* (*Potter* 1985, no. 798, pl. XXVII) was preceded by a closely observed and more highly finished drawing of three onions (*Potter* 1972, p. 114, repr.).

The subject of the present drawing has been identified by John F. Reed as an orchid cactus (*Epiphyllum phyllanthus;* correspondence, 16 February 2000). Although native to Central and South America, it thrives as a houseplant in more temperate climates. Given Potter's inscription—*At Camfield*, her grandparents' country home in Hertfordshire, north of London—it likely was in such a setting that she encountered the plant.

This drawing has not been connected to any of the artist's books for children, the earliest of which—*The Tale of Peter Rabbit*—was published in 1901. Potter's exuberant handling of the watercolor over quick notations in pencil suggests an artist enthralled with her subject, which she may have deemed too exotic for inclusion in a children's story. The Miss Hammond referred to in the drawing's inscription was Potter's last governess, with whom she stayed in contact into her twenties. KS

MAX LIEBERMANN

German, Berlin 1847–1935 Berlin

119

View of the Birch Alley in the Artist's Garden at Wannsee

Pastel.

10³⁄₁₆ x 15½ in. (258 x 343 mm).

Signed at lower left, in pencil, *mlieberman*.

PROVENANCE: Private collection, Switzerland.

Liebermann studied first in Weimar and Düsseldorf, where he became enthusiastic about seventeenth-century Dutch art and realism. By 1873, in the interest of accelerating his development, he had established himself in Paris. While there he became acquainted with the outdoor painters of the Barbizon school and the early Impressionists. He made the first of what were to become almost yearly trips to Holland in 1875; Dutch art was to prove a lifelong influence. By 1878 he had settled in Munich. His style was now fully established as a synthesis of Impressionism and realism, and he enjoyed success in Paris and elsewhere. Liebermann decided to return permanently to his native Berlin in 1884. He became president of the newly founded Berliner Sezession in 1898. Opposed to the new artistic movement, German Expressionism, he eventually resigned from the Sezession group.

This drawing is typical of Liebermann's work in the second and third decades of the twentieth century in its idiosyncratic palette of yellow-green, ocher, and reddish brown. It is one of the artist's studies for the 1918–20 painting of his garden that is now in the Niedersächsisches Landesmuseum, Hannover (Bremen 1995–96, p. 106, repr. in color). It resembles seven other pastels datable to the same period; for example, the nearly identical one that was sold in Berlin in 1932 (repr. sale, Berlin, Ball and Paul Graufe, 21 March 1932, no. 50). Since it is similar in size and tonality to the present work and depicts the same stand of trees and path, from a vantage a little farther to the left, it, too, must be preparatory for the Hannover painting. In *Allee in Sakrow,* another work of the same period, now in the Wallraf-Richartz Museum, Cologne (Cologne 1967, no. 75, repr.), the artist was intrigued by the contrast between the dark brown of the trunks of the trees and bright sunlight of the unshaded areas. According to Dr. Margreet Nouwen, who is preparing a catalogue raisonné of the pastels, watercolors, and gouaches of Max Liebermann, the view in the present work shows the villa and birch alley from the northwest. Apparently a little forest of birch trees was on the land when Liebermann bought the property, and he reduced this to a narrow alley. CDD

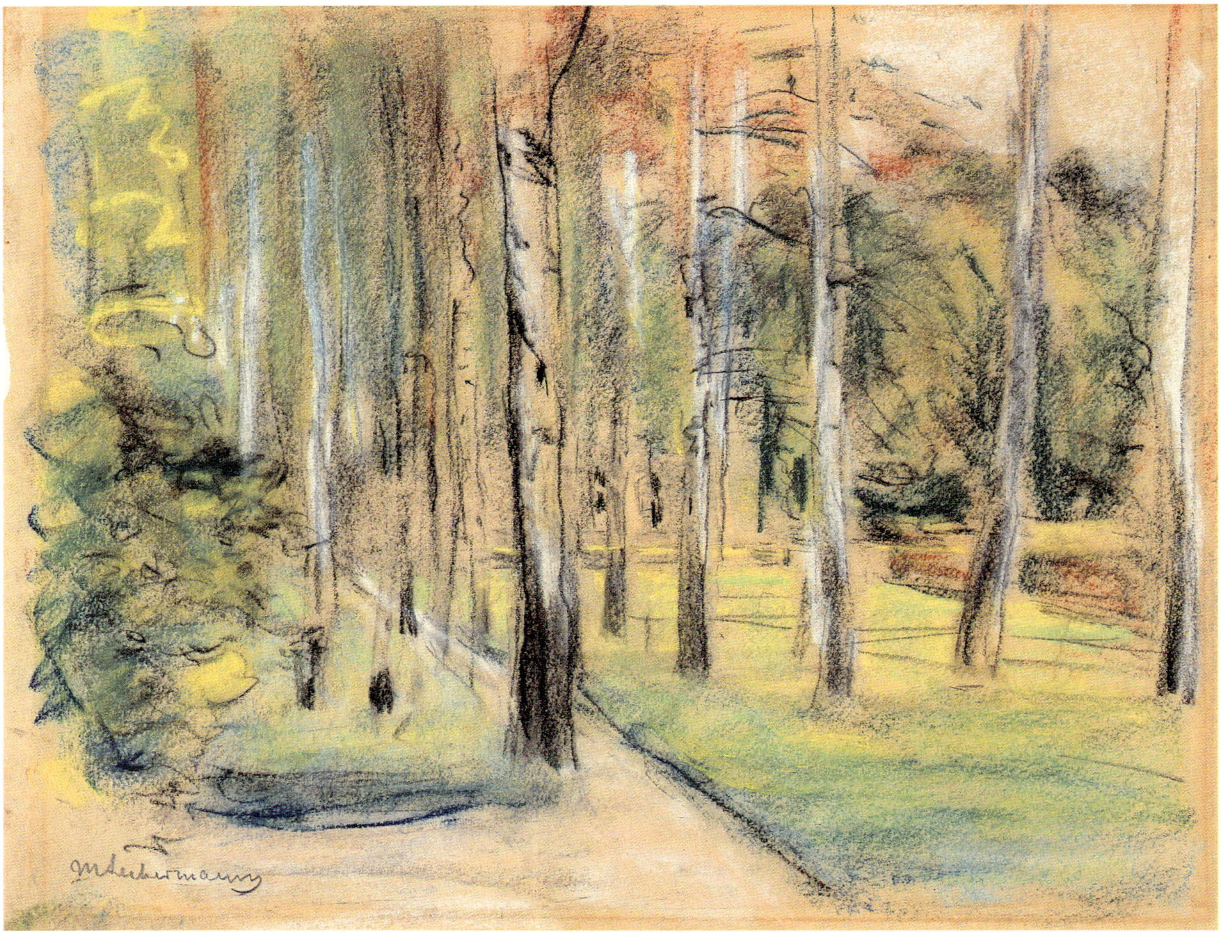

119

LLOYD REES

Australian, Yeronga, Brisbane, 1895–1988 Hobart

120

Lane Cove, Sydney

Pencil on cream wove paper.

7¾ x 11 in. (197 x 278 mm).

Signed and dated at lower left, in pencil, *L Rees / 1937.*

PROVENANCE: Martin Browne, Sydney.

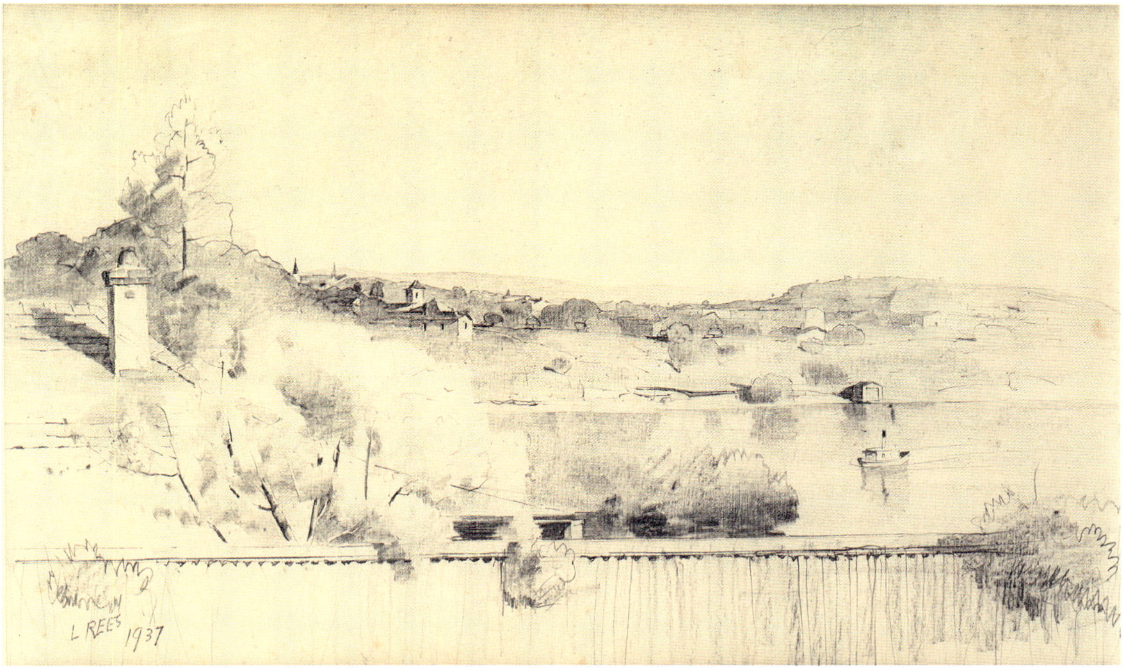

120

One of Australia's preeminent modern landscape painters, Rees was a prolific draftsman throughout his career. At age seventeen, he was diagnosed with a serious kidney disease that forced him to give up his job at a bank. To escape the emotionally depressing effects of his illness and as a respite from remaining indoors, Rees began exploring Brisbane and its environs, depicting their architecture and landscape. His practice of making keenly observed, sensitively executed drawings of his immediate environment was to characterize his draftsmanship for the remainder of his career, which lasted more than seventy years.

Having settled in Sydney in 1917, between 1931 and 1937 Rees concentrated on views of Sydney Harbor and the surrounding area. His pencil drawings from this period are the most accomplished in his oeuvre. Working directly from nature, he rendered precisely described yet poetic views, with an emphasis on careful observation but not strict realism. Although they appear to document particular sites objectively, Rees's drawings are carefully constructed compositions. In sheets such as this, the artist achieved a wide variety of tonal effects through the alternate use of the broad side of the pencil to shade and its sharp point to pick out details with a fine, crisp line. JT

ANDREW ZEGA AND BERND H. DAMS

American, born 1961
German, born 1963

121

Elevation of a Bronze Vase at the Parterre du Midi, Versailles

Watercolor on card.

13¼ x 8½ in. (337 x 213 mm).

Inscribed and dated on verso, in pencil, *A Bronze Vase at Versailles / ca. 1668, by Claude Ballin / © 1999 Edward Andrew Zega / & Bernd H. Dams*; signed by the artists and inscribed, *for Charles Ryskamp*.

PROVENANCE: Commissioned by Charles Ryskamp, 1999.

LITERATURE: Zega and Dams 2000, pp. 92–93, repr.

Since 1991, Andrew Zega, an architectural draftsman, and Bernd Dams, an architect and historian, have worked together to produce watercolor elevations of historic European garden architecture and sculpture. Because of the ravages of time and weather on outdoor sculpture, Zega and Dams undertake extensive archival research in order to accurately recreate damaged or destroyed garden decorations.

A particular interest in garden vase sculpture has inspired drawings such as this sheet depicting a verdigris bronze vase containing an orange tree. This vase was one of six commissioned by Louis XIV in 1666 from the royal silversmith Claude Ballin to ornament the low retaining wall along the Parterre des Fleurs, later called the Parterre du Midi, at Versailles. These baroque vases were intended to display the king's orange trees during the summer. With a precise, refined watercolor technique, the artists carefully recreated the vase as a record of the lost garden decoration at Versailles and an homage to the often forgotten virtuosity of garden sculpture. At the request of Charles Ryskamp, the artists included the orange tree that the vase was originally intended to contain.

In addition to the present sheet, Mr. Ryskamp's collection includes a drawing of the front gate of the Frick Collection that was given to him by Zega and Dams in 1994. JT

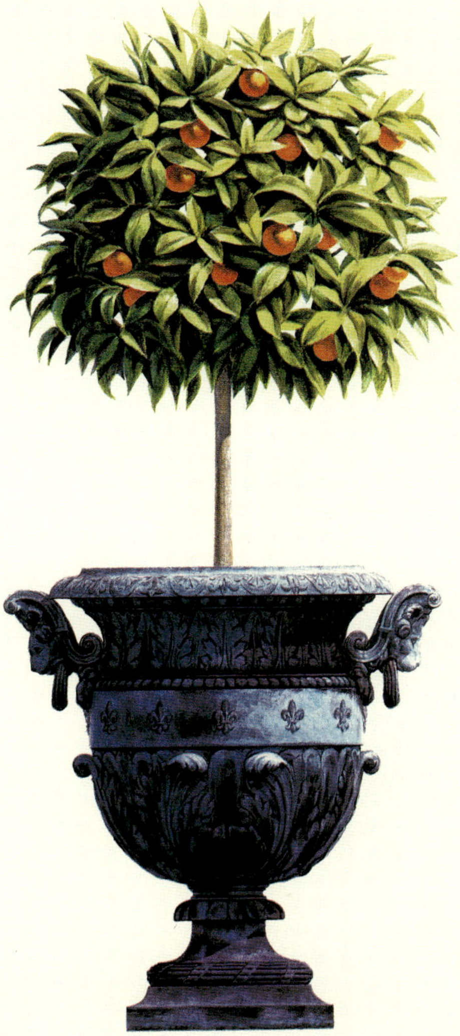

121

WORKS CITED IN ABBREVIATED FORM

LITERATURE

Arisi 1986
Ferdinando Arisi, *Gian Paolo Panini e i fasti della Roma del '700*, Rome, 1986.

Aubrun 1977
Marie Madeleine Aubrun, "Pierre Athanase Chauvin," *Bulletin de la Société de l'Histoire de l'Art Français*, 1977, pp. 191–216.

Baruch 1994
Maurice Baruch, *Portraits russes á l'aquarelle (1825–1855)*, Paris, 1994.

Baskett and Snelgrove 1978
John Baskett and Dudley Snelgrove, *The Drawings of Thomas Rowlandson in the Paul Mellon Collection*, New York, 1978.

Benesch 1928
Otto Benesch, *Die Zeichnungen der Niederländischen Schulen des XV. und XVI. Jahrhunderts*, vol. 2, *Beschreibender Katalog der Handzeichnungen in der Graphischen Sammlung Albertina*, Vienna, 1928.

van Berkum 1762
H. van Berkum, *Beschryving der stadt Schoonhoven . . .*, Gouda, 1762.

Bernt 1958
Walther Bernt, *Die Niederländischen Zeichner des 17. Jahrhunderts*, 2 vols., Munich, 1958.

Bindman 1977
David Bindman, *Blake as an Artist*, Oxford and New York, 1977.

Blake 1927
[Author unknown], *William Blake: The Description of a Small Collection of His Works in the Library of a New York Collector*, New York, 1927.

Blunt and Stearn 1994
Wilfrid Blunt and William T. Stearn, *The Art of Botanical Illustration*, revised edition, Woodbridge, Suffolk, 1994.

Bonzi 1964
Mario Bonzi, *Sinibaldo Scorza e Antonio Travi*, Genoa, 1964.

Brame and Reff 1984
Degas et son oeuvre, A Supplement, compiled by Philipe Brame and Theodore Reff, New York, 1984.

Brünniche 1953
Eigel H. Brünniche, *Vejledende tekst til J. Th. Lundbyes skitsebog Troldom og Huletanber*, Copenhagen, 1953.

Butlin 1981
Martin Butlin, *The Paintings and Drawings of William Blake*, 2 vols., New Haven, 1981.

Byam Shaw 1983
James Byam Shaw, *The Italian Drawings of the Frits Lugt Collection*, Paris, 1983.

Chatelet-Lange 1972
Liliane Chatelet-Lange, "Michaelangelos Herkules in Fontainebleau," *Pantheon* 20, no. 6, 1972, pp. 455–68.

Christensen 1923
H. Chr. Christensen, *P. S. Krøyer. Fortegneese over hans olienmalerier*, Copenhagen, 1923.

De Grazia 1995
Diane De Grazia, review of *Sixteenth-Century Italian Drawings in New York Collections* by William M. Griswold and Linda Wolk-Simon, *Master Drawings* 33, no. 2, 1995, pp. 175–77.

Di Giacomo 1988
Salvatore di Giacomo, *Gemito*, Naples, 1988.

Dunbar 1972
Burton L. Dunbar, "Some Observations on the 'Errera Sketchbook' in Brussels," *Bulletin, Musées Royaux des Beaux-Arts de Belgique*, 1972, pp. 53–82.

Engel 1967
E. P. Engel, *Anton Mauve (1838–1888)*, Utrecht, 1967.

Ewan 1968
Joseph Ewan, *William Bartram, Botanical and Zoological*

Drawings, 1756–1788, Philadelphia, 1968.

Feuchtmüller 1987

Rupert Feuchtmüller, *Friedrich Gauermann*, Rosenheim, 1987.

Gentleman's Magazine 1758

"Explanation of the Miscellaneous Plate," *Gentleman's Magazine*, 28, October 1758, p. 428.

Giovannoni 1980

Simona Lecchini Giovannoni, "Di uno 'scartafaccio' ed altri disegni inediti di Alessandro Allori," *Paragone* 31, no. 365, 1980, pp. 64–83.

Giovannoni 1991

Simona Lecchini Giovannoni, *Alessandro Allori*, Turin, 1991.

Glück 1933

Gustave Glück, *Rubens, Van Dyck unk ihr kreis*, Vienna, 1933.

Greindl 1944

Edith Greindl, *Corneille de Vos, portraitiste flamand (1584–1651)*, Brussels, 1944.

Grönvold 1915

Bernt Grönvold, *Friedrich Wasmann*, Leipzig, 1915.

Hannover 1898

Emil Hannover, *Maleren C. W. Eckersberg studie i dansk Kunsthistorie,* Copenhagen, 1898.

Haskell and Montagu 1997

Francis Haskell and Jennifer Montagu, general eds., Henrietta McBurney, assistant general ed., *The Paper Museum of Cassiano dal Pozzo. Catalogue Raisonné of Drawings and Prints in the Royal Library at Windsor Castle, the British Museum, the Institut de France and Other Collections* (London, 1994–), David Freedberg, series ed., *Series B: Natural History,* David Freedberg and Enrico Baldini, eds., *Part One: Citrus Fruit*, 1997.

Haskell and Montagu (forthcoming)

Francis Haskell and Jennifer Montagu, general eds., Henrietta McBurney, assistant general ed., *The Paper Museum of Cassiano dal Pozzo. Catalogue Raisonné of Drawings and Prints in the Royal Library at Windsor Castle, the British Museum, the Institut de France and Other Collections* (London, 1994–), David Freedberg, series ed., *Series B: Natural History. Part Four: Birds,* 2 vols. (forthcoming).

Haverkamp-Begemann et al. 1999

Egbert Haverkamp-Begemann, Mary Tavener Holmes, Fritz Koreny, and Donald Posner, *The Robert Lehman Collection, VII, Fifteenth- to Eighteenth-Century European Drawings*, New York, 1999.

Hofstätter 1974

Hans Hofstätter, *Caspar David Friedrich: Das gesamte graphische Werk,* Munich, 1974.

Hollstein

Hollstein, *Dutch and Flemish Etchings, Engravings and Woodcuts ca. 1450–1700*, XXXIII, *Jan van de Velde II to Dirk Vellert*, compiled by Ger Luijten and Christiaan Schuckman, Roosendaal, Netherlands, 1989.

Housted 1994

Erik Housted, *Fattig-Holm: Tre guldalderskaebner,* Copenhagen, 1994.

Ives et al. 1997

Colta Ives et al., *The Private Collection of Edgar Degas: A Summary Catalogue,* New York, 1997.

Joannides 1983

Paul Joannides, "Colin, Delacroix, Byron and the Greek War of Independence," *Burlington Magazine* 125, no. 965, 1983, pp. 495–500.

Joannides 1992

Mariannne Joannides, "Mandevare's Drawings: Le Rouge et le noire," *Phillips Preview*, London, autumn 1992, pp. 6–7.

Kauffmann 1984

C. M. Kauffmann, *John Varley, 1778–1842*, London, 1984.

Kent 1993

Neil Kent, "Christen Købke's Drawings. Assessing a Little-Known Master," *Apollo* 137, no. 373 (new series), March 1993, pp. 175–77.

Keynes 1970

Geoffrey Keynes, *Drawings of William Blake, 92 Pencil Studies*, New York, 1970.

Leeuwenberg 1966

Jaap Leeuwenberg, "The Grotesques Ascribed to Arent van Bolten," *Apollo* 83, no. 50 (new series), April 1966, pp. 272–77.

Legrand 1963

Francine Claire Legrand, *Les peintres flamands de genre au XVIIe siècle*, Brussels, 1963.

Linnell 1994

David Linnell, *Blake, Palmer, Linnell and Co.: The Life of John Linnell*, Sussex, 1994.

Madsen 1895

Karl Madsen, *Johan Thomas Lundbye, 1818–1848,* Copenhagen, 1895.

Madsen 1905

Karl Madsen, *Wilhelm Marstrand,* Copenhagen, 1905.

Maës 1998

Gaëtane Maës, *Les Watteau de Lille: Louis Watteau (1731–1798), Francois Watteau (1758–1823)*, Paris, 1998.

Massar 1970

Phyllis Dearborn Massar, "Costume Drawings by Stefano della Bella for the Florentine Theater," *Master Drawings* 8, no. 3, 1970, pp. 243–66.

McBurney 1989

Henrietta McBurney, "The Later History of Cassiano dal Pozzo's 'Museo Caraceo,'" *Burlington Magazine* 131, August 1989, pp. 549–53.

van Mosselveld and van Ham 1973

J. H. van Mosselveld and W. A. van Ham, *Tekeningen van Bergen-op-Zoom*, Maastricht, 1973.

Nathan 1954

P. Nathan, *Friedrich Wasmann, Sein Leben und Sein Werk*, Munich, 1954.

Nève 1913

J. Nève [de Mévergnies], *Inventaire des dessins et aquarelles donnés à l'État Belge par Madame la douairière de Grez*, Brussels, 1913.

Nørregård-Nielsen 1996

Hans Edvard Nørregård-Nielsen, *Christen Købke,* 3 vols., Copenhagen, 1996.

Parker 1956

K. T. Parker, *Catalogue of the Collection of Drawings in the Ashmolean Museum. Volume II: Italian Schools,* Oxford, 1956.

Popham 1932

A. E. Popham, *Catalogue of Drawings by Dutch and Flemish Artists in the British Museum*, vol. 5, London, 1932.

Potter 1972

The Art of Beatrix Potter, London, 1972.

Potter 1985

Beatrix Potter, The V&A Collection: The Leslie Linder Bequest of Beatrix Potter Material, Watercolours, Drawing, Manuscripts, Books, Photographs, and Memorabilia, catalogue compiled by Anne Stevenson Hobbs and Joyce Irene Whalley, London, 1985.

Poulsen 1991

Ellen Poulsen, *Jens Juel: Malerier og pasteller,* 2 vols., Copenhagen, 1991.

Reynolds 1984

Graham Reynolds, *The Later Paintings and Drawings of John Constable*, 2 vols., New Haven and London, 1984.

Roethlisberger 1993

Marcel G. Roethlisberger, *Abraham Bloemaert and His Sons, Paintings and Prints*, 2 vols., Doornspijk, 1993.

Roland-Michel 1970

Marianne Roland-Michel, *Anne Vallayer-Coster, 1744–1818*, Paris, 1970.

Rossetti 1863

William Michael Rossetti, *Annotated Catalogue of Blake's Pictures and Drawings*, in Alexander Gilchrist, *Life of William Blake*, 2 vols., London, 1863.

Rossetti 1880

William Michael Rossetti, *Annotated Catalogue of Blake's Pictures and Drawings*, enlarged, in Alexander Gilchrist, *Life of William Blake*, new and enlarged edition, 2 vols., London, 1880.

Ryskamp 1990

Charles Ryskamp, "A Cornelius Varley Sketchbook in the Morgan Library," *Master Drawings* 28, no. 3, 1990, pp. 344–59.

Schatborn 1973

Peter Schatborn, "Olieverfschetsen van Dirck Hals," *Bulletin van het Rijksmuseum*, vol. 21, no. 3, November 1973, pp. 107–16.

Scrase 1997
David Scrase, *Flower Drawings*, Cambridge, 1997.

Segal 1998
Sam Segal, introduction to the catalogue *Tulip Mania*, Sotheby's, Amsterdam, 16 June 1998, pp. 11–12.

Smith 1982
Hammond Smith, *Peter De Wint, 1784–1849*, London, 1982.

Smith 1994
Roberta Smith, "The Intimate Grandeur of Old Italian Drawings," review of *Sixteenth-Century Italian Drawings in New York Collections* by William M. Griswold and Linda Wolk-Simon, *New York Times*, 14 January 1994, p. C29.

Stampfle 1991
Felice Stampfle, *Netherlandish Drawings of the Fifteenth and Sixteenth Centuries and Flemish Drawings of the Seventeenth and Eighteenth Centuries*, New York, 1991.

Stampfle and Turner (forthcoming)
Felice Stampfle and Jane Turner, *Dutch Drawings of the Seventeenth to the Nineteenth Century in The Pierpont Morgan Library*, New York (forthcoming).

Sumowski 1980
Werner Sumowski, *Drawings of the Rembrandt School*, vol. 3, New York, 1980.

Thienemann 1856
Georg August Wilhelm Thienemann, *Leben und Wirken des unvergleichlichen thiermalers und kupferstechers Johann Elias Ridinger*, Leipzig, 1856.

Thomas 1982
Denis Thomas, "Peter De Wint: A Small Collection of Watercolours, Drawings and Paintings," exhibition review in *The Connoisseur* 202, no. 811, 1982, pp. 70–71.

Thomas and Bennett 1971
Denis Thomas with Ian Bennett, eds., *The Price Guide to English Watercolours*, London, 1971.

Van der Stighelen 1989
Katlijne Van der Stighelen, "Cornelis de Vos as a Draughtsman," *Master Drawings* 27, no. 4, 1989, pp. 322–40.

Van der Stighelen 1990
Katlijne Van der Stighelen, *De portretten van Cornelis de Vos (1584/5–1651): Een Kritische Catalogus*, Brussels, 1990.

Waldmann 1919
Emil Waldmann, *Wilhelm Leibl in Künst und Künstler*, Leipzig, 1919.

Wark 1975
Robert Wark, *Drawings by Thomas Rowlandson in the Huntington Collection*, San Marino, 1975.

White and Crawley 1994
Christopher White and Charlotte Crawley, *The Dutch and Flemish Drawings of the Fifteenth to the Early Nineteenth Centuries in the Collection of Her Majesty the Queen at Windsor Castle*, Cambridge, 1994.

Wirth 1965
Irmgard Wirth, *Mit Adolph Menzel in Berlin*, Munich, 1965.

Witt 1982
John Witt, *William Henry Hunt (1790–1864) Life and Work*, London, 1982.

Zega and Dams 2000
Andrew Zega and Bernd H. Dams, *Garden Vases*, introduction by Gérard Mabille, Paris, 2000.

Zwollo 1965
An Zwollo, "De Landschaptekeningen van Cornelis Massys," *Nederlands Kunsthistorisch Jaarboek* 16, 1965, pp. 43–65.

EXHIBITIONS

Amsterdam 1988
Van Gogh Museum, Amsterdam, *Anton Mauve aquarellen*, 1988.

Amsterdam 1993–94
Rijksmuseum, Amsterdam, *Dawn of the Golden Age: Northern Netherlandish Art, 1580–1620*, catalogue edited by Ger Luijten and Ariane van Suchtelen, 1993–94.

Amsterdam and elsewhere 1991–92
Rijksprentenkabinet, Rijksmuseum, Amsterdam, Graphische Sammlung Albertina, Vienna, The Pierpont Morgan Library, New York, The Fogg Art Museum, Harvard University, Cambridge, *Seventeenth Century Dutch*

Drawings: A Selection from the Maida and George Abrams Collection, catalogue by William W. Robinson, 1991–92.

Århus 1992

Kunstmuseum, Århus, *P.S. Kroyer: Tradition modernitet,* 1992.

Basel 1943

Kunsthalle, Basel, *Ausstellung von Werken des 19. Jahrhunderts aus Basler Privatbesitz,* 1943.

Basel 1956

Kunstmuseum, Basel, *Sammlung Richard Doetsch-Benziger,* 1956.

Basel 1987

Claude Kuhn, Basel, *Handzeichnungen alter Meister,* 1987.

Basel and elsewhere 1988

Kunstmuseum, Basel, Museum für Kunst und Kulturgeschichte der Hansestadt, Lübeck, Staatsgalerie, Stuttgart, *Ein Zeichner der Romantik: Friedrich Salathé, 1793–1858,* 1988.

Berlin 1890

Nationalgalerie, Berlin, *Ausstellung der Werke von Wilhelm Gentz und Carl Steffeck in der Königlichen National-Galerie,* 1890.

Berlin 1955

Nationalgalerie, Berlin, *Adolph Menzel Zeichnungen,* catalogue by Werner Schmidt, 1955.

Bonn and elsewhere 1968–69

Rheinisches Landesmuseum, Bonn, Saarländisches Museum, Saarbrücken, Städtische Kunstgalerie, Bochum, *Niederländische Zeichnungen des 17. bis 19. Jahrhunderts aus der Sammlung Hans van Leeuwen, Utrecht,* catalogue by E. K. J. Reznicek et al., 1968–69.

Bremen 1995–96

Kunsthalle, Bremen, *"Nichts trügt weniger als der Schein:" Max Liebermann der deutsche Impressionist,* 1995–96.

Brussels 1994–95

Musée d'Ixelles, Brussels, *Gainsborough to Ruskin: British Landscape Drawings & Watercolors from the Morgan Library,* 1994–95.

Brussels and elsewhere 1968–69

Bibliothèque Albert Ier, Brussels, Boijmans Van Beuningen Museum, Rotterdam, Institut Néerlandais, Paris, Musée des Beaux-Arts, Bern, *Dessins de paysagistes hollandais du XVIIe siècle,* 1968–69.

Cambridge 1930

Fogg Art Museum, Harvard University, Cambridge, *Loan Exhibition of Works of William Blake,* 1930.

Cambridge 1998

Busch Reisinger Museum, Harvard University, Cambridge, *Classicism, Romanticism, Realism: German Drawings from Mengs to Menzel in the Harvard University Art Museums,* Gallery Series no. 23, catalogue by William W. Robinson, 1998.

Cleveland 1980

Cleveland Museum of Art, *The Realist Tradition, French Painting and Drawing, 1830–1900,* 1980.

Cologne 1967

Wallraf-Richartz Museum, Cologne, *Handzeichnungen und Aquarelle,* 1967.

Copenhagen 1989

Statens Museum for Kunst, Copenhagen, *Sommerrejsen til Vejby 1843: J. Th. Lundbye og P.C. Skovgaard,* catalogue by Bente Skovgaard, Else Lofthus, and Kirsten Stromstad, 1989.

Copenhagen 1994

Thorvaldsens Museum, Copenhagen, *Johan Thomas Lundbye, 1818–48: . . . at male det kjære Danmark,* 1994.

Copenhagen 1996

Statens Museum for Konst, Copenhagen, *Christen Købke, 1810–1848,* catalogue by Hans Edvard Nørregård-Nielsen and Kasper Monrad, translated by W. Glyn Jones, 1996.

Copenhagen 1998–99

Den Hirschsprungske Samling af Danske Kunstneres Arbejder, Copenhagen, *Tegninger & Huletanker: Johan Thomas Lundbye, 1818–1848,* catalogue by Marianne Saabye et al., 1998–99.

Düsseldorf 1987

Galerie Sabrina Förster, Düsseldorf, *Katalog Nr. 14, Handzeichnungen und Aquarelle 1500–1900,* 1987.

Frankfurt 1998–99

Städelsches Kunstinstitut und Städtische Galerie, Frankfurt, *Innenleben: Die Kunst des Interieurs Vermeer bis Kabakov*, 1998–99.

Genoa 1990

Galleria di Palazzo Rosso, Genoa, *Maestri del disegno nelle civiche collezioni genovesi*, edited by Pietro Boccardo, 1990.

Hamburg 1987

Thomas le Claire Kunsthandel, Hamburg, *Handzeichnungen und Aquarelle, 1500–1900*, IV, 1987.

Hamburg 1989

Thomas le Claire Kunsthandel, Hamburg, *Meisterzeichnungen, 1500–1900*, VI, 1989.

Hertogenbosch 1977

Noordbrabants Museum, Hertogenbosch, *J. A. Knip, 1777–1847*, catalogue by Ellinoor Bergvelt and Margriet van Boven, 1977.

Kassel 1930–31

Hessischen Landesmuseum, Kassel, *Meisterliche Handzeichnungen aus Privatbesitz: Sammlung Deiker*, 1930–31.

Laren 1963

Singer Museum, Laren, *Nederlandse Tekeningen, Collectie Hans van Leeuwen*, 1963.

Leipzig 1934

C. G. Boerner, Leipzig, *Die Handzeichnungens-Samlung Prof. Paul Arndt-München, Deutsche Meister des XIX. Jahrhunderts*, 1934.

London 1963

Colnaghi, London, *Exhibition of Old Master Drawings*, 1963.

London 1966

Sotheby's, London, *Old Master Drawings*, 7 July 1966.

London 1970

John Baskett Ltd., London, *Exhibition of Old Master and English Drawings*, 1970.

London 1970a

Colnaghi, London, *Exhibition of Old Master and English Drawings*, 1970.

London 1976

Baskett and Day, London, *Exhibition of Fifty Old Master Drawings*, 1976.

London 1976a

Tate Gallery, London, *Constable Landscape Watercolours & Drawings*, catalogue by Ian Fleming-Williams, 1976.

London 1977

Hazlitt, Gooden and Fox, London, *Nineteenth-Century French Drawings*, 1977.

London 1978

Covent Garden Gallery Ltd., London, *"The Ingenious Mr. Seymour," James Seymour 1702–1752*, catalogue by William Drummond, 1978.

London 1979

Sotheby's, London, *An Exhibition of Old Master and English Drawings and European Bronzes from the Collection of Charles Rogers [1711–1784] and the William Cotton Bequest on loan from the City Museum and Art Gallery, Plymouth*, 1979.

London 1979a

Andrew Wyld, London, *Peter de Wint, 1784–1849: Watercolours, Drawings and Oil Paintings*, 1979.

London 1980

Covent Garden Gallery Ltd., London, *"All the World's a Stage" or What Can They Be Doing?* catalogue by William Drummond, 1980.

London 1981

Baskett and Day, London, *Exhibition of Fifty Old Master Drawings*, 1981.

London 1981a

Covent Garden Gallery Ltd., London, *Portrait, Figure & Genre Watercolours & Drawings: From Kneller to Epstein*, 1981.

London 1984

Niall Hobhouse, London, *Botanical Watercolours*, 1984.

London 1984a

Yvonne Tan Bunzl, London, *Old Master Drawings*, 1984.

London 1987

Harari and Johns, London, *Meisterzeichnungen/Master Drawings, 1500–1900*, 1987.

London 1987a

Lindsay Stainton and Christopher White, *Drawings in England from Hilliard to Hogarth*, London, 1987.

London 1987b

Spink and Son, London, *English Watercolour Drawings, Annual Exhibition*, 1987.

London 1989

Smithson and Williams, London, *Old Master Drawings. Recent Acquisitions*, 1989.

London 1990

Hazlitt, Gooden and Fox, London, *Natural History Drawings*, 1990.

London 1995

Peter Nahum at The Leicester Galleries, London, *A Century of Master Drawings, Watercolours & Works in Egg Tempera*, 1995.

London 1996

Grosvenor House, London, [Title unknown], 1996.

London 1999

National Gallery, London, *A Brush with Nature: The Gere Collection of Landscape Sketches*, catalogue by Christopher Riopelle and Xavier Bray, 1999.

London and New Haven 1984–85

Tate Gallery, London, and Yale Center for British Art, Yale University, New Haven, *George Stubbs 1724–1806*, catalogue by Judy Egerton, 1984–85.

London and New York 1976

Anthony Reed, London, and Davis and Long Company, New York, *David Cox: Drawings and Paintings*, 1976.

London and elsewhere 1972

Victoria and Albert Museum, London, Institut Néerlandais, Paris, Kunstmuseum, Bern, Royal Library of Belgium, Brussels, *Flemish Drawings of the Seventeenth Century from the Collection of Frits Lugt, Institut Néerlandais, Paris*, 1972.

Munich 1995

Galerie Arnoldi-Livie, Munich, *Sehnsucht zur Kindheit: Kinderdarstellungen in der Romantik und ihre Vorläufer*, 1995.

Munich 1999

Galerie Arnoldi-Livie, Munich, *Deutsche Kunst, 1600–1925*, 1999.

Munich and Cologne 1994

Neue Pinakothek, Munich, and Wallraf-Richartz Museum, Cologne, *Wilhelm Leibl zum 150. Geburtstag*, 1994.

Munich and New York 1992

Galerie Arnoldi-Livie, Munich, and Jill Newhouse, New York, *Baron François Gérard (1770–1837): Exhibition and Sale of Paintings and Drawings*, 1992.

Newark 1961

Newark Museum, Newark, New Jersey, *Nineteenth Century Master Drawings*, 1961.

New Brunswick 1983

Jane Voorhees Zimmerli Art Museum, Rutgers University, New Brunswick, New Jersey, *Haarlem, The Seventeenth Century*, 1983.

New Haven and Raleigh 1987

Yale Center for British Art, Yale University, New Haven, and North Carolina Museum of Art, Raleigh, *Sir David Wilkie of Scotland (1785–1841)*, catalogue by Hamish Miles and David Blayney Brown, 1987.

New York 1905

Grolier Club, New York, *Books, Engravings, Watercolours & Sketches by William Blake*, 1905.

New York 1948

Schaeffer Galleries, New York, *Drawings: Bruegel to Cézanne*, 1948.

New York 1969

Davis Gallery, New York, *Nineteenth-Century English Watercolors and Drawings*, 1969.

New York 1974

Grolier Club, New York, *William Blake and His Followers*, 1974.

New York 1982

Colnaghi, New York, *Aspects of Neoclassicism: Drawings and Watercolors, 1760–1840*, 1982.

New York 1984

The Pierpont Morgan Library, New York, *French Draw-*

ings, 1550–1825, catalogue by Cara Dufour Denison, preface by Charles Ryskamp, 1984.

New York 1985

Davis and Langdale, Inc., New York, *British Drawings: 1760–1925,* 1985.

New York 1986

Salander O'Reilly Galleries, New York, *Corot/Delacroix,* 1986.

New York 1987

Colnaghi, New York, *Old Master Drawings Presented by Jean-Luc Baroni,* 1987.

New York 1988

The Pierpont Morgan Library, New York, *The Romantic Spirit, German Drawings from the German Democratic Republic,* 1988.

New York 1989

Colnaghi, New York, *1789: French Art During the Revolution,* catalogue by Alan Wintermute, 1989.

New York 1989a

William H. Schab Gallery, New York, *Fiftieth Anniversary Issue,* 1989.

New York 1989b

W. M. Brady and Co., New York, *Master Drawings 1700–1890,* 1989.

New York 1990

Day and Bird, at E. J. Landrigan, Inc., New York, 1990.

New York 1991

Metropolitan Museum of Art, New York, *Eugène Delacroix (1798–1863): Paintings, Drawings, and Prints from North American Collections,* 1991.

New York 1992

Salander O'Reilly Galleries, New York, *William Blake, Paintings, Watercolors and Drawings,* essays and catalogue by Martin Butlin and Robin Hamlyn, 1992.

New York 1992a

W. M. Brady and Co., New York, *French Drawings 1770–1880,* 1992.

New York 1992b

The Pierpont Morgan Library, New York, *Sketching at Home and Abroad: British Landscape Drawing, 1750–1850,* 1992.

New York 1993

Richard Feigen Gallery, New York, *Sir Thomas Lawrence and Sir David Wilkie: Two Romantics,* 1993.

New York 1994

William H. Schab Gallery, New York, *Catalogue 80,* 1994.

New York 1994a

Metropolitan Museum of Art, New York, *Sixteenth-Century Italian Drawings in New York Collections,* catalogue by William M. Griswold and Linda Wolk-Simon, 1994.

New York 1994b

W. M. Brady and Co., New York, *Master Drawings 1500–1900* (IX), exhibition organized by Thomas le Claire Kunsthandel, Hamburg, 1994.

New York 1995

Trinity Fine Art Ltd., at Newhouse Galleries, New York, *An Exhibition of Old Master Drawings and European Works of Art,* 1995.

New York 1995a

The Pierpont Morgan Library, New York, *Fantasy and Reality: Drawings from the Sunny Crawford von Bülow Collection,* 1995.

New York 1995b

Frick Collection, New York, *Danish Drawings from the Collection of Charles Ryskamp,* an exhibition held in conjunction with *The Golden Age of Danish Art, Drawings from the Royal Museum of Fine Arts, Copenhagen,* 1995.

New York 1997

Adelson Galleries, New York, *Flavia Ormond Fine Arts Limited, London. Italian Old Master Drawings, 1500–1850,* 1997.

New York 1997–98

The Pierpont Morgan Library, New York, *Romanticism to Realism: Nineteenth-Century German Drawings,* 1997–98.

New York 1997–98a

Metropolitan Museum of Art, New York, *The Private Collection of Edgar Degas,* catalogue by Ann Dumas et al., 1997–98.

New York 1998

The Pierpont Morgan Library, New York, *To Observe*

and Imagine: British Drawings and Watercolors, 1600–1900, catalogue by Stephanie Wiles, 1998.

New York 1998a

Adelson Galleries, New York, *Flavia Ormond Fine Arts Limited, London. Old Master Drawings, 1500–1800*, 1998.

New York 1998b

James MacKinnon at W. M. Brady and Co., Inc., New York, *Paintings and Sketches 1780–1870*, 1998.

New York 1999

Metropolitan Museum of Art, New York, *Eighteenth-Century French Drawings in New York Collections*, catalogue by Perrin Stein and Mary Tavener Holmes, 1999.

New York 1999a

Artemis Fine Arts, Inc., New York, *Danish Paintings of the Golden Age*, catalogue by Suzanne Ludvigsen, 1999.

New York 1999b

Adelson Galleries, New York, *Flavia Ormond Fine Arts Limited, London, Old Master Drawings*, 1999.

New York 2000

Adelson Galleries, New York, *Flavia Ormond Fine Arts Limited, London, Old Master Drawings 1500–1890*, 2000.

New York 2000a

Hall and Knight Ltd., New York, *Fearful Symmetry. George Stubbs, Painter of the English Enlightenment*, catalogue edited by Nicholas H. J. Hall, 2000.

New York and London 1982

Galerie Arnoldi-Livie, Munich, *A Collection of Nineteenth-Century French Drawings*, organized by Colnaghi, New York and London, 1982.

New York and London 1988

Richard Day at E. J. Landrigan, Inc., New York, and Richard Day Ltd., London, *An Exhibition of Old Master Drawings*, 1988.

New York and London 1992

Colnaghi, New York and London, *An Exhibition of Master Drawings Presented by Jean-Luc Baroni*, catalogue edited by Stephen Ongpin, 1992.

New York and elsewhere 1975–76

The Pierpont Morgan Library, New York, Cleveland Museum of Art, Art Institute of Chicago, National Gallery of Canada, Ottawa, *Drawings from the Collection of Mr. and Mrs. Eugene V. Thaw*, 1975–76.

Nijmegen and elsewhere 1969–70

Waag, Nijmegen, Stedelijk Museum de Lakenhal, Leiden, Toneelmuseum, Amsterdam, *Johannes Jelgerhuis Rzn.: Acteur-schilder, 1770–1836*, 1969–70.

Oxford and London 1996–97

Ashmolean Museum, Oxford, and Hazlitt, Gooden and Fox, London, *Drawings by the Carracci from British Collections*, catalogue by Clare Robertson and Catherine Whistler, 1996–97.

Palm Beach and elsewhere 1983–84

Society of the Four Arts, Palm Beach, Cedar Rapids Museum of Art, Academy of Natural Sciences, Philadelphia, The Pierpont Morgan Library, New York, Beaumont Art Museum, Beaumont, Texas, Wadsworth Atheneum, Hartford, *Flowers of Three Centuries: One Hundred Drawings and Watercolors from the Broughton Collection*, circulated by the International Exhibitions Foundation, Washington, D.C., catalogue by David Scrase, 1983–84.

Paris 1920

[Venue unknown], Paris, *Exposition de petits-maîtres du XVIIIe siècle*, 1920.

Paris 1974–75

Musée du Louvre, Paris, *Dessins du Musée Atger conservés à la Bibliothèque de la Médecine de Montpellier*, 1974–75.

Paris 1976–77

Musée de l'Orangerie, Paris, *La Peinture allemande à l'époque du Romanticisme*, 1976–77.

Paris 1991

Galerie Michel Meyer, Paris, *Dessins Anciens*, 1991.

Paris 1992–93

Musée du Louvre, Paris, *Les Dossiers du musée du Louvre. Pannini*, catalogue by Michael Kiene, 1992–93.

Paris and New York 1993–94

Musée du Louvre, Paris, and The Pierpont Morgan Library, New York, *French Master Drawings from The Pierpont Morgan Library*, catalogue by Cara Dufour Denison, 1993–94.

Paris and elsewhere 1979–80

Institut Néerlandais, Paris, Koninklijk Museum voor Schone Kunsten, Antwerp, British Museum, London, The Pierpont Morgan Library, New York, *Rubens and Rembrandt in Their Century: Flemish & Dutch Drawings of the 17th Century from The Pierpont Morgan Library*, catalogue by Felice Stampfle, 1979–80.

Philadelphia 1939

Philadelphia Museum of Art, *Works of William Blake Selected from Collections in the United States,* 1939.

Princeton 1967

The Art Museum, Princeton University, Princeton, New Jersey, [Title unknown], 1967.

Princeton 1969–70

Princeton University Library, *William Blake: Engraver. A Descriptive Catalogue of an Exhibition*, catalogue by Charles Ryskamp, introduction by Geoffrey Keynes, 1969–70.

Princeton 1997

The Art Museum, Princeton University, Princeton, New Jersey, *In Celebration: Works of Art from the Collections of Princeton Alumni and Friends of the Art Museum,* 1997.

Rennes 1994

Musée des Beaux-Arts, Rennes, *De Dürer a Friederich: Dessins allemands du Wallraf-Richartz-Museum de Cologne,* 1994.

Rome 1991

Palazzo Ruspoli, Rome, *Il Segno del Genio: Cento disegni di grandi Maestri del passato dall'Ashmolean Museum di Oxford*, catalogue by Christopher White, Catherine Whistler, and Colin Harrison, 1991.

Rotterdam 1994–95

Boijmans Van Beuningen Museum, Rotterdam, *Nederlandse tekeningen uit de negentiende eeuw 1, 1800–1850: Keuze uit de verzameling van het prentenkabinet (Nineteenth-century Dutch Drawings 1, 1800–1850: Drawings from the Collection of the Printroom),* catalogue by Saski de Bodt and Manfred Sellink, 1994–95.

Salt Lake City 1964

Salt Lake City Art Centre, *John Linnell,* 1964.

Utrecht 1959–60

Genootschap Kunstliefde, Utrecht, *Catalogus der tentoonstelling van tekeningen uit de collectie van de heer Hans van Leeuwen te Amsterdam*, 1959–60.

Washington and New York 1986–87

National Gallery of Art, Washington, D.C., and The Pierpont Morgan Library, New York, *The Age of Bruegel: Netherlandish Drawings in the Sixteenth Century,* catalogue by John Oliver Hand et al., 1986–87.

Washington and elsewhere 1996–97

National Gallery of Art, Washington, D.C., The Brooklyn Museum, Saint Louis Museum of Art, *In the Light of Italy: Corot and Early Open-Air Painting*, catalogue by Philip Conisbee et al., 1996–97.

Wellesley and elsewhere 1969

Hopkins Center Art Galleries, Dartmouth College, Hanover, New Hampshire, Wellesley College Museum, Jewett Arts Center, Wellesley, Massachusetts, Museum of Art, Rhode Island School of Design, Providence, Rhode Island, Museum of Art, University of Connecticut, Storrs, Connecticut, *Selections from the Collection of Dutch Drawings of Maida and George Abrams*, catalogue by Franklin W. Robinson, 1969.

Zurich 1984

Kurt Meissner, Zurich, *100 Meister Zeichnungen*, 1984.

INDEX OF ARTISTS

PUBLISHED BY THE PIERPONT MORGAN LIBRARY

Karen Banks, *Publications Manager*
Patricia Emerson, *Senior Editor*
Deborah Winard, *Associate*
Jami Vodoklys, *Assistant*

PROJECT STAFF

Drawings and Prints
William M. Griswold, *Charles W. Engelhard Curator*
Cara Dufour Denison, *Curator*
Jennifer Tonkovich, *Assistant Curator*
Kathleen Stuart, *Frank Strasser Administrator*

Marilyn Palmeri, *Manager, Photography and Rights*
Anita Masi, *Director of Institutional Development and Membership*

Patricia Reyes, *Mellon Conservator*
Reba Snyder, *Conservator*
Gary Wright, *Art Preparator*

Designed by Jerry Kelly
Printed and bound by The Studley Press

PHOTOGRAPHIC CREDITS

Billy Cunningham, ii; Schecter Lee, Nos. 1–29, 32–42, 44–45, 47–104, 106–108, 110, 112–121;
Joseph Zehavi, Nos. x, 30–31, 43, 46, 105, 109, 111